USING STATISTICS IN SMALL-SCALE LANGUAGE EDUCATION RESEARCH

Assuming no familiarity with statistical methods, this text for language education research methods and statistics courses provides detailed guidance and instruction on principles of designing, conducting, interpreting, reading, and evaluating statistical research done in classroom settings or with a small number of participants. While three different types of statistics are addressed (descriptive, parametric, and non-parametric), the emphasis is on non-parametric statistics because they are appropriate when the number of participants is small and the conditions for use of parametric statistics are not satisfied. The emphasis on non-parametric statistics is unique and complements the growing interest among second and foreign language educators in doing statistical research in classrooms. Designed to help students and other language education researchers to identify and use analyses that are appropriate for their studies, taking into account the number of participants and the shape of the data distribution, the text includes sample studies to illustrate the important points in each chapter and exercises to promote understanding of the concepts and the development of practical research skills. Mathematical operations are explained in detail, and step-by-step illustrations in the use of R (a very powerful online freeware program) are provided to perform all calculations.

A companion website extends and enhances the text with PowerPoint presentations illustrating how to carry out calculations and use R; practice exercises with answer keys; data sets in Excel MS-DOS format; and quiz, midterm, and final problems with answer keys.

Jean L. Turner is Professor, TESOL/TFL Program, Monterey Institute of International Studies, USA.

ESL & Applied Linguistics Professional Series

Eli Hinkel, Series Editor

Braine • *Nonnative Speaker English Teachers: Research, Pedagogy, and Professional Growth*

Burns • *Doing Action Research in English Language Teaching: A Guide for Practitioners*

Nation/Macalister • *Language Curriculum Design*

Birch • *The English Language Teacher and Global Civil Society*

Johnson • *Second Language Teacher Education: A Sociocultural Perspective*

Nation • *Teaching ESL/EFL Reading and Writing*

Nation/Newton • *Teaching ESL/EFL Listening and Speaking*

Kachru/Smith • *Cultures, Contexts, and World Englishes*

McKay/Bokhosrt-Heng • *International English in its Sociolinguistic Contexts: Towards a Socially Sensitive EIL Pedagogy*

Christison/Murray, Eds. • *Leadership in English Language Education: Theoretical Foundations and Practical Skills for Changing Times*

McCafferty/Stam, Eds. • *Gesture: Second Language Acquisition and Classroom Research*

Liu • *Idioms: Description, Comprehension, Acquisition, and Pedagogy*

Chapelle/Enright/ • *Building a Validity Argument for the Test of English as* **Jamieson, Eds.** • *a Foreign Language™*

Kondo-Brown/ • *Teaching Chinese, Japanese, and Korean Heritage Language* **Brown, Eds.** • *Students Curriculum Needs, Materials, and Assessments*

Youmans • *Chicano-Anglo Conversations: Truth, Honesty, and Politeness*

Birch • *English L2 Reading: Getting to the Bottom, Second Edition*

Luk/Lin • *Classroom Interactions as Cross-cultural Encounters: Native Speakers in EFL Lessons*

Levy/Stockwell • *CALL Dimensions: Issues and Options in Computer Assisted Language Learning*

Nero, Ed. • *Dialects, Englishes, Creoles, and Education*

Basturkmen • *Ideas and Options in English for Specific Purposes*

Kumaravadivelu • *Understanding Language Teaching: From Method to Postmethod*

McKay • *Researching Second Language Classrooms*

Egbert/Petrie, Eds. • *CALL Research Perspectives*

Canagarajah, Ed. • *Reclaiming the Local in Language Policy and Practice*

Adamson • *Language Minority Students in American Schools: An Education in English*

Fotos/Browne, Eds. • *New Perspectives on CALL for Second Language Classrooms*

Hinkel • *Teaching Academic ESL Writing: Practical Techniques in Vocabulary and Grammar*

Hinkel/Fotos, Eds. • *New Perspectives on Grammar Teaching in Second Language Classrooms*

Hinkel • *Second Language Writers' Text: Linguistic and Rhetorical Features*

Visit **www.routledge.com/education** *for additional information on titles in the ESL & Applied Linguistics Professional Series*

USING STATISTICS IN SMALL-SCALE LANGUAGE EDUCATION RESEARCH

Focus on Non-parametric Data

Jean L. Turner

Routledge
Taylor & Francis Group

NEW YORK AND LONDON

First published 2014
by Routledge
711 Third Avenue, New York, NY 10017

and by Routledge
2 Park Square, Milton Park, Abingdon, Oxon OX14 4RN

Routledge is an imprint of the Taylor & Francis Group, an informa business

© 2014 Taylor & Francis

Library of Congress Cataloging-in-Publication Data

Turner, Jean L.
Using statistics in small-scale language education research : focus on non-parametric data / Jean L. Turner.
        pages cm. — (ESL & Applied Linguistics Professional series)
    Includes bibliographical references and index.
    1. Applied linguistics—Statistical methods.   2. Applied linguistics—Research.   3. Linguistics—Statistical methods.   4. Computational linguistics.   5. Corpora (Linguistics)   I. Title.
P138.5.T87   2014
418.0072'7—dc23   2013030128

ISBN: 978-0-415-81993-0 (hbk)
ISBN: 978-0-415-81994-7 (pbk)
ISBN: 978-0-203-52692-7 (ebk)

Typeset in Bembo
by Apex CoVantage, LLC

CONTENTS

PREFACE

My decision to write *Using Statistics in Small-Scale Language Education Research: Focus on Non-parametric Data* was motivated by two observations. First, there is a growing number of language educators who do research, the systemic inquiry done by "classroom practitioners investigating some aspect of their own practice" to gain a better understanding of and improve both learning and teaching (Nunan & Bailey, 2008, p. 17). Teacher–researchers like my colleagues, former students, and friends—Pablo Oliva, Nataliya Borkovska, Jennifer Grode, Derek Yiu, Rebecca Noreen, Maiya Saunders, and many others—are designing and conducting research to explore aspects of their professional practice and gain a deeper understanding of their learners and their learning environments.

I've taught research methods and statistics for language educators a while now and it seems to me that second and foreign language teachers, perhaps because of their focus on the humanities in their own education, missed out on the classes on designing and conducting quantitative research that professionals in the physical sciences were required to take. As a consequence, these language professionals hesitate to engage in research that involves collecting and analyzing numerical data, even when they recognize that numerical information can be useful. These researchers need to be able to understand and critique published statistical research as a foundation for their own work, and they also need the knowledge, skills, and confidence to design and carry out their own research. *Using Statistics in Small-Scale Language Education Research* addresses these needs through practical discussion of the principles of statistical analysis, which are illustrated with step-by-step examples from language education studies.

My second observation is closely related to the first: These teacher–researchers are often doing research in their own classrooms and schools with their own learners participating in the research—not simply because their students are convenient and willing, but because the primary goal of the research is to gain a deeper understanding of *those* learners and *those* learning environments. Though the researchers share what they learn from their research with other educators and those educators may be able to use that information in their own practice, the primary function of the research is not to draw conclusions about language learners and language learning in general. The emphasis in this text is on the use of non-parametric statistics, which suit the focus and the small, local scale of the work these researchers do. Unlike parametric statistics, whose use requires large numbers of anonymous participants and test scores distributed neatly in a bell-shaped curve, non-parametric statistics are designed to be used in conditions precisely like those in small-scale language education research. They're not only the right tools for the job, they're also *better* tools for the job because they're less likely to result in error than their parametric pals.

This book addresses three different types of statistics: descriptive, parametric, and non-parametric. I believe a thorough understanding of descriptive statistics is essential for any professional who regularly deals with tests and test scores, as many teachers do. I address parametric statistics not because I think researchers doing small-scale language education studies should use them, but because being able to read, understand, and critique research that does use them is an important skill—quite a bit of research in language education has used them. However, the focus of the text is on non-parametric statistics with the goal of assisting small-scale language education researchers in identifying and using analyses that are appropriate for their studies. To assist these researchers with the mathematical side of doing statistical research, I provide instruction in how to use a powerful, free, statistical software program called *R* to do calculations.

This book is intended as a course textbook and resource for undergraduate and graduate students in applied linguistics and language education, for language teachers, language-teachers-in-training, and language education professionals who are engaged in or planning small-scale language education research. The book is organized in four sections.

Section I (Chapters One through Five) establishes a foundation for doing statistical research. In Chapter One, I define research and give an overview of some of the features of various types of research. The five characteristics of sound statistical research are explored, including what I consider to be the most important, a study's readability by its intended audience.

In Chapter Two, I define the concept of *variable* and introduce the idea of variables being defined, or measured, by different types of scales. I introduce the reader to various ways of presenting data graphically and calculating and understanding the implications of descriptive statistics. The normal distribution model is introduced, as is the concept of standardized scores. The use of *R* is introduced in this chapter with a focus on data entry, the calculation of descriptive statistics, and the generation of various types of graphic data displays. The companion website (www.routledge.com/cw/turner), which includes datasets, additional practice problems, answer keys, and other resources is introduced in this chapter.

In Chapters Three and Four, I introduce and explain the roles that variables can be assigned in statistical research. I discuss the process of forming research questions and discuss considerations in the design of research that increase its soundness and usefulness. The structure of a research report is addressed in detail in Chapter Four, illustrated by a study conducted by Nataliya Borkovska. In Chapter Five, I introduce statistical logic as a set of rules to be followed when using and interpreting inferential statistics.

Section II (Chapters Six and Seven) focuses on statistics used to analyze differences between two sets of data. In Chapter Six, I address the three parametric *t*-test formulas. I discuss the conditions for their appropriate use and how they're calculated, whether the researcher does calculations with a handheld calculator or *R*. In Chapter Seven, I introduce non-parametric premises and the two non-parametric Wilcoxon statistics. The discussion is illustrated with research questions and data from small-scale research in language education, including studies done by Pablo Oliva and Jennifer Grode.

Section III (Chapters Eight and Nine) focuses on statistics used to analyze differences among more than two sets of data. In Chapter Eight, I introduce the family of analysis of variance (ANOVA) statistics, focusing on the between-groups, 1-way formula to provide sufficient information for critical reading of studies that use one of the formulas in this large family. Though I illustrate how to use *R* to carry out the ANOVA calculations, the emphasis in this chapter is on understanding the conditions for appropriate use of the ANOVA statistics and reading studies that use an ANOVA statistic. In Chapter Nine, I discuss the non-parametric Kruskal-Wallis and Friedman's Test statistics and the conditions for their appropriate use. As in other chapters, example studies serve as a context for illustrating the use, calculation, and interpretation of the statistics.

In Section IV (Chapters Ten through Twelve), the focus of each chapter is on analyzing patterns within variables or relationships between variables. In Chapter Ten, I introduce the parametric Pearson's product moment correlation coefficient and explain and illustrate the foundation of correlations. I explain the correlational premise and mathematical operations using both a calculator and *R*. In Chapter Eleven, I introduce the non-parametric Spearman's rho and Kendall's tau, illustrating the discussion with data I collected recently in one of my own classes. As in the previous chapters, I explain the mathematical foundation and operations before illustrating how to carry out the calculations using *R*. In Chapter Twelve, I introduce and discuss the 1-way chi-squared and 2-way chi-squared statistics and their usefulness in analyzing frequency count data. I explain the mathematical operations in calculating the statistics before illustrating how *R* can be used to carry out the calculations. The discussion is illustrated with data collected by Maiya Saunders, who must have spent a lot of time observing people order sandwiches!

ACKNOWLEDGMENTS

I wrote this book for language educators and with their help. I'd like to acknowledge the contributions, efforts, and endurance of the students in my research methods and statistics classes who have worked and played with me as I created this text; the questions they asked, the blank stares they gave me, and the solutions they proposed have made this text more useful. I'd like to thank in particular those who gave me permission to incorporate their data and research into this text: Jennifer Grode, Derek Yiu, Rebecca Noreen, Maiya Saunders, and Nataliya Borkovska.

I'd like to recognize my colleague Pablo Oliva for the pleasure of talking with him about his research on providing feedback to learners that enhances their motivation and autonomy. His feedback on my work was splendid—and enhanced my motivation. I thank Ruth Larimer and Renée Jourdenais for their support in getting me started and keeping me going. My colleague Philip Murphy did me one of the greatest professional favors anyone ever has by asking me why I wasn't using R. Well, the fact that I didn't know how to use it wasn't a good enough reason, and I greatly appreciate the push he gave me, his clever solutions, and his enthusiasm for research—and R.

I thank Huili Jiang for her careful reading and enthusiastic support of the book. I admire her intellect, her open mind, and her thoroughness; her insightful (and very tactful) comments and questions improved the book immensely.

Finally, I thank John Farley for his careful attention to my grammar, my punctuation, my words, my goals, and my coffee supply. And on days when I feel I have no trace of humor left, oh, how I appreciate that man's wit!

SECTION I
Foundations

1

WHAT IS RESEARCH?

What is research? When Professor Nataliya Borkovska was teaching technical English, she realized her students were challenged by the task of learning so much new terminology. She systematically tried out several different graphical approaches to presenting new vocabulary to see if they helped her students retain new technical vocabulary (Borkovska, 2007). Is her systematic trial of these techniques research, though it was done by a teacher in her own classroom, using techniques and data collection tools she had designed, with the primary purpose of gaining a deeper understanding of that learning environment? Professor Pablo Oliva teaches Spanish to graduate students who use Spanish in their workplaces. He wants to help them develop a habit of lifelong learning (Oliva, 2011) and provides feedback on their written assignments that he designed to promote their autonomy. He collected and analyzed questionnaire data to determine whether his students' autonomy was enhanced by the special feedback. Can his investigation be considered research, though the only participants were his students and the questionnaire data he collected consisted of students' self reports?

Professor Jennifer Grode wrestled with deciding whether to use language textbooks or authentic materials as the basis for her English language lessons. She had read a lot of expert opinion and theory but decided she really needed a sense of learners' opinions. She designed an online questionnaire to collect language learners' perceptions of the usefulness of these two types of materials and their degree of enjoyment of them (Grode, 2011). She used her findings to guide her decisions about when and how to use textbooks and authentic materials. Is her investigation research because she collected information from learners she didn't know?

Language educators' daily lives are filled with complex, professional decisions. Like Professors Borkovska, Oliva, and Grode, I believe that when educators make decisions about their pedagogical practices, the outcomes of those decisions are more useful when the decisions are based on knowledge of the students and the specific educational settings in which the decisions will be implemented. As McMillan (2000) writes, "[I]n fields such as education, where practice is heavily influenced by complex interactions among students, environments, and teachers, there is room for experts to disagree about what is known" (p. 3). In such complex environments, teachers who rely simply on what an authority has said or written, or even on their own past experiences, may not make the best decisions for their students. I believe that decision making should be informed by teachers' deep knowledge of the contexts in which they practice their profession as well as by their familiarity with current theory and practice. I also believe that teachers' decision making is best guided by a combination of careful study and thoughtful reflection in three areas: (1) their personal experiences and observations, (2) consideration of information from theory and experts or authorities, and (3) evidence gained from the systematic collection and analysis of information from specific learning environments.

The third of these perspectives is examined in this book; the systematic collection and analysis of information for the purposes of seeking answers to questions about specific learning environments, exploring the effectiveness of practice, or forming hypotheses and theories. This systematic process is *research*, though it doesn't involve large numbers of randomly selected, anonymous participants and the primary goal is a deeper understanding of the local learning environment rather than drawing conclusions about learners in general. Nunan and Bailey (2009) and Burns (2010) noted that research planned and carried out by teachers in the educational contexts in which they work and having the primary goal of improving practice is becoming increasingly important as a basis for informed practice. The work of educators such as Professors Borkovska, Oliva, and Grode reflects this trend.

In this text, I focus on *statistical research* with the goal of assisting language education researchers and others in reading and understanding statistical research and in planning and performing research that involves the statistical analysis of quantitative information. I recognize that language education researchers often collect and analyze qualitative data too. However, in this text I address the analysis of quantitative data because many of the teachers I've worked with in my research methods classes have told me they're not confident doing research that involves what they call "numbers." They recognize that quantitative information is useful, but they're unfamiliar with or uncomfortable reading statistical studies and doing math themselves, or they simply mistrust statistical research. If they previously took a statistics class, the focus was usually on formulas designed to be used in large-scale research, with the primary goal of applying the findings to people outside the study. This research requires anonymous participants and test scores distributed neatly in a bell-shaped curve; teachers may not see the relevance of this type of statistical analysis to their smaller, local investigations.

Though I address some of these statistics for large-scale research in this text, the emphasis is on non-parametric statistics, formulas that accommodate the features of small-scale language education research. These features include the relatively small number of participants and the fact that they're not anonymous recruits from a vast population of learners. Non-parametric statistics are also appropriate for analyzing information from tests, questionnaires, and other data collection tools designed to measure students' learning or opinions, regardless of whether the outcomes fall in a bell-shaped curve.

To help teacher/researchers who have concerns about math, I include step-by-step explanations of how to carry out the calculations and I illustrate how to use a powerful, free statistical software program called R. I appreciate the fact that it's free, but what's really great is that it's powerful and flexible enough to be used for almost all of the calculations I discuss in this textbook. I like the program's graphics capabilities too. (R can be used to make many different types of useful charts, graphs, and tables, though honestly, one feature I particularly like is the range of color options.)

Types of Research

One of the important defining characteristics of all types of research is systematicity. Some of the systematicity of statistical research is embodied in rules, of which there are two types. The first type is a set of procedural steps known as *statistical logic*, the platform for the probability statements that characterize statistical research. The second type of rules consists of mathematical operations embedded in formulas. Before studying either the rules of statistical logic or the mathematical rules expressed in statistical formulas, it's important to have a general understanding of what statistical research is, what it's not, and how statistical research differs from other types of research, because there are a lot of adjectives used with the term *research*. Some of these adjectives indicate the philosophy that underlies the research approach. Others designate the venue for the research, who does the research, or who might be included as participants. Some of the adjectives highlight the purpose of the research or the tools or techniques used to conduct the research or data analysis. Others indicate the types of models that are used in performing analyses and interpreting the results.

Consider the term *action research*. Bailey (2005) describes *action research* as systematic inquiry with "a reiterated cycle of procedures . . . taken in an attempt to improve a situation" (p. 25), so the term indicates the purpose of a research study. Burns (2010) notes that *action research* involves a teacher's "self-reflective, critical, and systematic approach" to identifying and exploring an issue in his or her educational context (p. 2). So another characteristic of *action research* is who does it—practitioners of a profession rather than people who are trained primarily as researchers. In language education, action research is typically done by teachers, typically to investigate the impact of an innovation or change in their usual practice on students' learning or well-being. Professor Oliva's research can be categorized as *action research* for several reasons. First, he himself identified an issue that he considers relevant and important—how features of the feedback he provides his students might impact their autonomy as learners and long-term interest in and commitment to studying Spanish. Second, he designed and carried out the research, though he'd probably tell you that he's not trained primarily as a statistician or researcher. Third, he made changes in his practice both as part of his investigation and as a result of his investigation. Finally, the goal of his investigation was to enhance his practice.

Like the term *action research,* the terms *exploratory research* and *confirmatory research* indicate the purpose of the research. People who do exploratory research conduct their studies to gain a deeper or broader understanding of the phenomena present in a particular learning environment or to form hypotheses. Confirmatory research is conducted to collect evidence to support a theory or hypothesis. Unlike the adjective *action,* the terms *exploratory* and *confirmatory* give no indication of who the researchers are, but much of the research in language education has features of exploratory or confirmatory investigation. I believe that both Professor Borkovska's and Professor Oliva's research can be considered *exploratory*—they conducted their studies to gain a deeper understanding of factors that might contribute to their students' learning.

Survey research, defined by Johnson (1992) as research done "to learn about characteristics of an entire group of interest (a population) by examining a subset of that group (a sample)" (p. 104), is a term that indicates the type of instrument used to collect information from the participants, a survey. The term *survey research* tells us something about the tool used to collect information and the information itself, because we know the data collection tool is a survey or questionnaire. The term also tells readers something about the participants; they are probably a representative subgroup of a larger group of people. Professor Grode's research is survey research; she used a questionnaire to collect language learners' perceptions of their enjoyment and the usefulness of both authentic and textbook-based instructional materials. She indicates how she recruited the 238 language learners who participated in her study and to what extent they can be considered representative of language learners in general (Grode, 2011).

Experimental research, described by Johnson (1992) as research conducted "to establish a cause-and-effect relationship between two phenomena" (p. 165) and having a *treatment,* a carefully planned manipulation of one of the phenomena, is a term that indicates something about the venue in which the research is conducted, a laboratory or a controlled or constrained environment of some sort. The term also indicates something about the researchers' underlying philosophy. Researchers and readers of experimental research must hold the underlying belief that something of value can be learned through the manipulation of phenomena in a controlled setting and that the new, deeper understanding gained through the research can be applied outside the conditions of the controlled setting. Professor

Borkovska's (2007) study on the relative effectiveness of two different types of graphic organizers on learners' retention of new vocabulary can be considered an experimental study—she carefully designed two different techniques for presenting new technical terminology and collected data to examine whether the learners who experienced the different techniques had similar retention of new vocabulary. Though she did not conduct the research in a laboratory, she did constrain the learning environment, as you'll see when you read the Procedures section of her study in Chapter Four.

The term *observational research* designates research with no manipulation of phenomena. Within the general category of observational research, the term *retrospective research* indicates that the researcher collects and analyzes information on actions or events that occurred in the past. The term *prospective research* indicates that the researcher identifies the participants in the research and then collects information as it occurs (De Veaux, Velleman, & Bock, 2008).

The term *statistical research* indicates both the type of information collected and how the information is analyzed. In statistical research, the information that's systematically collected is *quantitative*; it consists of numbers—scores, rankings, or frequency counts. This systematically collected quantitative information is referred to as *data*. (Systematically collected qualitative information is referred to as data too.) The studies conducted by Professors Borkovska, Oliva, and Grode all involve the collection and analysis of quantitative data. (Professors Oliva and Grode also collected and analyzed qualitative data in the form of their participants' written responses to survey questions or oral responses in interviews.) Professor Borkovska examines vocabulary retention scores and Professor Oliva examines his participants' self-reported level of motivation. Professor Grode examines several qualities—her participants' perception of their enjoyment of both authentic materials and textbook-based materials and their perceptions of the usefulness of the two types of materials.

Types of Statistical Formulas

There are three different types of statistical formulas addressed in this text: descriptive statistics, parametric statistics, and non-parametric statistics. *Descriptive statistics* are formulas (and the values they yield) used to characterize the midpoint and spread of a set of scores with mathematical qualities. Several of these descriptive statistics will be familiar to most readers, specifically the mean, or mathematical average of a set of scores, and the standard deviation, the average distance of the scores in the set from their mathematical mean. Descriptive statistics will be explored in Chapter Two.

Parametric statistics include a number of formulas used to analyze quantitative data when a set of general conditions are met. The first four of the conditions presented below are summarized from Corder and Foreman (2009). To each point I add some remarks in "Jean-speak." (Jean-speak is the language I use when I'm trying *not* to use technical terminology I haven't yet defined. It includes generic terms and phrases like *conditions, quality, thing, bell-shaped curve,* and *information.* I assure readers who object to imprecise language that I define and use technical terms in the next chapters.)

1. The data to be analyzed have mathematical properties; that is, the information must be represented by interval-scale scores (p. 2).

    Remarks: In Chapter Two, I explain what interval scales are and discuss how the design of different types of tests or other data collection tools relates to characteristics of the information we get from them. For now, take this point about interval scales to mean that parametric statistics should be used only when the data are numerical scores.

2. The participants or objects of study are "randomly drawn from a normally distributed population" (p. 2).

    Remarks: There are three important points here. First, in the context of statistical analysis, a population is a very large group of people or things. Second, random selection means that there's no pattern to how the research study participants are identified and chosen from the population. Third, a graph of the population's scores on the quality the researcher wants to investigate would make a bell-shaped curve, referred to as a normal distribution.[1]

    About populations—they're big. In statistics, populations are all of the people or things that share a set of relevant characteristics; for example, all of the Japanese university students who are studying English could be considered a population. In fact, a population may be infinitely large, like the population of people who graduate from high school in Japan—there are more people graduating every year, so we can't possibly identify everyone in the population. However, all 23 students in my educational research methods class this term are not a population, even though they represent the entire universe of people in that class, because there aren't enough of them to be considered a population in the statistical sense. I suppose, though, that there are enough language teachers and language-teachers-in-training who have taken, are taking, or will take a course on research methods that they might be considered a population.

    The idea of random selection of research study participants from a population implies that the names of all the hundreds or thousands of members of the population were put into an imaginary hat. An imaginary person wearing a blindfold then chose a specified number of people from this population to participate in the study. Note that the person taking the names out of the hat doesn't choose them alphabetically, by height, by weight, by whether they want to participate in research, or any other characteristic, including whether they are in the researcher's classroom or school—or in the researcher's friends' classrooms or schools. (All of these ways of selecting participants imply some pattern to identifying them as participants in the study.) Note, too, that strictly speaking, if we allow any of the randomly selected participants to decline to participate, we no longer have a randomly selected sample of the population—the only people who remain as participants are those who agreed to take part in the research. These people aren't completely representative of the population because people who don't want to participate aren't included! In language education research, participants are rarely selected from a population—researchers don't typically have access to a population of language learners from which to select their participants.

As for the bell-shaped curve, in Chapter Two I describe important features of this shape and discuss some of its uses in statistics.

3. The number of participants or objects is "adequately large" (p. 2).

Remarks: I don't know what you think about the phrase "adequately large," but it seems really vague to me! In the chapters that follow, I attempt to clarify what "adequately large" means for the different statistical procedures I discuss.

4. The data are collected in such a way that each piece of information is independent of the other pieces of information (except for a number of formulas that allow paired values) (p. 2).

Remarks: Because I'm haunted by a memory from middle school of a math test I failed, I think the idea of independence is best illustrated by questions on a math test that *aren't* independent of one another. On one of my sixth-grade math tests, the first question required me to calculate something. I don't remember exactly what I was supposed to calculate, but I *do* remember that once I'd done the calculation, I was supposed to use my answer when I answered the next questions. So I used it, and because I had made a mistake in the first calculation, my answers to the next questions were wrong and I failed the test. These math questions weren't independent. I'm still a little grumpy about the test—I don't think the test fairly measured my knowledge of what we were studying, though I guess it did measure my ability to check the accuracy of my calculations (I evidently had very little of that ability at that time). It's probably time for me to get over my lingering feelings about this test, and I'll certainly work on it, but I hope my sixth-grade math misadventure helps you remember that one of the conditions for the appropriate use of a parametric statistic is independence of the pieces of information.

Field, Miles, and Field (2012) identify another assumption that must be met when using a parametric statistic; my remarks are added here too:

5. The *variances* in the outcomes must be approximately equal for all comparison groups when examining differences between groups, or at all levels of comparison when examining relationships between two different sets of information (p. 168).

Remarks: What this idea of variance means is that the spread of scores for each of the groups you want to compare has to be about the same. More on this point in Chapter Six.

These five requirements reflect a particular philosophical stance—that the primary purpose of experimental research is to gain a better understanding of a population through investigations of random samples from the population. When a study is well designed and carefully conducted, and the assumptions for the use of parametric statistics are met, these useful analytic tools support assertions that researchers make about the population based on the outcomes of the participants.

However, as I noted earlier, many researchers in language education do research primarily to gain a deeper or broader understanding of the phenomena present in a particular learning environment—their primary goal is not generalization of their findings to a population. The number of participants in language education research may be rather small (rather than "adequately large") and the participants are those who are in the learning environment—they're not randomly chosen from a population of learners. The tools the researchers use to collect their data are often designed to measure students' learning, attitudes, or feelings rather than being designed to yield normally distributed scores. These features reflect their research purposes but throw into question the use of parametric statistics for analysis of their data. *Non-parametric statistics*, the third type of formulas addressed in this text, are often exactly the right tools.

Non-parametric statistics are statistical formulas designed for use when the participants are not randomly chosen from a population and the samples may be small or of unequal sizes. Non-parametric formulas are useful for analyzing data that consist of rankable scores or frequency counts and don't require that the data be normally distributed. Though some researchers—and readers of research—consider parametric statistics to be more powerful than non-parametric ones, this is true only when the data are normally distributed. The power of a parametric statistic is related to its ability to identify a statistically significant outcome when there is one. When data are not normally distributed, the power of a parametric statistic cannot be calculated because the calculation relies on characteristics of the normal distribution model. More importantly, when data are not normally distributed non-parametric statistics are less likely than parametric statistics to result in a specific type of error when interpreting the outcomes of the analyses (Field et al., 2012, p. 667).[2] This type of error, a *Type II error,* means that the researcher concluded that there was *no* statistically significant outcome when there probably was one.[3] Additionally, when data aren't normally distributed, the likelihood of a *Type I error* is affected. A Type I error means that the researcher concluded that there was a statistically significant outcome but there probably wasn't—exactly how probable is ambiguous. Moreover, as Field and colleagues (2012) noted, because the likelihood of a Type I error is ambiguous, the *effect size* of the findings (p. 58) can't be accurately calculated. *Effect size* is important because it's "an objective and (usually) standardized measure of the magnitude of the observed effect" (p. 57). Given these concerns, non-parametric statistics *should* be used when the five conditions for parametric analysis aren't met.

I was planting some flower bulbs (daffodils) recently and realized that the two tools I used illustrate the distinction between parametric and non-parametric statistics. The first tool option was a garden trowel; a garden trowel is a small, handheld digging device, like a small shovel or spade. A garden trowel can be used for many different kinds of gardening jobs as long as two general conditions are met: the garden job requires digging, and the digging is best done by hand. Parametric statistics are like garden trowels—they're useful general purpose tools, though certain conditions, those that I discussed above, have to be met.

My second tool option was a bulb planter. A bulb planter is also a small, hand-held gardening tool, but it's designed for a very specific type of small-scale digging: making holes in which to plant bulbs. Because it's designed for this specific job, it isn't useful for other types of small-scale digging jobs, but it's the *perfect* tool for digging holes for bulbs. Non-parametric statistics are the bulb planters of the statistics world—they're formulas designed to be used when data *aren't* normally distributed and when generalization of research findings to a population *isn't* the goal of the research. In these conditions, the non-parametric statistics are better—less likely to result in error than the parametric ones (Field et al., 2012, p. 654).

Language education researchers do often want to collect and analyze quantitative data, just as Professors Borkovska, Oliva, and Grode did. Though their quantitative data may not meet the conditions for parametric analyses, they may wish to read and evaluate studies in which these statistics have been used. The emphasis in the discussion of parametric statistics in this textbook is therefore on understanding them and the studies in which they're used rather than on using them. The focus on non-parametric statistics in this text is intended to assist researchers in analyzing their quantitative data with tools that are designed specifically for their purposes and the types of data they're likely to collect.

After you finish reading this section of the chapter, I'd like you to listen to a song by Marcia Ball called "The Right Tool for the Job."[4] Aside from the fact that I like the song and her performance, her words carry an important message: Why not use the right tool for the job?

Characteristics of Statistical Research

Brown (1988) discussed five characteristics of good statistical research regardless of the type of statistic used: systematicity, evidence of statistical logic, variables that are made tangible, reductiveness, and replicability. His discussion was the starting point for creating the list of critical characteristics of sound statistical research that I present here:

- Good statistical research shows evidence of systematicity throughout.
- Good statistical research includes definitions of the phenomena in the study that make them observable and countable, rankable, or measurable.
- Good statistical research uses appropriate mathematical formulas to reduce quantitative information and make patterns and trends more easily observed.
- Good statistical research includes enough detail that the study could be replicated.
- Good statistical research is readable by members of the intended audience.

Let's take a close look at each of these features.

Systematicity is a defining characteristic of research; it's the systematicity of research that distinguishes research from an anecdotal account of events. Systematicity is represented in research by evidence of clear procedures being established and followed. Regardless of the type of research, there should be clear evidence of systematicity in all procedures, from designing the study, to collecting the data, to analyzing the data, to interpreting and reporting the findings. A review of Professor Borkovska's research report, presented on the companion website (www. routledge.com/cw/turner) and discussed in Chapter Four, reveals systematicity throughout her study, particularly in the detailed description she gives of how she developed the two different approaches to graphic organizers that her participants use, how she designed the test of vocabulary retention she used, and how she analyzed the data she collected.

Another critical characteristic of sound statistical research is that the phenomena investigated in the study, the variables,[5] are defined in ways that make them observable and countable, rankable, or measurable. For example, if I want to investigate the relationship between the two variables *musical training* and *language proficiency*, I have to first carefully define both. I might define musical training as *hours spent in music classes* and determine the total number of hours each participant has spent in music classes. Alternatively, I might define musical training by *type*, perhaps *voice* and *instrumental*, categorize the participants according to whether their training in music has focused on singing or playing an instrument, and count how many participants fall into each of the two categories. To define language proficiency, I might use published descriptors, such as the *ACTFL Proficiency Guidelines—Speaking* (American Council on the Teaching of Foreign Languages, 1999), and administer the Oral Proficiency Interview (Language Testing International, 2004) so that I have a language proficiency score for each participant. Or I might develop a list of can-do statements that allow the participants to characterize their language proficiency based on self-assessments of their abilities. The approach I take to defining the variables is informed by the nature of my research question and characteristics of the participants in my study. Regardless of the approach a researcher takes, in sound statistical research the variables are clearly defined and the manner in which they're made observable and countable, rankable, or measurable is clearly explained and makes good sense.

One of the problems in research, and one of the goals of good research, is to systematically reduce a large amount of data so relationships between variables and differences among groups can be easily seen and studied. Thus, another feature of sound research is that there's systematic reduction of information. In statistical research, this reduction is accomplished through the use of mathematical formulas. In sound statistical research, a rationale is given for the type of formula(s) used. Additionally, the conditions that must be satisfied for the use of that particular formula are noted and met. For example, Professor Borkovska (2007) writes in the Analysis and Results section of her study, presented in Chapter Four, that she "plotted the scores that the participants received on the test and found that their results did not yield a normal distribution. Hence, the non-parametric statistical procedure of the Mann–Whitney U-test was performed to compare the two groups rather than the parametric t-test formula." She explains that she made a graph of her data and examined it to guide her decision about what statistic to use. The Mann–Whitney U test,[6] the non-parametric statistic she used to analyze her data, reduces the participants' scores to a single number that allows analysis of the pattern within the data. (More on this statistic in Chapter Seven.)

The fourth characteristic of sound statistical research is that there's a very thorough description of the study's setting, procedures, and participants. This description should contain enough detail that another researcher could replicate the study. In experimental research in the physical sciences, replicability is what ultimately leads to other researchers' acceptance or lack of acceptance of a specific outcome. Demonstrable replicability in the physical sciences serves two purposes—it shows first that there's sufficient, accurate detail in the original research report to replicate the precise conditions of the original experiment. The second purpose, confirmation of the research findings, is satisfied when the experiment is conducted again, usually by another researcher in another setting, with precisely the same outcome. For example, my brother, John Turner, who is a physicist, was funded for postdoctoral work at the University of California at Berkeley in the 1980s. His task was to replicate a study in which the original researcher reported on the potential of producing hydrogen from sunlight, water, and iron oxide as a renewable, inexpensive, non-polluting source of power. John studied the original research report thoroughly, worked carefully to replicate the conditions of the original study, and felt confident that he had done so. However, despite maintaining the same conditions as had been described in the original study, he didn't have the same outcomes. Ultimately, because researchers like John couldn't achieve the same outcomes as reported in the original study despite having replicated the described conditions, the idea of exploiting sunlight, water, and iron oxide as an alternative power source was abandoned. The fact that the research could not be replicated outside the environment of the original experiment was accepted as evidence that the original study wasn't sound.

In language education research, where much of the research takes place in the classrooms, schools, and other environments where the events we study occur rather than in carefully controlled laboratory settings, the notion of replicability is viewed differently. The participants in our research are those who happen to be in settings at the time the research is conducted, so it's very unlikely that the exact conditions of a previous study could be replicated. When we do attempt to redo a study, we generally don't expect exactly the same outcomes; instead we anticipate that the subtle or deliberate differences in the conditions of the original research environment and the new research environment will result in clearer outcomes, or outcomes that add to our collective knowledge by demonstrating how the differences impact the outcomes. Replicability is not typically viewed as an avenue for showing the soundness of one's study, as replicability is viewed in the physical sciences. Instead, a reader's evaluation of the possible replicability of a study is viewed as a way of checking the thoroughness of the original report or as an avenue for building knowledge through investigating the inevitable differences that occur in recreating an experiment in a non-controlled setting.

Finally, sound statistical research is readable. Research is done to expand our individual and collective knowledge, so research is valuable only when it can be understood by its intended audience. Sound, useful research reflects authors' awareness of the background of the anticipated readers (or listeners) and consequently includes sufficiently clear explanation and discussion to facilitate their understanding. A sound research study follows the conventions of the genre, all of the critical concepts are defined, and the procedures are explained in detail. I should add a caveat here and say I don't mean to imply that good statistical research is understandable by everyone. For example, years ago, I decided that I'd try to read my brother's doctoral dissertation in physics, but I got no farther than the title, which had only one word I understood, *cobalt*.[7] Though I'm a competent reader of research in language education, I've never completed a course on physics and I'm definitely not representative of my brother's intended audience of physicists. However, his work was very well received within his community of physicists. With this book, I hope to enable you to be successful in reading the research of others and in describing your research to like-minded colleagues.

Notes

1 A normal distribution of scores looks sort of like this:
2 "Outcomes" in this context is a sadly generic word—what I really mean to say is "there is no statistically significant difference" among the groups that are examined, or "there is no statistically significant relationship" between the two variables that are investigated. These phrases will make sense after you've studied Chapters Five through Twelve!
3 When the five conditions for appropriate use of parametric statistics *are* met, parametric statistics are more powerful in the sense that there is less chance of being wrong if the researcher asserts that there is no difference between groups when there probably is a difference. This type of mistake in interpreting the outcome of a statistical analysis is known as a Type II error. (For a very detailed explanation, please refer to Field, Miles, & Field, 2012, p. 667.)
4 Here's a link to a video of Marcia performing "The Right Tool for the Job": www.youtube.com/watch?v=vbVO3xkGbZQ.
5 There's more information on how to define variables in Chapter Two.
6 The Mann–Whitney U test is discussed in Chapter Nine, though I refer to it as a Wilcoxon Rank Sum statistic because the formula R uses is the same as the Mann–Whitney U-test formula but the R command is wilcox.test.
7 I know the word *cobalt*. And I know that cobalt is an element, though I don't think about cobalt very often, and when I do I usually associate the word with a vibrant shade of blue. I like colors, you know.

2

DEFINING AND DESCRIBING VARIABLES

In Chapter One, I noted that one of the characteristics of good statistical research is that it "includes definitions of the phenomena in the study that make them observable and countable, rankable, or measurable" (p. 11). These "phenomena" are more precisely known as *variables*; in fact, when phenomena are defined in a manner that makes them observable and countable, rankable, or measurable, they become variables.

According to Shavelson (1996), a variable is "an attribute (characteristic or property) of an object or person that can change from one object to another or from person to person" (p. 12). Hatch and Lazaraton (1991) note, too, that a variable might change within a person or object across time (p. 51). They add that a variable might be an attribute of a piece of text. A feature or attribute of an environment might also be a variable. *Language ability*, for example, is a variable; an attribute of people that can change within an individual across time and also varies across different people. *Number of languages spoken* is a variable, too; one that varies across different people and could change for an individual as well. *Type of cohesive devices* is a variable; an attribute of texts. Similarly, *amount of natural light in a classroom* is a variable, as is *age*, although the state of being 10 years old is a level of a variable, not a variable itself, as I explain below.

Because variables vary, they have more than one level. Some variables have only a few levels, like the variable *sex,* which varies across only two levels, male and female. Some variables have many levels. *Class rank,* for example, might have as many levels as there are students in a class—from first to last. Language ability, if it is measured by a test, has as many levels as there are scoring points on the test. For example, if a researcher defined language ability as the ability measured by the Combined English Language Skills Assessment in a Reading Context (CELSA) (Association of Classroom Teacher Testers, 1993), the variable *language ability* would have 76 levels because there are 75 points on this test and it's possible for a test taker to receive a score of zero—that's a total of 76 levels.

Types of Scales for Expressing Variable Levels

Did you notice that the levels of the three variables I mentioned seem different in nature from one another? Don't the two levels of the variable *sex* seem to have different properties than the levels of class rank or language ability? In fact, the levels of sex, class rank, and language ability are defined by different types of *scales*. Sex is a *nominal scale* variable, class rank is an *ordinal scale* variable, and language ability (as it's discussed here) is an *interval scale* variable.

The different types of scales—nominal, ordinal, and interval—carry different amounts and kinds of information about variables and their levels. Nominal scales are the simplest type of scale; they carry information about only the category. Ordinal scales carry the category information plus information about the order of the categories; that is, which of the variables' ordered categories are highest, lowest, and so on. Most readers are probably familiar and comfortable with the idea that someone ranked first has more of the attribute in question than someone ranked second, and the person ranked second has more of that quality than the person ranked third. Because rankings are ordinal in nature, we don't know exactly how much difference there is among the three individuals when the only information we have about them is their rank, though we can put them in order. Ordinal scales don't allow us to *measure* how much difference there is because ordinal scales don't have equal intervals. Interval scales carry the most information about variable levels—not only about category and order, but they also tell us that the intervals between the ordered categories are equidistant. This idea of equidistance is what gives an interval scale mathematical properties and allows us to measure precise differences. For example, Olympic swimmers' times are measured on an interval scale that has equal intervals of a hundredth of a second. In 2012, Dana Vollmer finished first in the 100-meter butterfly competition. Her time of 55.98 seconds was a world record for this event and was 0.89 seconds faster than the time for Lu Ying (56.87), who placed second in the event. Alicia Coutts was third. Her time of 56.94 was 0.07 seconds slower than Lu Ying's (ESPN, 2012). In the sections that follow, I explain each type of scale in more detail.

Nominal Scales

The levels of a nominal scale variable represent categories. There's no hierarchy in the levels, meaning that the levels of a nominal variable aren't ordered in any way. Consider the variable *native language*. Native language is a nominal variable; individuals can be categorized according to their specific native languages. The variable of native language has two or more levels, depending on these factors: (1) how a researcher defines native language and (2) the specific characteristics of the researcher's participants. When native language is a variable in a research project, it must have at least two levels because variables vary. To illustrate, imagine we want to know whether the native language of a group of students is related to their degree of success in an English reading class, and we choose to include native speakers of Spanish, Portuguese, and Cantonese in our study. In this study on reading success, the variable of native language has three levels: Spanish, Portuguese, and Cantonese. The three levels of the variable could be labeled numerically (Spanish = 1, Portuguese = 2, Cantonese = 3), but they represent only categories. It's important to keep in mind that the three levels of this variable have no mathematical properties even when they're given numerical labels. People familiar with the concept of a mathematical average who have an intuitive understanding of nominal scales know it's nonsensical to calculate the average native language of a group of people. The idea of calculating the average of a nominal variable is incomprehensible, maybe even laughable, because nominal scales don't have mathematical properties.

Ordinal Scales

Ordinal scales carry categorical information, but they also show ordering of the categories. There are two varieties of ordinal scale. The first is a simple ranking—the levels of the variable in question indicate the category and rank of each level in comparison with the others. For example, imagine that there are 12 English language learners in a teacher's class and we ask the teacher to order them from highest to lowest in terms of their *speaking skills* in group work. When the teacher ranks them, she compares the students with one another and creates an ordinal scale. If she can't distinguish among some of the students, she assigns them the same rank. In the ranks shown below, the teacher decided that two of the students were tied for Rank 4 and two others were tied for Rank 7. Her ranking of her students based on her perception of their *speaking skills* looks like this:

> Alice is first.
> Bao is second.
> Charlie is third.
> Danielle and Emily are tied for fourth place.
> Frances is fifth.
> Gi is sixth.
> Hillary and Ike are tied for seventh place.
> Jennifer is eighth.
> Kevin is ninth.
> Laura is tenth.

The ordinal variable, speaking skills, as defined by this teacher, has ten ordered levels (first through tenth). We know by the nature of ordinal scales that people who are ranked first, second, and third have more of the ability in question than people who are ranked fourth or fifth. And we know that people ranked sixth or seventh, regardless of how many people might be placed at a particular level, have more of the ability than anyone who is ranked eighth, ninth, or tenth.

Tests and assessments that are scored using a holistic scale yield the second type of ordinal information. A holistic rating scale consists of a set of sequenced descriptions of test-taker performance designed so scorers can characterize and rank learners' performance. These descriptions typically take into account several specific features at once but yield one general or global score at each level of the scale. Instead of asking the teacher to rank her students against one another, I could provide her with a holistic scale like the Holistic Scale for Evaluating Students' Speaking Skills in Group Work immediately below, give her some training so she can use it consistently, and ask her to give each of her students a holistic speaking skills score.

Holistic Scale for Evaluating Students' Speaking Skills in Group Work

3 Student has sufficient knowledge of vocabulary and grammar to actively participate in group work with classmates. Student can ask and answer questions and can express and support an opinion.

2 Student has sufficient knowledge of vocabulary and grammar to participate in group work with classmates as an active listener. Student can answer most questions directed to him/her and when prompted by others' questions, can express his/her opinion using simple sentences.

1 Student has sufficient knowledge of vocabulary and grammar to understand questions that are presented to him/her by classmates during group work. Student can give short, contextually accurate responses that are several words in length to others' questions.

On the basis of her careful, systematic observation of the students' participation in group work, she might award scores of 3 to Alice, Bao, Charlie, and Danielle; scores of 2 to Emily, Frances, Gi, Hillary, Ike, and Jennifer; and scores of 1 to Kevin and Laura. Though the holistic scores don't tell us exactly how much more effective a student who is a 3 is at participating in group work than a student who is a 2 or a 1, because the descriptions represent points on an ordinal scale we know the speaking skills of students ranked at 3 *are* better than the speaking skills of 2s and 1s. Ordinal scales don't tell us exactly how much more of the attribute in question the higher-ranked people have; we simply know that they have more because the levels of the variable are ordered. Many teacher-made tests yield ordinal scores, as do some commercial tests, such as the Oral Proficiency Interview (OPI) developed by the American Council on the Teaching of Foreign Language (ACTFL) (Language Testing International, 2004).

Another type of scale that I'd like to mention here is a Likert scale, a fairly common approach to compiling responses to a particular type of questionnaire item. A Likert-type item measures the extent to which respondents agree or disagree with a statement, like the items in Figure 2.1.

Depending on how finely the researcher wants to measure, the Likert-type items might have three to nine levels. To create a Likert scale score, the numbers an individual chooses for each item are added together; the total possible for this 4-item Likert scale ranges from 4 to 24. Likert scales are ordinal in nature because the distance between the points isn't really equal—at least not measurably equal. However, it's generally accepted that the more levels there are within an item, and the more items there are within a scale, the more closely a Likert scale moves toward being interval in nature.

Variables defined by the first type of ordinal scale, where the students are ranked by comparing them with one another, don't have mathematical properties—so, for example, we can't calculate the average of the 12 students' rankings. However, some researchers treat the scores from Likert scales and the second type of ordinal scale, where students are given an ordinal score based on their comparison to a set of sequenced descriptions, as though they have mathematical properties because the scale is *continuous* (Hatch & Lazaraton, 1991). The ordered descriptions

I feel comfortable speaking English with my classmates in my English conversation class.										
very strongly disagree		strongly disagree		disagree		agree		strongly agree		very strongly agree
1		2		3		4		5		6

I feel comfortable speaking English with other students in my English language school.										
very strongly disagree		strongly disagree		disagree		agree		strongly agree		very strongly agree
1		2		3		4		5		6

I feel comfortable speaking English with my English teacher.										
very strongly disagree		strongly disagree		disagree		agree		strongly agree		very strongly agree
1		2		3		4		5		6

I feel comfortable speaking English with other English teachers in my English language school.										
very strongly disagree		strongly disagree		disagree		agree		strongly agree		very strongly agree
1		2		3		4		5		6

FIGURE 2.1 Example Likert-Type Items

in the Holistic Scale for Evaluating Students' Speaking Skills in Group Work are continuous because a score of 3 indicates more skill or ability than 2, and a score of 2 indicates more than 1. The average class rank of the teacher's 12 students can't be calculated and interpreted meaningfully, but the average speaking skills score for the 12 students can be calculated—the average is 2.17. The teacher has to interpret this average very carefully, though. She can't really characterize the abilities of her students on the basis of this average because the holistic scale doesn't have a description for 2.17. The average simply provides a sense of the mathematical midpoint of the students' speaking skills in group work.

Interval Scales

Like ordinal scales, interval scales carry categorical information and show ordering of the categories. However, interval scales allow us to measure things exactly because the ordered levels are equidistant from one another. When I had to do some repairs to my fence recently, I discovered that I had 1½-inch nails and 3-inch nails, but I needed 2-inch nails to do the job. The type of nail that I needed to repair my fence is sold by length. *Nail length* is an interval scale variable with levels that are exactly ½ inch apart; at the hardware store, I found bins of 1-inch nails, 1½-inch nails, 2-inch nails, 2½-inch nails, and 3-inch nails. I bought what I needed and fixed the fence. The levels of an interval scale are the same size—a half-inch for this type of nail.

When I was at the local farmers' market a little later and bought some tomatoes I noticed that the tomato merchants priced their tomatoes on an interval scale too—*tomato diameter.* However, tomato diameter is measured with less precision than nails: The levels on the nail length scale are each exactly ½ inch; the levels on the tomato diameter scale are exactly 1 inch. Tomatoes that are between 0.5 and 1.5 inches in diameter are considered 1-inch tomatoes; tomatoes between 1.51 and 2.5 inches are considered 2-inch tomatoes; 3-inch tomatoes are between 2.51 and 3.5 inches in diameter, and anything over 3.5 inches is considered a 4-inch tomato—at least in this discussion! The venders sorted their tomatoes into bins and sold them according to diameter. Because tomato diameter is an interval variable and the unit of measurement is 1 inch, the difference in diameter between a tomato in the 1-inch bin and a tomato in the 2-inch bin is considered 1 inch—though honestly, to my eye, the tomatoes in a particular bin didn't all look the same size. When we know how many tomatoes are placed in each bin, we can calculate the average diameter of the tomatoes, because the levels of the variable are on a scale where the intervals are the same size, 1 inch. A 1-inch difference in tomato diameter is the same, regardless of whether we are comparing a tomato from the 1-inch bin with a tomato from the 2-inch bin, or comparing a tomato from the 3-inch bin with one from the 4-inch bin.

Some readers may be troubled by the fact that the tomatoes in a particular bin don't all look like they're the same size. This concern is related to the precision of measurement. Consider how people in the United States conceptualize the *age of adults*—each level of the variable is considered to be a 12-month period of time. My niece just celebrated her 21st birthday and will be considered 21 years old for a period of 1 year. Her sister is 23 years old—2 years older, though if we defined age of adults in intervals of a month instead of a year, we'd see that she's really only 18 months older than her sister, not 24. For different variables and purposes, interval size is defined differently. For most purposes, it makes sense to characterize the variable age of adults using one year as the unit of measurement that defines its levels—we don't need greater precision. For Olympic swimmers, it makes sense to characterize time using a hundredth of a second as the unit to define its levels, and apparently it makes sense to tomato merchants to sort tomatoes using a scale with 1-inch intervals.

Physical attributes of nails and tomatoes, such as length and diameter, are typically defined and measured by interval scales, as are physical attributes of people, such as swimmers' time, as well as some less tangible attributes, such as language aptitude and language ability.

Language aptitude, that is, the potential ability to learn a second or foreign language, can be measured by a language aptitude test, such as the Modern Language Aptitude Test Elementary Version (MLAT-E) (Carroll & Sapon, 2002). The scores for the MLAT-E range from 0 to 130 on an interval scale. There are 131 levels, each level representing a possible score, and the levels of the scale are considered to be equidistant from one another, just like scales that measure length and diameter, or age. Because the points on the interval scale MLAT-E are equidistant, the 3-point differences between the scores of 83 and 86 and the scores of 114 and 117 are comparable; a 3-point difference is the same magnitude, regardless of where on the scale it occurs. The fact that the MLAT-E scale is interval in nature, that the levels or points on the scale are equidistant, means that meaningful mathematical operations can be performed on the variable values. We can calculate the average aptitude of a group of children or find the difference in aptitude between two children because the variable is defined using an interval scale.

Final Comments on Scale Types

Scales can carry up to three kinds of information—category (nominal scales), order of category (ordinal scales), and whether the intervals between ordered categories are equidistant (interval scales). Researchers can convert the most complex type of scale, an interval scale, to an ordinal scale or even a nominal scale if doing so makes sense for their purposes. Using tomato diameter as an example, instead of pricing the tomatoes as some merchants did, using an interval scale with four levels, a merchant might decide to use an ordinal scale with three levels, less than 1 inch (tiny), 2 to 4 inches (medium), and more than 4 inches (giant). Some information is lost when tomato diameter is defined as tiny, medium, and giant and we can't retrieve that information unless we go back to the tomatoes and measure them again using the four-level interval scale. However, for the purpose of selling tomatoes, the three-level ordinal variable may be more sensible and efficient than the four-level interval scale variable. If there's a strong demand for 2-inch tomatoes (when sliced, they fit very neatly on a sandwich), merchants might even reduce the tomato diameter variable to a nominal scale with two levels, *2-inch* and *not 2-inch*, and charge a higher price for the sandwich-sized, 2-inch tomatoes.

When researchers define and describe a variable, they provide a definition that indicates the type of scale for the levels of the variable. There may be practical reasons for changing the scale of a variable, such as language aptitude, which begins as an interval scale variable, to an ordinal or even a nominal variable, just as tomato merchants may find pricing and selling their tomatoes an easier, more-efficient task when they reduce the diameter variable from a four-level interval scale to a simpler two-level nominal scale—thus needing only two prices instead of four. As you've seen, the type of scale has an impact on whether mathematical operations can be done; in later chapters, you'll see that the type of scale also determines the type of statistical formula that can be used to analyze the data. I'll often return to the issue of type of scale in the following chapters.

If you'd like to practice defining and describing variables before reading about graphic and statistical tools for organizing and reporting variable characteristics, take a look at Practice Exercises 1 and 2 at the end of the chapter.

Introducing *R*

Throughout the textbook, I illustrate how to use the free online statistical program called *R* to create the charts, graphs, and figures that are displayed (*R* Foundation for Statistical Computing, 2010). I also illustrate how to use *R* to do all of the calculations. Information about how to use *R* is presented in numbered gray text boxes. At the end of each chapter is a summary of the *R* commands that were introduced.

Graphic and Statistical Tools for Organizing and Reporting Variable Characteristics

Once data have been collected, researchers can organize and present them in various ways, depending on the nature of the data. Probably the simplest and most familiar approach to organizing and presenting data is reporting frequency, the number of occurrences for each level of a variable. For nominal variables, reporting frequency is often as straightforward as a chart indicating the number of occurrences at each level of the variable. Do you recall the study I described earlier in the chapter about the relationship between students' native language and their degree of English reading success? The nominal scale variable, native language, has three levels, Spanish, Portuguese, and Cantonese. I might make a graphic like Table 2.1 to show the number of participants for each of the levels of the variable.

TABLE 2.1 Table for Number of Participants at Each Level of Nominal Variable *Native Language*

Spanish	Portuguese	Cantonese	Total
11	16	15	42

Alternatively, the information can be presented graphically in a *bar chart* (also referred to as a *bar graph* or *bar plot*). By tradition, the horizontal axis of the chart, the *x-axis*, presents the levels of the variable. The vertical axis, the *y-axis*, presents the frequency information, as shown in Figure 2.2.

Of course, there are other ways of presenting frequency information, such as a pie chart (Figure 2.3). Pie charts are particularly useful for representing relative frequencies, proportions, but are less effective for highlighting differences (Verzani, 2005, p. 37). (When presented in gray scale, as in this text, a pie chart may be even less effective for highlighting differences than when

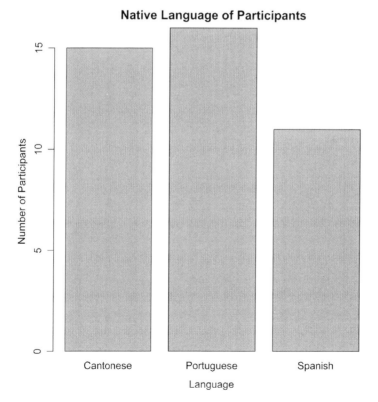

FIGURE 2.2 Bar Chart for Number of Participants at Each Level of Nominal Variable *Native Language*

Native Language of Participants

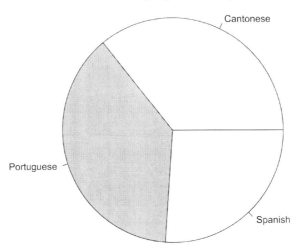

FIGURE 2.3 Pie Chart for Number of Participants at Each Level of Nominal Variable *Native Language*

presented in color.) As Verzani noted, though pie charts are commonly used in some newspapers and other media, they don't present information as transparently to the human eye as a bar chart does, so in research studies, graphic representations such as Table 2.1 or Figure 2.2 are usually a better choice than pie charts.

Using *R* to Create a Table, a Bar Chart, and a Pie Chart

Information about how to use *R* is presented in numbered, gray boxes. In the first gray box below, I show a simple way to enter nominal data (in later chapters, I describe how to import files). In the gray boxes that follow, I show how to make a bar chart and how to make a pie chart. Note that *R* commands are always bolded.

Box 2.1 Entering Nominal Data Directly Into *R* and Creating a Simple Table

Annotation	**R command**
Open *R*. The *R console* gives an arrow prompt, >.	>

(Continued)

Box 2.1 (*Continued*)

At the arrow prompt, type the name of your variable, followed by an equal sign.[1] Note: Give your variable a simple, transparent name. *R* is case sensitive and doesn't auto-correct like many word processors, so keep the name simple and check your spelling.	> **native.language =**
After the equal sign, type a lowercase **c.** (You can think of "**c**" as "collect" because you are collecting the data when you type this command.) Then the opening parenthesis (Yes, *parenthesis* is the singular form of *parentheses*.).	> **native.language = c (**
When entering the values for a nominal variable, the name of the level for each datum (yes, the singular of *data*) is presented in double quotation marks. The data are separated by commas outside the quotation marks. After the final datum, type the closing parenthesis. Complete the data entry with the enter key.	> **native.language = c ("Spanish", "Spanish", "Spanish", "Spanish", "Spanish", "Spanish", "Spanish", "Spanish", "Spanish", "Spanish", "Spanish", "Portuguese", "Portuguese", "Portuguese", "Portuguese", "Portuguese", "Portuguese", "Portuguese", "Portuguese", "Portuguese", "Portuguese", "Portuguese", "Portuguese", "Portuguese", "Portuguese", "Portuguese", "Cantonese", "Cantonese", "Cantonese", "Cantonese", "Cantonese", "Cantonese", "Cantonese", "Cantonese", "Cantonese", "Cantonese", "Cantonese", "Cantonese", "Cantonese", "Cantonese")**
After you enter the data, use the **table** command to create a table like Table 2.1. First type the command, then indicate the variable you want to use by typing its name inside parentheses. Remember that when you complete a command, you must enter it using the enter key. Note: The default *R* output places the levels of the variable in alphabetical order rather than in the order the information was entered.	> **table (native.language)** The output for this command string looks like this: native.language Cantonese Portuguese Spanish 15 16 11

The commands for *R* can be elaborated to make a bar chart that looks like Figure 2.2.

Box 2.2 Using *R* to Make a Bar Chart of the Levels of a Nominal Variable

Enter the data as in Box 2.1. To make the bar chart, add the command **barplot** to the command string for the table, **table (native.language)**. Use the enter key to complete entry. Note: The **table (native.language)** command is embedded in the new command, **barplot**. Both the **barplot** and the **table** commands require parentheses—that's why there are so many parentheses in the command.	> **barplot (table (native.language))** The bar plot generated by this command looks like this: 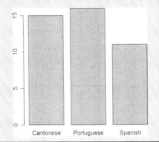
To label the *y*-axis, use **ylab=**. The label itself is included inside double quotation marks. Note: Whatever you type between the double quotation marks will be represented in the title; if you want an uppercase letter at the beginning of a word in the title, type it in uppercase.	> **barplot (table (native.language), ylab = "Number of Participants")** Note the label for the *y*-axis in the new bar plot. 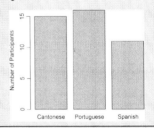
To label the *x*-axis, add **xlab =** to the command string. The label is included in double quotation marks.	> **barplot (table (native.language), ylab = "Number of Participants", xlab = "Language")** In this bar plot, both of the axes have labels. 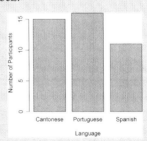

(*Continued*)

Box 2.2 (*Continued*)

To add a title to the bar plot itself, use **main =** and specify the title in double quotation marks inside the parentheses.	> **barplot (table (native. language), ylab = "Number of Participants", xlab = "Language", main = "Native Language of Participants")** Note that the new bar plot has a title. 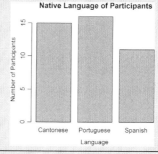
To change the color of the bars from the (boring) default gray to some other color, add **col =** and designate the color name inside double quotation marks. I chose purple because I like it, though you'll have to imagine what it looks like in purple until you make your own.	> **barplot (table (native. language), ylab = "Number of Participants", xlab = "Language", main = "Native Language of Participants", col = "purple")** (I wish you could see the barplot in purple, instead of boring gray. Why don't you make one?)

Making a pie chart requires a different command, **pie.**

Box 2.3 Using *R* to Make a Pie Chart of the Levels of a Nominal Variable

Enter the data as shown in Box 2.1. On the next command line, type **pie** followed by the **table** command with the variable name. Use the enter key to complete the command.	> **pie (table (native.language))**
If you want to give the pie chart a title, add **main =** and indicate the title inside double quotation marks.	> **pie (table (native.language), main = "Native Language of Participants")** The output from this command is presented as Figure 2.3.

Which type of chart most clearly and efficiently shows the number of participants in each level of the variable? For the nominal variable *native language*, I prefer a simple table like Table 2.1 or a bar chart like Figure 2.2 because to my eye, they allow easy comparison of the number of participants at each level of the variable. For other types of variables, other graphic representations might be clearer.

The levels of interval scale variables can be displayed graphically too. For example, Figure 2.4 presents the frequency distribution, also known as a *histogram,* for the reading scores of the 42 participants in the study on native language and reading outcomes. The dependent variable, success in the reading class, was operationalized as reading ability and measured by a teacher/researcher-developed test. The teacher's reading test yields interval-scale data and has 31 levels (zero through 30). Note that the lowercase letter *n* is used in Figure 2.4 to indicate the number of participants in the study. The lowercase italicized *k* is used to indicate the total possible number of points on the assessment instrument.

Note, too, that the horizontal x-axis displays a subset of the variable levels, from a score of 10 through a score of 23. The vertical y-axis displays the number of participants who achieved the score at each of the reported variable levels. Each of the levels of the variable between 10 and 23 is displayed even when there are no individuals who have scores at a particular level, as is the case for 13, 15, 16, and 21. The bins for values 0 through 9 and 24 through 30 are not shown. (When many

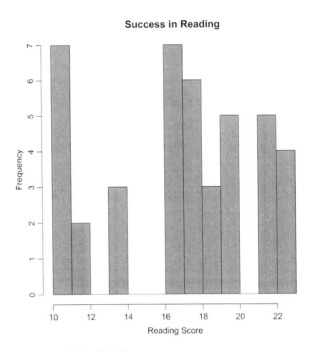

FIGURE 2.4 Histogram of Reading Scores
Note: *n* = 42; *k* = 30.

levels of the variables at the top or bottom of the distribution are empty, the scale can be truncated by omitting these empty categories, but the empty categories between the lowest and highest scores can't be eliminated.)

In Box 2.4 below, I describe how to make a simple frequency distribution of the interval data, a histogram, using *R*, and then provide information about a few additional features that can be used with the histogram command.

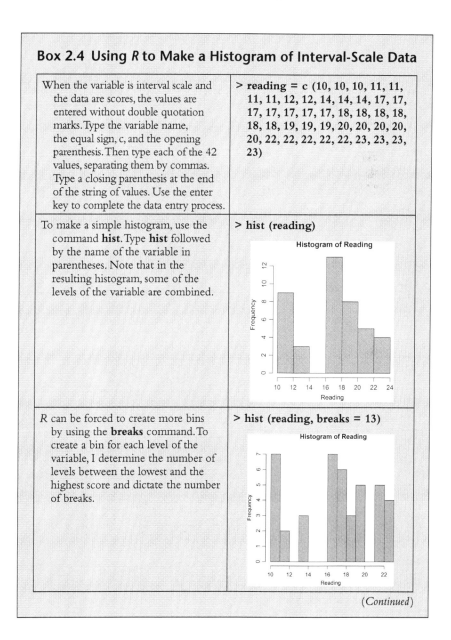

Box 2.4 Using *R* to Make a Histogram of Interval-Scale Data

When the variable is interval scale and the data are scores, the values are entered without double quotation marks. Type the variable name, the equal sign, c, and the opening parenthesis. Then type each of the 42 values, separating them by commas. Type a closing parenthesis at the end of the string of values. Use the enter key to complete the data entry process.	> **reading = c (10, 10, 10, 11, 11, 11, 11, 12, 12, 14, 14, 14, 17, 17, 17, 17, 17, 17, 17, 18, 18, 18, 18, 18, 18, 19, 19, 19, 20, 20, 20, 20, 20, 22, 22, 22, 22, 22, 23, 23, 23, 23)**
To make a simple histogram, use the command **hist**. Type **hist** followed by the name of the variable in parentheses. Note that in the resulting histogram, some of the levels of the variable are combined.	> **hist (reading)**
R can be forced to create more bins by using the **breaks** command. To create a bin for each level of the variable, I determine the number of levels between the lowest and the highest score and dictate the number of breaks.	> **hist (reading, breaks = 13)**

(Continued)

Box 2.4 *(Continued)*

I think the bins, or breaks, are easier to see if I add color to the histogram, so in this step I add the **col** command (and ask you to imagine blue instead of gray).	> **hist (reading, breaks = 13, col = "blue")** 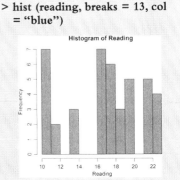
To add my own title, I use the **main** command. The default *x*-axis label is the name of the variable. In this step, I change the default label for the *x*-axis using the **xlab** command.	> **hist (reading, breaks = 13, col = "blue", main = "Success in Reading", xlab = "Reading Score")** 
Alternatively, I could spread the distribution out a little more, by requesting more breaks.	> **hist (reading, breaks = 20, col = "blue", main = "Success in Reading", xlab = "Reading Score")** 

A Warning About Interpreting Histograms

Researchers and readers of research need to be aware that the number of levels presented on the *x*-axis of a histogram affects the visual impact of the image, as does the manner in which values are combined. In Figure 2.5, I present three histograms of the same data, the 42 reading scores. To my eye, Histogram A emphasizes distinctions among the participants and approximates a bell curve, or normal distribution. (I discuss the characteristics of the normal distribution model later in this chapter.) I think Histogram B gives the impression of four clusters of participants, while Histogram C gives the impression of two separate groups of participants. Isn't it a little scary that these three histograms give such different impressions of the data?

Some researchers make choices in creating figures that disguise the true characteristics of their data, though they may not do so intentionally. Researchers and readers of research should be aware that changing the features of the *x*-axis or the *y*-axis changes the appearance of a distribution, but does not change the facts. When attempting to understand the characteristics of a set of interval scores, it's useful to consider not only the shape of the distribution, but also two additional

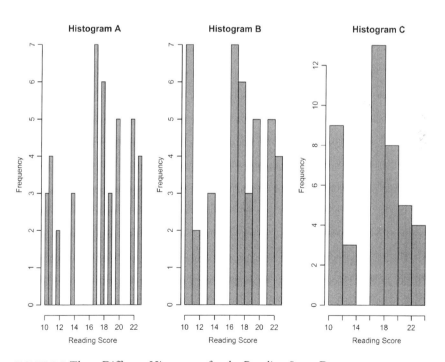

FIGURE 2.5 Three Different Histograms for the Reading Score Data

characteristics: its central tendency and its dispersion, characteristics I define in the next section. I believe the measures of central tendency and dispersion can be considered "truth in packaging," because they eliminate some of the subjectivity of a visual representation!

Central Tendency

There are three measures of central tendency for an interval-scale frequency distribution—*mode, median,* and the average, which I'll now refer to as the *mean.*

Mode

The first measure of central tendency is the mode. The mode is simply the level of the variable (the score) that occurs most frequently in a specific distribution of scores. In the distribution of reading scores in Figure 2.4, the most frequently occurring score is 17; there are seven participants who have scores of 17, so in this particular frequency distribution the mode is 17. A distribution might be bimodal or even trimodal if there is a tie for most frequently occurring score, though the distribution shown in Figure 2.4 has only one mode.

Median

The median is the level of the variable (the score) that's located at the physical center of the distribution. When there's an even number of scores, as in this example with 42 participants, the score that's physically in the center is located between the two scores in the middle. To determine the median when there's an even number of scores, start at one end of the distribution and count the scores toward the middle—in this case, count 21 scores toward the middle. I'm starting from the low end of the distribution with the first score of 10 . . .

10 10 10 11 11 11 11 12 12 14 14 14 17 17 17 17 17 17 17 18 18 . . .

It looks like the twenty-first score is 18 and the twenty-second score is 18 too. The score that's physically in the middle of the distribution is halfway between the twenty-first and twenty-second scores. To find the point halfway between the two scores in the middle, simply add the two scores and divide the outcome by 2, that is, $18 + 18 = 36$, and 36 divided by 2 = 18. So the score that's located in the physical center of this distribution, the median, is 18. When there's an odd number of scores, the score in the middle of the set of scores is the median.

Mean

The third measure of central tendency is the mean. The mean is the score located at the mathematical center of the distribution. The mathematical rules for calculating the mean are expressed in this formula:

$$\bar{X} = \frac{\sum X}{n}$$

In this formula,[3] the symbol $\bar{X}$ indicates *mean*. The symbol X refers to an individual *score*. The symbol $\sum$ means *sum* (or *add*) all of the values of X—add up the scores. The symbol n refers to the total number of participants in the group. To calculate the mean, I first find the sum of all 42 scores, which is 726. Then I divide the sum by the total number of people, 42.

$$\frac{726}{42} = 17.2857$$

When rounded to the hundredth place, the mean is 17.29.[4]

R can be used to carry out these mathematical steps, as I illustrate in Box 2.5 using the reading scores from the study introduced above.

Box 2.5 Using *R* for Each Step in the Calculation of the Mean for a Set of Interval-Scale Scores

Enter the interval-scale data as shown in the first step in Box 2.4.	**> reading = c (10, 10, 10, 11, 11, 11, 11, 12, 12, 14, 14, 14, 17, 17, 17, 17, 17, 17, 17, 18, 18, 18, 18, 18, 18, 19, 19, 19, 20, 20, 20, 20, 20, 22, 22, 22, 22, 22, 23, 23, 23, 23)**
R can be used to carry out each step in the calculation of the mean. The command **sum** followed by the variable name in parentheses gives the sum of the 42 reading values.	**> sum (reading)** The R output is presented below. The bracketed [1] in the output simply indicates the first (and only) piece of information in the output. The sum of the reading values is 726. [1] 726
To divide the sum by the total number of values, first verify that there are really 42 values in the dataset. The command **length** yields the number of values for a variable.	**> length (reading)** The output is the number of values. [1] 42
To carry out the division of the sum of the scores by the number of scores, use **sum(reading)** and **length(reading)**. The symbol that indicates division is /.	**> sum(reading)/length(reading)** The output is the mean. [1] 17.28571

R can be used to perform each step in the calculation of the mean, but R also has shortcut commands, like **summary**, which gives the mean and median. The mode is found using an elaboration of the **table** command.

Box 2.6 Using R Shortcuts and Commands to Calculate the Mean, Mode, and Median for a Set of Interval-Scale Scores

The **summary** command in R provides both the mean and the median. First, type **summary** and add the name of the variable in parentheses.	> **summary (reading)** The output provides the median and the mean (bolded). Min.　1st Qu.　**Median**　**Mean**　3rd Qu.　Max. 10.00　14.00　**18.00**　**17.29**　20.00　23.00
For small datasets such as the reading dataset, the **table** command gives information that allows easy identification of the mode. In the **table** output, locate the score (in the upper line of information) that occurs most frequently (use the frequency data in the second row of information); the score and its frequency are bolded.	> **table (reading)** The output is a simple table. reading 10 11 12 14 **17** 18 19 20 22 23 3 4 2 3 **7** 6 3 5 5 4
For larger datasets, identifying the most frequent score isn't quite as easy. Use the **subset** command with the **table** command to find the mode. Note that the command includes *two* equal signs with no space between them.	> **subset (table (reading), table (reading)==max (table (reading)))** The output indicates that the mode is 17 and that there are seven scores of 17. 17 7

All three measures of central tendency provide information about the mid-point of a distribution of interval scores; the mode indicates the most frequent score, the median indicates the score located at the physical center of the set, and the mean indicates the score located at the mathematical center of the set. These three measures are useful, but the mean, mode, and median don't give any indication of how widely dispersed the scores are. The two measures of dispersion—range and standard deviation—provide important information about the spread of the distribution.

Dispersion

There are two measures of dispersion, *range* and *standard deviation*.

Range

Range, which is the spread of a set of scores expressed in number of points, is easy to calculate. It's simply the difference between the highest score in the distribution and the lowest. In the reading score distribution, the highest score is 23 and the lowest is 10, so the range is 13 points, 23 minus 10.[5] All of the scores fall within this range.

Standard Deviation

Standard deviation provides us with more information than range does. The standard deviation is the average distance of the scores in a distribution from the mean of that distribution, so calculating the mean for the set of scores is the first step in determining standard deviation.

The formula for standard deviation looks like this:

$$\sqrt{\frac{\sum (X - \bar{X})^2}{n - 1}}$$

Before demonstrating how R can be used to calculate the standard deviation of a set of scores, I demonstrate how to calculate standard deviation using a handheld calculator—some people appreciate seeing the steps and find that reviewing the steps helps them understand the statistic. (The rest of you can skip to Box 2.7 to review the explanation of how to use R to calculate the standard deviation of a set of scores.) In this explanation, I use the reading scores displayed in Figure 2.4 and shown in Box 2.4.

The first steps in calculating the standard deviation for a set of interval-scale scores involve creating a chart similar to Table 2.2. Each of the scores is entered in the first column. In the second column, the difference between each score and the mean for the group is recorded. The mean for this group of scores is 17.29, remember? When I complete this step, some of the values in the second column are negative and some are positive. If I added these values, the negative and positive values would cancel one another out. I don't want this to happen; I want each person's score to count, so in the next step I transform each of the $X - \bar{X}$ values by squaring it.[6]

The squared values are presented in the third column in Table 2.2. The magic of math made all of the squared values positive. When I add the squared values I find:

$$\sum (X - \bar{X})^2 = 696.40$$

TABLE 2.2 Steps in Calculating Standard Deviation

X	$X - \overline{X}$	$(X - \overline{X})^2$
10	$10 - 17.29 = -7.29$	$+53.14$
10	$10 - 17.29 = -7.29$	$+53.14$
10	$10 - 17.29 = -7.29$	$+53.14$
11	$11 - 17.29 = -6.29$	$+39.56$
11	$11 - 17.29 = -6.29$	$+39.56$
11	$11 - 17.29 = -6.29$	$+39.56$
11	$11 - 17.29 = -6.29$	$+39.56$
12	$12 - 17.29 = -5.29$	$+27.98$
12	$12 - 17.29 = -5.29$	$+27.98$
14	$14 - 17.29 = -3.29$	$+10.82$
14	$14 - 17.29 = -4.12$	$+10.82$
14	$14 - 17.29 = -3.12$	$+10.82$
17	$17 - 17.29 = -0.29$	$+0.08$
17	$17 - 17.29 = -0.29$	$+0.08$
17	$17 - 17.29 = -0.29$	$+0.08$
17	$17 - 17.29 = -0.29$	$+0.08$
17	$17 - 17.29 = -0.29$	$+0.08$
17	$17 - 17.29 = -0.29$	$+0.08$
17	$17 - 17.29 = -0.29$	$+0.08$
18	$18 - 17.29 = +0.71$	$+0.50$
18	$18 - 17.29 = +0.71$	$+0.50$
18	$18 - 17.29 = +0.71$	$+0.50$
18	$18 - 17.29 = +0.71$	$+0.50$
18	$18 - 17.29 = +0.71$	$+0.50$
18	$18 - 17.29 = +0.71$	$+0.50$
19	$19 - 17.29 = +1.71$	$+2.92$
19	$19 - 17.29 = +1.71$	$+2.92$
19	$19 - 17.29 = +1.71$	$+2.92$
20	$20 - 17.29 = +2.71$	$+7.34$
20	$20 - 17.29 = +2.71$	$+7.34$
20	$20 - 17.29 = +2.71$	$+7.34$
20	$20 - 17.29 = +2.71$	$+7.34$
20	$20 - 17.29 = +2.71$	$+7.34$
22	$22 - 17.29 = +4.71$	$+22.18$
22	$22 - 17.29 = +4.71$	$+22.18$

(*Continued*)

TABLE 2.2 (*Continued*)

X	$X - \overline{X}$	$(X - \overline{X})^2$
22	22 − 17.29 = +4.71	+22.18
22	22 − 17.29 = +4.71	+22.18
22	22 − 17.29 = +4.71	+22.18
23	23 − 17.29 = +5.71	+32.60
23	23 − 17.29 = +5.71	+32.60
23	23 − 17.29 = +5.71	+32.60
23	23 − 17.29 = +5.71	+32.60

When I replace $\Sigma\,(X - \overline{X})^2$ with 696.40 in the formula, it looks like this:

$$\sqrt{\frac{696.40}{n-1}}$$

Once I have the sum of the squared values, I divide that sum by $n-1$. In this case, n is 42, so $n-1$ is 41:

$$\sqrt{\frac{696.40}{41}} = \sqrt{16.99}$$

The last step is finding the square root of 16.99, which is 4.12.

$$\sqrt{16.99} = \mathbf{4.12}$$

The standard deviation, the average distance from the mean for this set of scores, is 4.12 points.

In Box 2.7, I show how to use R to carry out the steps in calculating the standard deviation for a set of scores; in Box 2.8, I present a shortcut.

Box 2.7 Using R to Carry Out the Steps in Calculating the Standard Deviation of a Set of Interval-Scale Scores

Enter the interval data. (I use the data from the reading test displayed in Figure 2.4 and shown in Box 2.4.)	> **reading = c (10, 10, 10, 11, 11, 11, 11, 12, 12, 14, 14, 14, 17, 17, 17, 17, 17, 17, 17, 18, 18, 18, 18, 18, 18, 19, 19, 19, 20, 20, 20, 20, 20, 22, 22, 22, 22, 22, 23, 23, 23, 23)**

(*Continued*)

Box 2.7 (*Continued*)

Calculate the mean for the set of scores.	> **mean (reading)**
Calculate the difference between each score and the mean.	> **(reading)mean (reading)**
Use **^2** to square each of the differences.	> **((reading)mean (reading)) ^2**
Use **sum** to find the sum of these squared differences.	**sum (((reading)mean (reading)) ^2)**
Use **length** to check the number of scores and verify the *n* size.	> **length (reading)**
Subtract 1 from the *n*.	> **length (reading) −1**
Put these commands together in the formula for standard deviation.	> **sum (((reading)mean (reading)) ^2)(length (reading) −1)**
And find the square root of the value using the command **sqrt**.	> **sqrt (sum (((reading)mean (reading)) ^2)/ (length (reading) −1))** The output is the standard deviation. [1] 4.121838

The standard deviation for a set of scores can be calculated following the steps in Box 2.7 but there's also a single word command, **sd**, as shown in Box 2.8. Even if you had some mathematical and *R*-related fun carrying out the steps outlined in Box 2.7, I suspect you'll eventually find the **sd** command to be a valuable shortcut.

Box 2.8 Using *R*'s sd Command to Calculate the Standard Deviation of a Set of Interval-Scale Scores

Enter the interval data, as shown in Box 2.4.	> **reading = c (10, 10, 10, 11, 11, 11, 11, 12, 12, 14, 14, 14, 17, 17, 17, 17, 17, 17, 17, 18, 18, 18, 18, 18, 18, 19, 19, 19, 20, 20, 20, 20, 20, 22, 22, 22, 22, 22, 23, 23, 23, 23)**
Type the command **sd** followed by the variable name in parentheses.	> **sd (reading)** The output is the standard deviation. [1] **4.121838**

The standard deviation of a group of scores is typically reported along with the other descriptive statistics, but in some statistical formulas the concept of *variance* is very important. Variance is the sum of the differences between the scores and the mean, divided by $N - 1$. More simply, it's the squared value of the standard deviation (s^2). Like the standard deviation, variance reflects how much variability there is within a set of scores.

You'll find a few practice problems for the concepts presented in this part of the chapter at the end of this chapter—Practice Problems 3 through 14. In the section that follows, I discuss the usefulness of knowing the standard deviation of a distribution of scores.

Distribution Shapes and Characteristics

The mean, mode, median, range, and standard deviation are the descriptive statistics typically reported for interval-scale data. An understanding of descriptive statistics is important for educators, researchers, and statisticians alike. The ability to interpret the descriptive statistics of a set of scores is useful for practical reasons because this information helps us understand the characteristics of a group of learners. The concepts of central tendency and dispersion are also critical in defining the shape of a specific type of frequency distribution model, the bell shape that's an assumption in the use of parametric statistics and the foundation for interpreting the scores of people who have taken some types of standardized tests.

In thinking about the practical usefulness of understanding descriptive statistics, consider a situation like this one. The students in a fairly large intensive English program with a curriculum at three levels of proficiency take a test at the end of each term to determine whether they have the knowledge and skills to move to the next level in the curriculum or receive a certificate of completion. This term, there are enough students at the intermediate level to form two separate classes. Table 2.3 displays the descriptive statistics for the two classes (the individual scores for the people in the two classes are presented in the resource area of the companion website www.routledge.com/cw/turner).

The measures of central tendency—mean, mode, and median—indicate that the students in these two classes are very similar in terms of their abilities when they're viewed as groups; however, the measures of dispersion, range and standard deviation, show that the students in Class A are more diverse in their knowledge and

TABLE 2.3 Descriptive Statistics for Two Classes

Descriptive Statistics	Class A	Class B
n size	17	1
Mean	25.41	25.76
Mode(s)	25, 26	26
Median	26	26
Range	15 points	5 points
Standard deviation	*4.32*	*1.72*

Note: k = 35 points.

skills than are those in Class B. The teachers of these two classes may need to plan their lessons slightly differently to accommodate the students in these two classes.

The Normal Distribution Model

Not only do the measures of central tendency and dispersion provide a sense of the skills and abilities for a group of learners—but the concepts are also critical in defining the characteristics of a useful frequency distribution model, the *normal distribution*. The model's shape is defined by two features. First, the mean, mode, and median are equal and fall at the spatial and the mathematical centers of a symmetrical distribution, as shown by the vertical line in the middle of the distribution in Figure 2.6.

Second, the bell-like shape is achieved by the scores being distributed in a specific way. Approximately 34% of the scores in a normal distribution fall into the area between the mean and one standard deviation *above* the mean. Because the distribution is symmetrical, approximately 34% of the scores fall into the area between the mean and one standard deviation *below* the mean too. About 68% of the scores in a normal distribution fall between one standard deviation below the mean and one standard deviation above the mean. Approximately 14% of the scores in the distribution fall between one standard deviation and two standard deviations above the mean. And because the distribution is symmetrical, approximately 14% of the scores fall between one standard deviation and two standard deviations below the mean. About 96% of the scores in a normal distribution fall between two standard deviations below the mean and two standard deviations above the mean. Approximately 2% of the scores in the distribution fall between two standard deviations and three standard deviations above the mean. And because the distribution is symmetrical, approximately 2% of the scores fall between two standard deviations and three standard deviations below the mean. You can think of most of the scores in a normal distribution being included

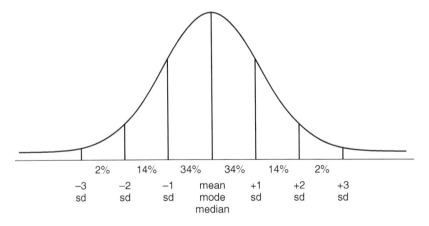

FIGURE 2.6 The Normal Distribution Model

within three standard deviations below the mean and three standard deviations above the mean, but I've indicated approximate percentages because the normal distribution model extends beyond three standard deviations above and below the mean. In fact, the tails of the distribution model extend into infinity, though practically, the lower end of a distribution of scores is limited by the fact that one typically can't have a score of less than zero, and the higher end is limited by the maximum number of points on the tool used to collect the data.

Tests Designed to Yield Normally Distributed Scores

The normal distribution is a useful model, and the distribution shape described above does actually occur in some sets of data, but the term *normal* does not imply that it is typical, nor are normal distributions inherently better than distributions with other shapes. The normal distribution shape is simply one that occurs when measuring some interval-scale variables in very large groups, or *populations*. For example, if we recorded the height of 10,000 randomly identified adults, we would probably find a normal distribution of height. Additionally, some tests are constructed so that when they're administered to the population for which they are designed, the scores fall in a normal distribution. The Graduate Records Exam (GRE) and the Paper-Based Test of English as a Foreign Language (Paper-Based TOEFL or PBT) are both *norm-referenced* tests, constructed to yield a normal distribution when administered to a large number of people from their intended population.

Tests Designed to Measure Students' Learning

In contrast, the tests that language teachers make for use in their own classes aren't designed to yield a normal distribution of scores and they usually don't, not even by chance. Teachers' tests are often designed to measure students' learning or mastery of particular content or areas of knowledge or skill. When students are correctly placed in their classes and they're well instructed, it isn't surprising if they all perform fairly well on such tests. Figure 2.7 shows a negatively skewed distribution—a distribution where the majority of the learners perform well.

FIGURE 2.7 A Negatively Skewed Distribution

Frequency
```
8
7  X  X  X  X
6  X  X  X  X   X  X
5  X  X  X  X   X  X  X
4  X  X  X  X   X  X  X  X
3  X  X  X  X   X  X  X  X
2  X  X  X  X   X  X  X  X  X
1  X  X  X  X   X  X  X  X   X  X  X  X  X  X  X        X
   1  2  3  4   5  6  7  8   9  10 11 12 13 14 15 16 17 18 19 20
                              Score
```

FIGURE 2.8 A Positively Skewed Distribution

In some situations, imagine, for example, a pretest administered *before* instruction on a particular topic. A distribution might be positively skewed, like the distribution shown in Figure 2.8.

The adjective *positive* or *negative* when used with the term *skewed distribution* indicates the direction to which the large mass of scores is pulled by the tail of the distribution.

Outliers

When researchers review the distribution of the scores they've collected, in addition to considering the shape of the distribution, some will check to see if there are any *outliers.* Outliers are individuals whose scores are so extremely different from the other participants' scores that they seem not to fit into the group. Sometimes what appears to be an outlier is simply a score that wasn't entered correctly; the error should be corrected before analyzing the data. In other cases, the outlier might truly be someone who's very different from the others in terms of background, experience, or personal characteristics. What to do with true outliers depends partly on whether the research is parametric or non-parametric.

The idea of being able to apply research findings to situations and settings beyond the research environment is called *generalization.* In most parametric research studies, one of the primary goals is generalizability, so the extent to which the participants in a particular study are representative of a larger population is very important. When using a parametric statistic, a histogram of the data should always be made to verify that there are no outliers. In Figure 2.9, notice the score on the far left; that person's performance is very different from the others'. The score would inflate the standard deviation, particularly given that the number of participants is rather small. If I were working in the parametric paradigm with the goal of generalizing the findings of my study to a population, before analyzing the data I'd first check this person's score to verify that a mistake hadn't been made in scoring the test or entering the data. If there were no error in the score or entry of the score, I'd verify that the person's background was similar to the others, but even if the person seemed quite similar, in a parametric study the outlier would almost certainly be omitted from the analysis because the learner is so different from the others.

Outliers are viewed differently in non-parametric language education research. The primary goal of much small-scale language education research is not generalizability, but a deeper understanding of the learners and learning in a particular educational context. There may be students who perform very differently from the others, but they're part of the group despite how differently they perform—they're learners in that environment, and a deeper understanding of their learning is valuable too. The researcher often collects additional information to attempt to understand why the outliers' performance is so different. Are they the same age as the other learners? Do they have a similar educational background? Did they begin their language studies at the same time as the others? Did they attend their language classes regularly? These are just a few of the questions the researcher might explore. In non-parametric studies, outliers are often included in the analysis, though in some cases—for example, if there's a group of outliers with a similar background and performance profile—their performance might be analyzed separately. The exception to retaining outliers might be if they joined the class much later than the other learners or missed an abnormal number of class sessions. The researcher decides whether to retain an outlier based on this additional information and provides an explanation in the research report.

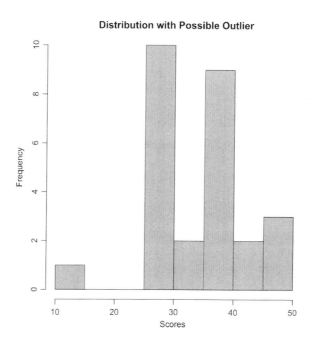

FIGURE 2.9 A Distribution With a Possible Outlier

Standardizing Scores

There are three types of distribution shapes with names—normal distribution, negatively skewed distribution, and positively skewed distribution—though there are many distribution shapes with no name. When interval-scale scores are normally distributed, the scores can be standardized—converted to a standard measuring scale—using the characteristics of the normal distribution model. I think it's important for educators to understand how standardized scores are derived because the scores of many of the high stakes tests students take are standardized and presented in the form of a *percentage*, a *percentile score*, a *z-score*, or a *T-score*. In the discussion that follows, I explain and illustrate these concepts through a practical example.

Imagine that like many score users, you want to compare a learner's performance on one interval-scale test with performance on another. My example learner is named John. John is an intermediate-level language learner. Along with the other 124 intermediate-level students at his school, he took a test before the new term started, the Initial Test. They all took a test at the end of the term too, the Final Test. The descriptive statistics for the Initial and Final tests for the entire group of 125 intermediate level students are displayed in Table 2.4, along with where John scored on each.

The Initial Test has 95 points and the Final Test has 110 points. To compare John's scores on the two tests, the scores might be converted to *percentages*. His Initial Test score of 77 out of 95 points is converted to 81% by dividing 77 by 95 and multiplying by 100; his Final Test score of 88 out of 110 points is converted to 80% by dividing 88 by 110 and multiplying by 100. The percentages, 81% and 80%, make John's performance on the two tests appear similar. However, when scores are normally distributed, the characteristics of the normal distribution model can be used to *standardize* scores, taking into account the performance of the entire group of learners, not merely the individual in question. Percentile scores, *z*-scores, and *T*-scores are different types of standardized scores based on the normal distribution model.

TABLE 2.4 Descriptive Statistics for Initial and Final Test and John's Scores

Initial Test	*Final Test*
Mean = 67	Mean = 82
Standard deviation = 10	Standard deviation = 3
$k = 95$	$k = 110$
John's score = 77	John's score = 88
John's percentage score = 77/95 = 81%	John's percentage score = 88/110 = 80%

Percentile Scores

Percentile scores are standardized scores expressed on an ordinal scale. A percentile score is derived from the defining characteristics of a normal distribution. To illustrate, when the scores for the Initial Test are normally distributed, the distribution looks something like Figure 2.10. The mean, 67, is at the center of the distribution, and because the standard deviation for the set of scores is 10 points, approximately 34% of the scores in the distribution are between 57 and 67; another 34% are between 67 and 77. Approximately 14% of the scores are between 47 and 57; another between 77 and 87. Approximately 2% of the scores are between 37 and 47; another 2% are between 87 and 95. (The highest value is 95 rather than 97 because there are only 95 points on the test.)

Percentile scores reflect the accumulation of scores in the distribution, moving from the lower end of the distribution to the higher end. In this set of scores, a score of 47, which is two standard deviations below the mean, is at the 2nd percentile, meaning that a person with a score of 47 scored as well as or better than 2% of the people in the normal distribution of scores. A person who has a score of 67 is at the 50th percentile and scored as well as, or better than, 50% of the people in the distribution. Figure 2.10 shows the percentile scores for the Initial Test that can be identified without doing any calculations, though percentiles can be calculated for any score in a normally distributed set of scores. I don't believe many small-scale education researchers would ever need to calculate percentile scores, which tend to be used for reporting scores on only large-scale, commercial,

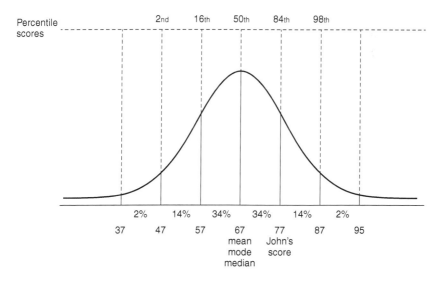

FIGURE 2.10 Percentiles and the Distribution of Scores for the Initial Test

norm-referenced tests, but if you have access to a normally distributed dataset and you want to report percentiles, you can find a formula and an explanation of how to use it in the text by Ware, Ferron, and Miller (2013, pp. 110–11).

In the distribution of scores for the Initial Test, John's raw score of 77 falls exactly at the 84th percentile. Check the distribution in Figure 2.11 to see where his raw score of 88 on the Final Test falls in the distribution of Final Test scores.

The raw score of 88 on the Final Test is at the 98th percentile—higher in the distribution than his percentile score on the Initial Test. In comparison with the 124 other learners who took the tests, he improved quite a bit from the Initial Test to the Final Test; he moved from a ranking of 84th to a ranking of 98th.

z-Scores

The ordinal percentile scale allows us to make a general comparison of scores, but if I want to express John's relative improvement in a number of points, I need to convert John's Initial Test and Final Test scores to the same *interval* scale, perhaps a *z*-scale or *T*-scale. To convert normally distributed scores to a *z*-scale, I mathematically adjust the mean of the distribution to zero and the standard deviation to one point using the following formula, where X indicates an individual's score, $\overline{X}$ is the mean of the scores, and s is the standard deviation of the scores.

$$z\text{-score} = \frac{X - \overline{X}}{s}.$$

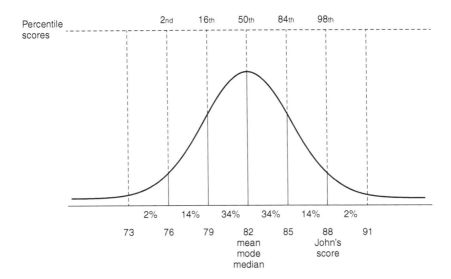

FIGURE 2.11 Percentiles and the Distribution of Scores for the Final Test

A z-score distribution looks like the model in Figure 2.12, though I've added John's Initial and Final test scores, converted to z-scores.

The calculation for transforming John's raw score on the Initial Test to a z-score is:

$$\frac{77-67}{10} = \frac{10}{10} = 1\mathbf{z}$$

The calculation for transforming his raw score on the Final Test to a z-score is:

$$\frac{88-82}{3} = \frac{6}{3} = 2\mathbf{z}$$

The Initial Test and Final Test scores can now be placed on the same z-scale, as I have done in Figure 2.12, and I can compare the z-scores mathematically, calculating the difference and expressing the difference as a number of z-scale points. John's z-score on the Final Test is 1 point higher than his z-score on the Initial Test.

By the way, an important feature of the z-scale is that 95% of the values in the distribution fall between −1.96 and +1.96, 99% of the values fall between −2.58 and +2.58, and 99.9% fall between −3.29 and +3.29. This information is useful in interpreting some statistical outcomes, as you'll see later in this chapter.

The z-distribution is a useful tool for researchers doing some types of statistical calculations, though z-scores aren't much good for reporting scores to students.

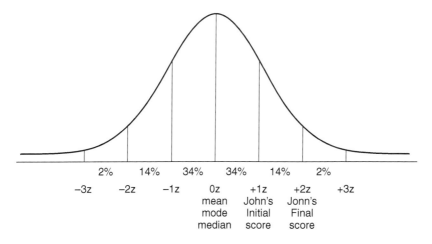

FIGURE 2.12 Model z-Score Distribution with John's Initial and Final Test z-Scores

John's Initial Test score of 1 doesn't sound very impressive, does it? And even his impressive gain from the Initial Test to the Final Test, one entire point on the z-scale, sounds dull. The situation could be worse, though—half of the z-scores are negative numbers—at least John's scores are positive! For actual score reporting, the T-scale may be more understandable and user friendly—at least everyone receives a positive score.

T-Scores *and CEEB Scores*

The formula for converting z-scores to T-scores adjusts the mean to 50 points and the standard deviation to 10 points, as shown in Figure 2.13. The formula for converting a z-score to a T-score looks like this:

$$T\text{-score} = 10z + 50$$

John's z-score on the Initial Test can be converted to a T-score like this:

$$[(10)\,(1)] + 50 = 10 + 50 = \mathbf{60}$$

His z-score on the Final Test can be converted to T-score like this:

$$[(10)\,(2)] + 50 = 20 + 50 = \mathbf{70}$$

The difference between John's performance on the Initial and Final Tests is 10 points on a T-scale. The 10-point difference sounds more impressive than the

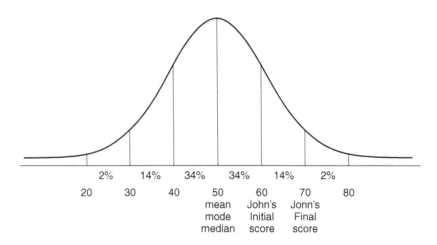

FIGURE 2.13 Model T-Score Distribution With John's Initial and Final Test T-Scores

1-point z-scale difference, doesn't it? Note that when scores are expressed on a T-scale, everyone who takes the test will have a score that's a positive number. Therefore, T-scores seem more like scores to many score users than z-scores. Scores can be standardized in other ways, too, such as the formula used by the College Entrance Examination Board (CEEB) (Educational Testing Service, 2010) for reporting scores on several of its tests, including the GRE. The CEEB formula adjusts the mean of the distribution to 500 points and the standard deviation to 100, as shown in Figure 2.14.

$$CEEB \text{ score} = 100z + 500$$

John's z-score on the Initial Test can be converted to a CEEB score like this:

$$[(100)\ (1)] + 500 = 100 + 500 = \mathbf{600}$$

His z-score on the Final Test can be converted to CEEB score like this:

$$[(100)\ (2)] + 500 = 200 + 500 = \mathbf{700}$$

The difference between John's performance on the Initial and Final Tests is 100 points on the CEEB scale. John tells me that even though he knows the CEEB scale is simply one of several ways of expressing normally distributed scores, the 100-point improvement in his performance is more satisfying than the 1-point improvement shown when a z-scale is used.

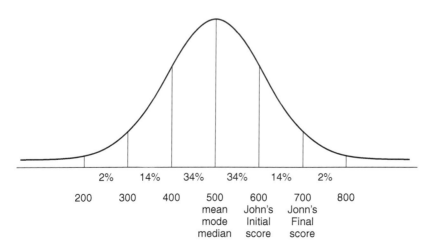

FIGURE 2.14 Model CEEB Score Distribution With John's Initial and Final Test CEEB Scores

If you'd like to practice calculating and interpreting descriptive statistics and standardized scores, take a look at Practice Problems 15 through 18 before continuing to the next part of the chapter.

Checking the Normality of a Dataset

In small-scale language education research, researchers are often more interested in gaining a deeper understanding of their learners and the learning environment in which they work than generalizing their findings to a population of learners. These researchers often use tests and questionnaires they've designed to measure specific areas of their students' learning, knowledge, skills, and opinions rather than norm-referenced data collection tools designed to yield normally distributed data. Non-parametric statistics are appropriate for analyzing the type of data their tests and questionnaires yield. However, as you may recall from Chapter One, one of the important requirements for researchers working in the parametric paradigm is that their data are normally distributed. Responsible researchers who are thinking of using a parametric statistic need to use data collection tools designed to yield normally distributed scores *and* check the distribution of their data to verify that this necessary condition is met.

To verify that their data are normally distributed, some researchers are satisfied by calculating the descriptive statistics, making a histogram of the data, and examining the descriptive statistics and the histogram to verify that the data approximate the normal distribution model.[7] However, it's difficult to make this eyeball judgment. Do you think the distribution of the 23 scores from a listening test shown in Figure 2.15 matches the normal distribution model closely enough to allow use of a parametric statistic?

Here are the descriptive statistics for the set of scores.

n	Range	Minimum	Maximum	Mean	Median	Mode(s)	Std. Deviation
23	14.00	16.00	30.00	24.91	26	24, 26, 27, and 29	3.63

The descriptive statistics show that the mean, modes, and median are somewhat similar, and when I examine the histogram I don't see any clear outliers, but it looks to me like the distribution is a bit negatively skewed—there's a slightly longer tail on the left side of the distribution than the right side. Is it too skewed to be considered normally distributed? And what about the highest point in the distribution? The distribution doesn't look completely flat, but is it too high—peaking like a very steep mountain? My eyeballing of the descriptive statistics and histogram doesn't convince even me that the data conform to the normal distribution model. Fortunately, there's a statistic called the Shapiro–Wilk test that allows a researcher to determine the likelihood of a dataset being normally

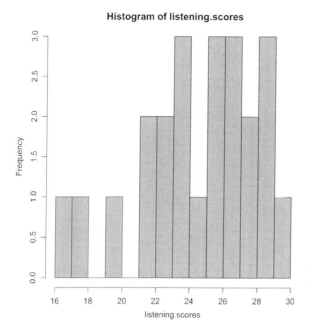

FIGURE 2.15 Frequency Distribution of 23 Listening Test Scores

distributed. The Shapiro–Wilk test statistic is appropriate with 200 or fewer participants (Field, Miles, & Field, 2012, p. 182), though when there's a very small number of participants, 30 or fewer, it isn't very rigorous and should be used in conjunction with careful review of the descriptive statistics and histograms of the data.

The Shapiro–Wilk Test of Normality

R can be used to calculate the Shapiro–Wilk test. It's represented by an uppercase W in the R output and is accompanied in the output by the *exact probability* of the W value. When the exact probability, indicated as p, is equal to or greater than .05, one can be 95% certain that the data *are* normally distributed.[8] When p is less than .05, one can be 95% certain that the data *are not* normally distributed (Field et al., 2012, p. 182). In Box 2.9, I demonstrate how to use R to calculate the Shapiro–Wilk test statistic for the set of 23 listening scores displayed in Figure 2.15 (the dataset itself can be found in the resource section of the companion website www.routledge.com/cw/turner).

The Shapiro–Wilk test value, W, is interpreted by examining its p-value. As I said, a p-value equal to or greater than .05 indicates we can be 95% certain that

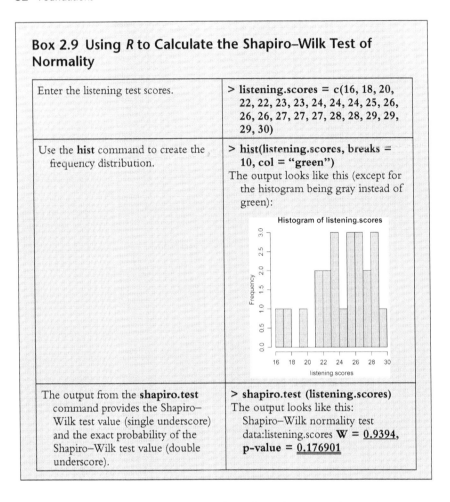

Box 2.9 Using *R* to Calculate the Shapiro–Wilk Test of Normality

Enter the listening test scores.	> **listening.scores = c(16, 18, 20, 22, 22, 23, 23, 24, 24, 24, 25, 26, 26, 26, 27, 27, 27, 28, 28, 29, 29, 29, 30)**
Use the **hist** command to create the frequency distribution.	> **hist(listening.scores, breaks = 10, col = "green")** The output looks like this (except for the histogram being gray instead of green):
The output from the **shapiro.test** command provides the Shapiro–Wilk test value (single underscore) and the exact probability of the Shapiro–Wilk test value (double underscore).	> **shapiro.test (listening.scores)** The output looks like this: Shapiro–Wilk normality test data:listening.scores **W = <u>0.9394</u>, p-value = <u>0.176901</u>**

the data *are* normally distributed; a *p*-value of less than .05 indicates that we can be 95% certain that the data *are not* normally distributed. The *p*-value 0.1746901 is greater than .05, so it indicates that there's 95% certainty the scores are normally distributed (Field et al., 2012, p. 182). If you'd like a practice problem for calculating and interpreting the Shapiro–Wilk test statistic, try Practice Problem 19.

The Test of Skewedness and the Test of Kurtosis

Field and colleagues (2012) note that the Shapiro–Wilk test is appropriate to use with small datasets, less than 200.[9] However, when there are more than 200 cases in a dataset, the researcher should check two features of the distribution separately rather than use the Shapiro–Wilk test. The first of these two features is *skewedness*, the extent to which the data are pulled toward one end of the distribution or the other. The second is *kurtosis*, which is the extent to which the shape of the distribution is too flat or too sharply peaked.

One of the things I like about *R* is that users contribute to its development. Many individual *R* users have created and shared command strings for calculating statistics. Some of these command strings are encapsulated in simple commands, like the **sd** command for calculating the standard deviation (see Box 2.3) and the **shapiro.test** command for the Shapiro–Wilk test (Box 2.9), and are automatically downloaded and installed with *R*. Other commands reside in packages that can be downloaded and added to *R*. In Box 2.10, I explain how to install a package called *pastecs* that can be used to calculate skewedness and kurtosis. The *pastecs* package includes the command **stat.desc**, which produces most of the descriptive statistics for a set of data as well as testing skewedness and kurtosis. In Box 2.10, I illustrate how to use *R* to calculate skewedness and kurtosis.

Regarding interpretation of both the skewedness and kurtosis statistics, Field et al. (2012) report that "the further the value is from zero, the more likely it is that the data are not normally distributed" (p. 176). Additionally, when the skewedness value is positive, there are more scores at the low end of the distribution than expected; when the skewedness value is negative, there are more scores at the high end than expected. When the kurtosis value is positive the peak of the distribution is higher than expected for a normal distribution; when the kurtosis value is negative, the distribution is flatter than expected. That's a lot of information, but how much difference from zero indicates that a distribution is *too* skewed or *too* peaked to be considered normally distributed?

The information about the z-scale that you encountered earlier in this chapter is relevant to interpreting *R*'s skewedness and kurtosis output. Recall that 95% of the values in a normal distribution fall between z-scores of -1.96 and $+1.96$. If you recall that fact, you probably also remember that 99% of the values in a normal distribution fall between z-scores of -2.58 and $+2.58$. Maybe you even remember that 99.9% fall between z-scores of -3.29 and $+3.29$. The skewedness and kurtosis values that *R* provides are converted to z-scores, and *R* provides a value labeled *skew.2SE* and a value labeled *kurt.2SE* to facilitate the interpretation of skewedness and kurtosis.[10]

To interpret either *skew.2SE* or *kurt.2Se*, the first step is to remove the positive or negative sign and look at the absolute value. When the absolute value of *skew.2SE* is greater than 1, there's about 95% certainty that the distribution is skewed. When the absolute value of *kurt.2SE* is greater than 1, there's about 95% certainty that the distribution is too peaked or too flat to be considered normally distributed. Field et al. (2012, p. 175) note that for small groups (fewer than 200 participants), interpreting kurtosis and skewedness at 95% certainty is sufficiently rigorous, though a researcher with 200 or more participants should interpret kurtosis and skewedness at 99.9% certainty. In Box 2.10, I explain how to use *R* to determine the skewedness and kurtosis of a set of scores.

Box 2.10 Adding a Package to *R* and Using *R* to Calculate Kurtosis, Skewedness, and the Shapiro–Wilk Statistic

Install the "pastecs" package. You'll need to select a Comprehensive R Archive Network (CRAN) site when *R* prompts you to do so. (I usually use one of the California sites because that's where I live.)	> **install.packages ("pastecs")** The **install.packages ("pastecs")** output will look something like this: package "pastecs" successfully unpacked and MD5 sums checked. The downloaded packages are in [file directory information for where the package is located]
Use the **library** command to put the downloaded package into *R*'s library of packages so it's available for use. Note: There are *no* double quotation marks in the **library** command!	> **library(pastecs)**
Enter the listening test scores.	> **listening.scores = c(16, 18, 20, 22, 22, 23, 23, 24, 24, 24, 25, 26, 26, 26, 27, 27, 27, 28, 28, 29, 29, 29, 30)**
Take a look at the frequency distribution using the **hist** command.	> **hist(listening.scores, breaks = 10, col = "green")** The output looks like this: Histogram of listening.scores Frequency / listening scores
The output from the **stat.desc** command string provides most of the descriptive statistics, a measure of skewness, a measure of kurtosis, *and* the Shapiro–Wilk statistic when **norm = TRUE** is specified. The **norm = TRUE** component of the command instructs *R* to perform analyses indicating whether the dataset is normally distributed.	> **stat.desc (listening.scores, norm = TRUE)** This command provides many statistics— among them are: minimum maximum range sum 16 30 14 573 median mean variance 26 24.9130435 13.1739130 standard deviation (std.dev) 3.6295886

(*Continued*)

Box 2.10 (*Continued*)

	skewednesss skew2SE −0.7241345 −0.7522121 kurtosis kurt2SE −0.2192648 −0.1172835 normtest.W (the Shapiro–Wilk statistic) 0.9394267 probability level for the Shapiro–Wilk value 0.1746901
Adding the **basic = FALSE** component to the command removes several basic statistics from the output so the output is a bit less cluttered.	**> stat.desc (listening.scores, norm = TRUE, basic = FALSE)** Among the statistics produced by this command string are: median mean std.dev 26.0000000 24.9130435 3.6295886 skewedness skew2SE −0.7241345 −0.7522121 kurtosis kurt2SE −0.2192648 −0.1172835 normtest.W (Shapiro–Wilk value) 0.9394267 normtest.p (probability of Shapiro–Wilk value) 0.1746901
Field et al. (2012, p. 176) give the command for rounding output to a specified number of places. I illustrate with a command specifying that the output be limited to two decimal places.	**> round (stat.desc (listening.scores, norm = TRUE, basic = FALSE), digits = 2)** The output includes this information: median mean std.dev 26.00 24.91 3.63 skewness skew2SE −0.72 −0.75 kurtosis kurt2SE −0.22 −0.12 normtest.W 0.94 normtest.p 0.17

To interpret the *R* output, I first take a look at skewedness. The skewedness value (rounded to two decimal places) is −0.72 and the skew2SE value is −0.75. The negative sign on the skewedness value indicates that there are slightly more scores at the high end of the distribution than there would be if the data were normally distributed—I think that skewedness can be seen in the frequency distribution itself (see Figure 2.15). The skew2SE value is interpreted by first removing the positive or negative sign; that is, the absolute value of the skew2SE value is interpreted. The absolute value of skew2SE, 0.75, is *less* than 1, so according to Field and colleagues (2012), there's 95% certainty that the listening scores are normally distributed, despite there being slightly more scores at the high end of the distribution.

The kurtosis value is −0.22 and the kurt2SE value is −0.12. The negative sign on the kurtosis value indicates that the distribution is slightly flatter than it would be if it were normally distributed, but I don't perceive this slight flattening when I examine the frequency distribution of the data in Figure 2.15, do you? The absolute value of kurt2SE is 0.12 (less than 1), so it indicates that the listening scores approximate to a normal distribution despite the distribution being slightly flatter than the normal distribution model. In summary, our interpretation of the skewedness and kurtosis confirms what the Shapiro–Wilk statistic told us—we can be reasonably confident that the listening scores conform to the normal distribution model.

If you'd like to try using *R* to calculate skewedness and kurtosis, see Practice Problem 20.

R Commands Introduced in Chapter Two (In the Order Introduced)

variable.name = c ("value 1", "value 2", "value 3") This command is used to enter nominal data directly into *R*.

variable.name = c (1, 2, 2) This command is used to enter ordinal or interval data directly into *R*.

table (variable.name) This command creates a table in the *R* output.

barplot (table (variable.name)) This command creates a barplot. A main title, a label for the x-axis, a label for the *y*-axis, and a color for the bars can be added.

barplot (table (variable.name), main = "Main Title", xlab = "Label for the x-axis", ylab = "Label for the y-axis", col = "color's.name") This command creates a barplot. A main title, a label for the *x*-axis, a label for the *y*-axis, and a color for the bars can be added.

pie (table (variable.name) This command creates a pie chart. A main title can be added.

pie (table (variable.name), main = "Main Title") This command creates a pie chart. A main title can be added.

hist (variable.name) This command creates a histogram. A main title, a label for the *x*-axis, a label for the *y*-axis, and color can be added. A specific number of breaks can also be added.

hist (variable.name, main = "Main Title", xlab = "Label for the x-axis", ylab = "Label for the y-axis", col = "color's.name", breaks = number) This command creates a histogram. A main title, a label for the *x*-axis, a label for the *y*-axis, and color can be added. A specific number of breaks can also be added.

sum (variable.name) The command adds the values of the variable and reports the sum.

length (variable.name) This command reports the number of values for the variable that's specified (the *n* size).

summary (variable.name) This command gives the minimum score, the maximum score, the mean, the median, and the 1st and 3rd quartile scores for a set of scores.

subset (table (variable.name), table (variable.name)==max (table (variable.name))) This command reports the mode for the variable. Note that the command includes two equal signs with no space between them.

mean (variable.name) This command reports the mean of the variable values.

sd (variable.name) This command reports the standard deviation of the variable values.

shapiro.test (variable.name) This command reports the observed value of the Shapiro–Wilk test and the exact probability of the observed value of the statistic. The Shapiro–Wilk statistic tests the data to determine whether the values are normally distributed.

install.packages ("name.of.package") This command is the first in a set of two that installs a package of additional commands (retrieved from the *R* site) into *R*.

library (name.of.package) This command is the second in a set of two that installs a package of additional commands (retrieved from the *R* site) into *R*. Note that there are no double quotation marks in the **library** command.

stat.desc (variable.name, norm = TRUE, basic = FALSE) This command resides in the *pastecs* package and, once installed, reports most of the descriptive statistics for the variable, an analysis of the skewedness of the distribution of scores, an analysis of the kurtosis of the distribution of scores, and the Shapiro–Wilk value.

round (stat.desc (variable.name, norm = TRUE, basic = FALSE), digits = 2) This command, when used with the **stat.desc** command, rounds the values of each reported statistic to two decimal places.

number ^2 This is a mathematical operation command and reports the squared value of the number that precedes it.

sqrt (number) This is a mathematical operation command and reports the square root of the number that follows it in parentheses.

Practice Problems for Chapter Two

An answer key is available on the companion website (www.routledge.com/cw/turner).

Practicing the Concepts—Variables and Scales

1. Here are some variables one might consider if doing research to explore the conditions for optimal language learning. Be prepared to discuss what type of scale might be used in defining the levels of each: nominal, ordinal, or interval.

Variable name	Type of scale
Native language of learner	_____
Language learning aptitude	_____
Language ability	_____
Learner's age	_____
Learner's sex	_____
Learner's personality	_____
Teacher's experience	_____
Teacher's education	_____
Teacher's personality	_____
Class meeting time	_____
Frequency of class	_____
Duration of class	_____
Configuration of seats	_____

2. Name two additional variables of each type (nominal, ordinal, and interval) that occur to you when you think about doing research in a classroom.

   Two nominal variables:
   Two ordinal variables:
   Two interval variables:

Practicing the Concepts—Measures of Central Tendency and Dispersion

Study A. A Spanish vocabulary test was given to a group of Spanish-speaking first-graders. The school district requires you to provide the mean and standard deviation for your students. Complete the chart below to guide your computation of these values.

X	$(X - \overline{X})$	$(X - \overline{X})^2$
41		
33		
32		
29		
27		
27		
26		
24		
19		
19		
18		
17		
14		

3. What is the mean? _____

4. What is the mode? _____

5. What is the median? _____

6. What is the range? _____

7. What is the standard deviation? _____

8. Draw the frequency distribution.

Study B. Here are the scores for a reading quiz you gave in your class. Use R for this problem.

88	87	54	97	34
78	56	99	87	73
74	69	85	87	86
87				

9. Make a frequency distribution of the data.

10. Calculate the mean.

11. Calculate the standard deviation.

12. Report the mode.

13. Report the median.

14. What is the range?

Practicing the Concepts—Standardized Scores

When scores are in a normal distribution, that fact can be used to regularize them; that is, to convert the scores from the raw score scale to a recognized standardized scale, so the scores from different tests (or test forms) can be directly compared even when the number of points on the different tests, the means, and the standard deviations are different. Keep in mind that scores can be standardized only when they are in a normal distribution because the process relies on the defined characteristics of a normal distribution.

Here is some test performance information.

Midterm test	Final test
Mean = 47	Mean = 51
$s = 3$	$s = 6$
$n = 45$	$n = 43$
$k = 100$	$k = 100$
Rob's score = 53	Rob's score = 53
Michael's score = 39	Michael's score = 49

15. Calculate percentages for Rob's and Michael's midterm scores and final scores.

16. Calculate the z-scores for Rob's and Michael's midterm scores and final scores.

17. Convert the z-scores to the T-scale or the CEEB scale—you decide which scale seems more useful.

18. Be prepared to discuss how you would explain the outcomes to Rob and Michael (and their parents) as well as to your colleagues.

Practicing the Concepts—Checking a Distribution for Normality Using R

19. Enter the Spanish vocabulary test scores from Practice Problem 1 and calculate and interpret the Shapiro–Wilk test to determine whether the data are normally distributed.

20. Load the *pastecs* package into *R* and calculate skewedness and kurtosis.

Notes

1 *R* users who are programmers will probably be more comfortable using > instead of the equal sign (=); however, in all of the examples presented in this text, the equal sign is unambiguous—and I am not a programmer by profession—so I use the equal sign.
2 When many levels of the variables at the top or bottom of the distribution are empty, the scale can be truncated by omitting these empty categories, but the empty categories between the lowest and highest scores can't be eliminated.
3 In some statistics texts, the formula for the mean includes additional information and looks like this:

$$\overline{X} = \frac{\sum_{i=1}^{n} X_i}{n}$$

The X_i and the $\sum_{i=1}^{n}$ components simply indicate that each individual's score is included in the calculation. I use the simpler style for most of the formulas in this text.
4 In-text explanations, I'll generally round decimal places to the hundredth position, so 17.2857 is rounded to 17.29.
5 Some people add one to the difference between the highest and lowest scores, but in *R* and several other statistical software programs, one isn't added to the difference. Because I'm using *R*, I decided to use the highest lowest definition of range as *R* does.
6 The sum of these squared values is called the *sum of squared errors*, an important concept in the calculation of some parametric statistics.
7 They need to confirm that the mean, mode, and median are approximately equal, the peak of the distribution isn't too high, the two tails of the distribution are similarly extended, and there aren't any outliers.
8 Readers who have studied statistical logic and understand the function of the null hypothesis and the alternative hypothesis in statistical reasoning will find it useful to know that the null hypothesis for the Shapiro–Wilk statistic is that the data are normally distributed. The alternative hypothesis is that the data are not normally distributed.
9 In psychology, Andy Field's discipline, 200 participants is considered "small;" many researchers in language education would consider 200 to be a huge number of participants!

10 The skewedness and kurtosis statistics are interpreted by converting them to z-scores. Field et al. (2012, pp. 174–5) note that the values of *skew.2SE* and *kurt.2SE* are, respectively, the value of the skewedness statistic divided by two standard errors and the value of the kurtosis statistic divided by two standard errors. (*Standard error* is a concept similar to *standard deviation* but refers to a population rather than a smaller sample.) Because the formula for converting the raw skewedness value to a z-score is $\dfrac{skewedness - 0}{SE_{skewed}}$

and the formula for converting the raw kurtosis value to a z-score is $\dfrac{kurtosis - 0}{SE_{kurtosis}}$,

when *skew.2SE* and *kurt.2SE* are less than approximately 1, there's about 95% certainty that the data are normally distributed. When they're less than 1.29, there's about 99% certainty that the data are normally distributed, and when they're less than 1.65, there's about 99.9% certainty that the data are normally distributed.

3

DESIGNING SOUND RESEARCH— VARIABLE ROLES, THREATS TO VALIDITY, AND RESEARCH DESIGN

As I noted in Chapter One, research should be readable by the intended audience. Well-written research conforms to the conventions of the genre so readers don't have to figure out how the information is structured as well as what the author did and discovered; well-written research also reflects the author's awareness of readers' background in the level of detail and the clarity of the explanations. However, readers are also concerned about the quality and usefulness of studies and the possible applicability of research findings to their own settings. Three topics related to research quality and usefulness are addressed in this chapter: (1) the types of roles variables may take in statistical research, (2) common threats to the soundness and usefulness of research and techniques for reducing their possible impact on research study validity, and (3) features of the major types of research design and the relationship between these features and the interpretation of research findings. I think familiarity with these design-related features of statistical research is important for both readers and authors so they can evaluate others' research and carry out and report sound research of their own.

Variable Roles

In statistical research, variables have specific roles because the goals of statistical research include investigating whether there is a relationship between variables or whether one or more variables have an effect on some other variable or variables. All but one of the statistical formulas[1] you'll study in this text require at least two variables—an *independent variable* and a *dependent variable*—and almost all statistical research has at least one independent and one dependent variable. Many statistical research studies have more than one independent or dependent variable.

In addition to the required independent and dependent variables, a study might also have one or more *moderator variables* and *control variables*. All studies have other variables too—variables that aren't studied but have an impact on the outcomes of the research. These unstudied variables, which have an unexamined impact on the outcomes of the research, are *confounding variables*. They present threats to the soundness and usefulness of a research study. In the discussion that follows, I define and illustrate each of the four types of assigned roles for variables and then discuss several named threats to the soundness and usefulness of research studies.

Independent Variables

An independent variable is one whose levels are systematically manipulated, identified, or selected by the researcher to determine its relationship to another variable or to investigate its effect on another variable. For example, for a researcher who wants to investigate the relationship between *student learning style* and *performance in an intensive foreign language program*, makes the independent variable *student learning style* when and because the researcher systematically selects or identifies people of different learning styles to participate in the study. In this example study, the researcher asked all of the students in an intensive language program to complete a learning style inventory to identify each learner's dominant learning style: visual, auditory, or kinesthetic. At the end of the intensive language program, the researcher administered a final language test as a measure of *performance in an intensive foreign language program*. The researcher sorted the participants into groups according to their dominant learning styles and compared the *performance* of the groups to determine whether there was a difference among the three groups formed by dominant learning styles. *Student learning style* is the independent variable in this study because the researcher systematically identified the learners' dominant style and investigated whether people with different learning styles tended to have different learning outcomes.

Another researcher might investigate the effect of *type of oral practice (paired versus threesome)* on *quality of students' performance in a role play*. In this study, *type of oral practice* is the independent variable when and because the researcher manipulates the type of oral practice the participants engage in, paired practice or threesome practice. In the first half of the course, some of the students practice their oral skills in paired activities and some of the students practice their oral skills in groups of three. In the second half of the course, the students who had paired practice work in groups of three and the students who had practiced in threesomes practice in pairs. At several points during the course, the researcher systematically observes and evaluates the students as they participate in role plays and compares the *quality of students' performance* when they're practicing in pairs to the *quality of students' performance* when they're practicing in threesomes. The independent variable is *type of oral practice* because the researcher manipulates the type of practice to determine whether it has an effect on the learners' performance in role plays.

Dependent Variables

The *dependent variable* in a statistical study is the variable that's systematically observed or measured to determine its possible relationship or response to the independent variable. The dependent variable outcomes are related to or affected by the independent variable. In the first study mentioned above, the dependent variable is *performance in an intensive foreign language class* because students' performance in the program is systematically measured to investigate the strength of the relationship between the independent variable (*student learning style*) and *performance*. The researcher explores whether performance in learning a foreign language is dependent upon student learning style. In the second study, the dependent variable is *quality of students' performance in a role play* because the quality of the students' performance is systematically observed to determine whether the *type of oral practice* has an impact or effect on *the quality of students' performance in role plays*.

Moderator and Control Variables

As Hatch and Lazaraton (1991) noted, researchers sometimes create special secondary independent variables. These secondary independent variables are known as *moderator variables*. For the study described above, in which the effect of *type of oral practice* on the *quality of students' performance in role plays* is investigated, the researchers' main interest is whether students who practice language in pairs ultimately perform differently in role plays than those who practice in threesomes. However, the researcher could add another variable, one that represents a secondary interest. The researcher might think, for example, that the sex of a student could interact with *type of oral practice*, resulting in different *quality of performance in role plays* depending on the participant's sex. If sex is a moderator variable in this study, both men and women must be included in each level of the independent variable, *type of oral practice*; there must be both men and women who work in pairs and men and women who work in threesomes. The researcher will collect data from both the men and the women so their relative success in the different *types of oral practice* can be investigated. *Sex* functions as a moderator variable, a secondary independent variable, one whose levels are systematically manipulated, identified, or selected to investigate the effect on the dependent variable.

A *control variable* is similar to a moderator variable in that the researcher believes it might have an impact on the outcome of the study. However, instead of systematically including participants representing all of the levels of the moderator variable (both men and women, for example), only one level of the variable is represented in the study. When sex is a *control variable,* only men or only women are participants in the study. When a control variable is created, the interpretation of the research results is necessarily limited, so if *sex* is a control variable and only women are included as participants, the interpretation of the findings should be limited to women. Of course, if *sex* is a control variable and only men are included in the study, the interpretation of the findings is similarly limited to men.

Threats to Research Study Soundness and Usefulness

Hatch and Lazaraton (1991) define *intervening variable* as "a variable that was not [intentionally] included in the study" (p. 67) but has an unstudied impact or effect on the dependent variable or variables. I prefer the term *confounding variable* for these unstudied variables. In the research on the possible effect of type of oral practice on students' performance in a role play, an additional variable, *amount of training in drama,* might be considered a confounding variable when the impact of the students' possible training in drama is neither moderated (investigated systematically) nor constrained (as would be the case if it were a control variable). Some participants might have had drama instruction and some might not—some might be completely unaccustomed to speaking before an audience and some might be professional performers! Whether the participants had previous training and experience is likely to have an effect on students' role play performance, regardless of the type of oral practice they have.

I think of confounding variables as the bad guys in research because they have an unstudied, unpredictable, and unwanted effect on the results of a research project. A confounding variable is by definition one that's not intentionally included in the study—it doesn't have an assigned role—though when designing a study, potentially confounding variables can be identified and constrained by turning them into moderator variables or control variables, or by the way participants are selected and through the design or configuration of the research setting. For example, in the study on the effect of type of oral practice on students' role play performance, if I think that a participant's dramatic training might have an impact on role play performance, I could ask participants whether they've had any dramatic training and make certain to include both experienced and inexperienced performers. I could then analyze whether experienced and inexperienced performers have different outcomes when they practice in pairs versus in threesomes. In this case, I've created a moderator variable, *amount of training in drama.* Alternatively, I could constrain the possible confounding effect of the variable *amount of training in drama* by excluding people with dramatic training from the study, thus creating a control variable.

This might be a good place to take a break and practice these concepts (Practice Problems 1 through 7) before reading about confounding variables and research study validity.

Research Study Validity

Confounding variables present threats to both the soundness and the usefulness of a research study, the two aspects of research study validity. Research study validity can be examined from two perspectives—*internal validity* and *external validity*. Internal validity relates specifically to the soundness or integrity of a study; that is, the extent to which the findings are due to the variables with assigned roles— the independent, dependent, moderator, and control variables. External validity relates to the usefulness of a study—the extent to which the findings of the study are applicable outside the context of the study. In small-scale language education research, external validity is usually not a great concern because the researchers' primary goal is to gain a deeper understanding of the local learning environment, but internal validity, the soundness of a study, is always an important consideration.

Threats to the internal validity, the soundness, of a study are numerous, and any threat to the internal validity of a study also limits the external validity of the study. Consider this example from the program evaluation of a new content-based language curriculum for a summer intensive language program at a university. The design of the evaluation research called for a pretest, and as the research assistant I traveled to Japan to administer the three-hour pretest to the Japanese participants in the study. I don't have words to express how hot and humid it was on the day of the pretest. The test was given in an auditorium with no ventilation or windows. Neither the testtakers nor the test administrator were allowed to drink or eat anything in the auditorium and no one was allowed to leave during the test. No one fainted—we all survived—but it was definitely not an ideal test administration environment! In contrast, the weather was perfectly pleasant on the day of the posttest, which was administered three months later, after the participants had completed the content-based course.

When the researchers compared the participants' pretest performance to their posttest performance, they found that most of the students showed an impressive gain in their language skills; the participants had *much* higher scores on the posttest than they did on the pretest. The researchers were excited, certain they had clear evidence of the effectiveness of the new content-based curriculum. I had to remind them that the pretest environment was so uncomfortable it could have had an adverse impact on the test takers' performance. The internal validity of the evaluation study was seriously threatened by this naturally occurring phenomenon, the high temperature and humidity on the day of the pretest. Due to this threat to the internal validity of the study, the generalizability of the study is also limited; we can't apply the findings of the study to other settings. We can't assume that completing a content-based course like the one in the study is going to result in a huge improvement in students' language skills because we can't be certain whether the results of the original study were due to the type of curriculum—or the weather.

Some threats to validity, primarily those related to the selection of the participants or features of the research setting, are directly related to the external validity, or generalizability, of a study. For example, in the past, research done on new pharmaceutical drugs was typically conducted with adults as opposed to children. Adults were identified or selected to participate in these studies for a number of ethical, legal, and practical reasons and it was assumed that the drugs would work for children as they do for adults, once dosages were adjusted for children's smaller size. Recent research has revealed, however, that some medicines work very differently for children than for adults, and a medicine determined to be safe and effective for adults can't be assumed to be safe and effective for children. Participant selection directly threatens the external validity of the results—we can't assume that the findings for adult participants can be applied to children.

Threats to validity come from three broad areas: characteristics of the participants (the manner in which they are selected and their feelings and behaviors); features of the data collection tools or procedures; and features of the environment or setting in which the research takes place. Some threats to validity occur so frequently or are so remarkable that they've been given names, though most threats are unnamed. In the discussion that follows, I discuss the three sources of threats and comment on some of the named threats and concerns in these areas.

Issues Related to the Participants

Participant-related threats to the internal and external validity of a study come from characteristics of the participants, the manner in which they were selected, and their feelings or behaviors.

Participant selection—how participants are selected—limits external validity to the extent that the selection process results in the participants being idiosyncratic. In some types of research, external validity isn't a concern, because the goal of the research is to gain a deeper understanding of a particular learning environment. However, in some research, the primary goal is to apply the findings to a population; in this research it's a problem if the researchers use a *convenience sample.* A convenience sample is a group of participants readily available for some reason, perhaps because they're in the researcher's or a colleague's class; the generalizability of the findings is limited by the extent to which the convenience sample, the class, is unique. Another researcher might try to avoid the limitations of a convenience sample and recruit volunteers, but the generalizability of research done with volunteer participants is limited by the fact that the participants *are* volunteers—they aren't representative of people who don't volunteer.

Random selection of participants from a population of possible participants, in combination with random assignment of the selected participants to the levels of the independent variable, minimizes the threat presented by how participants are selected, but random selection and random assignment usually aren't necessary in small-scale language education research because generalizability is not the primary goal. Instead, researchers often rely on detailed descriptions of the participants so readers can determine the extent to which they can incorporate what they learned from the study into their personal knowledge systems and decide whether they might apply the findings in their own teaching environments.

Differential attrition presents a threat to the internal validity of an experimental study and its generalizability because the number of participants who drop out of the study varies across the experimental conditions. Consider this example. A researcher is investigating whether using Total Physical Response (TPR) helps young children learn a second language and forms two instructional groups with 15 children in each class—one class receives TPR-based lessons and the other doesn't. At the conclusion of the study, the TPR class still has 15 students but the other class has only 8. If the researcher compares the performance of these two groups, differential attrition threatens the soundness of the findings, because the results may be impacted by the fact that more students stayed in one class than the other. Differential attrition may occur despite a researcher's efforts to prevent it. The extent to which the researcher can determine the reasons for participants' leaving the study and report this information, however, may be helpful for interpreting the results of the study.

Maturation is a named threat that relates to the extent to which the results of a study are due to the cognitive development of the participants as opposed to the variables with assigned roles. Though primarily a concern in longitudinal studies involving young participants, I think cognitive development may be a factor in some studies of adult learners of second languages, especially if one accepts that a possible benefit of learning a second language is enhanced cognitive abilities. The threat presented by maturation is often addressed by ensuring at the outset of a study that the participants in the non-experimental and experimental groups are similar in all relevant ways. The maturation threat is not removed, but we assume that participants in both the experimental and non-experimental conditions show similar maturation and any differences between the groups at the conclusion of the study are due to the variables with assigned roles.

History is another named threat. I think its name is deceptive, so I mention it here; the term refers to threats presented by participants' involvement in activities concurrent with rather than previous to the study in question. A history threat is presented, for example, if some participants in a study on rate of learning have private tutors *while* involved in the research; the participants' having had private tutors *before* their involvement in a study is not a history threat (though their having had tutors before their participation might threaten the validity of a study in different ways). History threats are an important factor in small-scale language education research because the research takes place in naturally occurring environments rather than in laboratories. The extent to which researchers can identify and report on participants' concurrent activities, perhaps through interviews with the participants, may help the researcher and readers of the research interpret the results of the study.

The *Hawthorne effect* is another named threat to validity. The Hawthorne effect operates when the participants' behavior in a study is affected positively either by the attention they receive as participants or by some other perceived benefit rather than by the variables with assigned roles. For example, imagine that I'm interested in exploring how to improve education in a developing country where a lack of easily accessible, inexpensive transportation to school prevents many children from attending regularly. I decide to give one group of children a simple, easy-to-maintain bicycle and bicycle riding lessons so they can ride to school. As the study unfolds, I notice that the children who received the bicycles seem be doing very well in school—better than their peers who weren't given bicycles. However, I notice that many of the children who received bicycles still have irregular attendance—so why are they doing better in school than their peers? It's possible that the Hawthorne effect threatens the validity of this study. Perhaps the children feel important, valued, and appreciated because they received something they perceive to be very valuable, the bicycle and the riding lessons, and their enhanced performance in school is due to their changed self-perception, their feeling appreciated, worthy, and special, rather than the fact that they can get to school regularly with less effort. One solution to the Hawthorne effect might be to identify children who don't have a transportation problem and compare their performance in school to those who do; participants who represent the different levels of the variable are identified and relevant data are simply collected and examined without the direct involvement of the participants. Other threats to the validity of the study are presented by this different design, but the Hawthorne effect would be eliminated.

The *halo effect* presents a threat to validity of a study when the participants respond or behave as they do because they like the researcher, or in the case of action research, they particularly like the teacher/researcher. In experimental research in which participants receive different types of instruction, the halo effect could be constrained by having the same teacher present each of the different types of instruction. Additional threats to validity are presented by this solution, though, including the possibility that teaching all of the different classes would be so exhausting that the teacher's personality would change for the worse. Alternatively, the researcher might recruit teachers who have similar experience and student evaluations, or perhaps a team-teaching approach could be used so that all of the participants encounter all of the teachers, reducing the impact of the halo effect.

When *participant expectancy* presents a threat to validity, participants change their behavior because they believe they've figured out what the researcher wants or expects, and they provide it (or deliberately don't provide it!) accordingly. When this threat occurs, the outcome of the study is impacted by these changes in the participants' behavior in addition to the variables with assigned roles. *Researcher expectancy* may have a similar impact; a researcher may see results from a particular group because he/she expects them. A *double-blind* technique is sometimes used in research in other fields, such as in pharmaceutical studies, with neither the participants nor the researchers knowing which participants receive the new medicine and which do not. This approach isn't feasible in small-scale language education research, though a researcher might be able to conduct the research at several different sites, with the participants in the different places unaware of what goes on at other sites.

Issues Related to Data Collection Tools and Procedures

The features of the tools or procedures used to collect data may also present threats to the validity of a study; two concepts are relevant—*test reliability* and *test validity*.[2]

Reliability

Because one of the defining features of research is its systematicity, the *reliability* of the data collection tools—the tests, interviews, or observation protocols that are used—is a great concern. Reliability refers to the tools' consistency of measurement. One type of reliability, *test–retest reliability,* reflects the extent to which a data collection tool is administered consistently. Clear, comprehensive directions for the administrator and research participants are essential to ensure consistency. In the Materials or Procedures section of both research proposals and research reports, relevant aspects of the administration and use of the data collection tools should be described, as Professor Borkovska did in her study that's discussed in Chapter Four.

Two additional types of reliability are related to the consistency of human scoring. Participants' scores should reflect their abilities and knowledge, not the ability of individual raters or groups of raters to apply scoring criteria equitably and consistently. *Intrarater reliability* is a measure of a single rater's consistency in applying a tool's evaluation criteria. *Interrater reliability* is a measure of the consistency of two (or more) raters. Poor intrarater or interrater reliability has an adverse impact on the internal validity of a study, and consequently on the external validity to the extent that the findings of the study are impacted. When a data collection tool is used that requires the subjective judgment of evaluators to determine participants' scores, the researcher should be certain that the evaluation criteria are clear and the evaluators are trained; evidence to support the rater reliability should be reported in the Materials section of research proposals and reports.

Consistency of measurement is also a concern when researchers use different forms of a test, such as Form A as a pretest and Form B of the same test as a posttest. The extent to which the two forms of a test measure similarly—the extent to which they're interchangeable—is a concept known as *equivalent form reliability.* When using multiple forms of a published, commercially available test, a researcher should review and report the publisher's information on the test's equivalent form reliability. When using multiple forms of an unpublished test, the researcher should describe how the equivalence of the forms was established. This information, too, is typically included in the Materials section of research proposals and research reports.

The fifth type of reliability, *internal consistency*, is particularly important when a researcher uses a norm-referenced test, which is designed to yield a normal distribution of scores when given to its intended audience. Conceptually, internal consistency is the extent to which the points on an interval scale measure consistently—the extent to which items on a test measure in a similar fashion. A practical example might help make this point clear. I have two tools that measure length—a metal tape I bought at a hardware store and an antique cloth tape my grandmother gave me. When measuring things, I usually use the cloth tape because it reminds me of my grandmother and it has a pretty embroidered case, but I use the metal tape as a backup. I wanted to replace a length of damaged baseboard, so I got out my grandmother's cloth tape and measured the damaged segment. When I measured and cut a length of new baseboard, I used the metal tape—I didn't want to cut my grandmother's tape by accident. When I tried to fit the new baseboard into place, I discovered it was too long. The problem could have been worse—the piece I cut could have been too short—but what had happened? I examined the cloth tape closely and discovered that it was showing its age—some parts of it had weakened and stretched. In one section of the tape, the inches had stretched to almost 1¼ inches; in another, they were only a little more than an inch, but all of the inches were slightly different lengths. The differences were small, but the measurement units, the inches marked on the tape, didn't measure consistently. I realized that when the internal consistency of the measurement units mattered, I would have to use the metal tape. With norm-referenced tests, the internal consistency matters and should be high, showing that the units of measurement are equidistant and measure similarly.[3] In the Materials section of a research report, the researcher should report evidence of the data collection tools' internal consistency when the tools are norm-referenced.

Validity

The appropriateness and accuracy, or *validity*, of the tools used to collect data are also a concern. The data that are collected must really tell us something about the variable in question. You may be familiar with the quantitative section of the Graduate Records Examination (GRE)—do you think it would be a good measure of the *mathematics skills* of high school sophomores? I don't—because although the GRE measures examinees' mathematics skills and quantitative abilities, the intended audience for the test consists of applicants to graduate studies, not sophomores in high school. There's research to support the usefulness of the GRE for admissions to some graduate programs (Kuncel, Hezlett, & Ones, 2001), but there's no evidence to support its use for measuring the mathematical skill of sophomores in high school. The appropriateness of the data collection tools chosen or developed by a researcher should be addressed in the Materials section of both the proposal and the research report through discussion of research that supports the relevance and usefulness of the tools—this information might also appear in the literature review. When the tools are developed by the researcher, the Materials section of the proposal and report should include a thorough description of the tools' development and any research that the researcher did to assemble evidence of their appropriateness.[4]

Other Tool-Related Concerns

Among the many other threats to research study validity presented by the data collection instruments is the *practice effect*. The practice effect is a concern in pretest-posttest designs that require participants to take the same test more than once. When the same form of a test is used as both the pretest and the posttest, some participants may perform better on the posttest simply because they previously encountered the material—for them, the pretest was a chance to practice, and as a consequence they perform differently on the posttest than they would have if they hadn't taken the pretest. The practice effect has a direct impact on the internal validity of a study because the findings are influenced by the participants' familiarity with the data collection tool rather than by the variables with assigned roles. Using equivalent forms of a test as the pretest and posttest is a strategy for reducing the threat presented by the practice effect, though as discussed above there must be evidence of equivalent form reliability. Alternatively, some researchers attempt to constrain the possibility of a practice effect by designing their studies with a rather long period of time between the pretest and posttest, though there is no consensus on the optimal length of the interval.

Another named threat presented by data collection tools is the *reactivity effect*. The reactivity effect is a threat when a data collection tool causes the participants in a study to behave differently than they would have if they hadn't encountered that tool. For example, asking participants in a study to complete a questionnaire on how they prepare for taking exams might raise the participants' awareness of their approach to exam preparation or present them with exam preparation options that wouldn't have occurred to them if they hadn't completed the questionnaire. This new awareness might result in the participants' changing their exam preparation approach and performing better on a test that's used later in the study than they would have if they hadn't completed the questionnaire. The reactivity effect threatens the study's internal validity to the extent that changes in the participants' performance are due to encountering the questionnaire rather than the variables in the study with assigned roles. To some unknown extent, the results of the study are contaminated by the fact that the participants completed the questionnaire, so both the soundness of the study and its generalizability are threatened. In an attempt to counteract a possible reactivity effect, researchers may include non-relevant tasks (distractors) on their data collection instruments to obscure what the instruments are really intended to measure. In some cases it may also be possible for researchers to collect data at the conclusion of a study rather than initially, thus avoiding a possible reactivity effect.

Issues Related to the Research Environment

Threats to the validity of research that come from features of the environment or setting in which the research takes place can be naturally occurring or artificial.

Naturally Occurring Threats

Naturally occurring threats to validity are a concern in small-scale language education research because much of the research is done in the environments where learning and teaching take place rather than in laboratories where the features of an environment can be controlled. Features of these natural environments such as temperature, lighting, time of day, noise level, etc., threaten the soundness of the research, much as the awful heat and humidity during the administration of the pretest threatened the internal and external validity of the program evaluation study I described above. Researchers generally attempt to constrain naturally occurring threats by careful consideration of the research setting before the study begins. This initial planning may allow the researchers to address possible threats before they occur; for example, if I'd checked the weather forecast the day before that testing day in Japan, I would have learned that record-breaking heat and humidity were expected. I could have requested a room with air conditioning for the test administration site or rushed out to purchase small, battery-operated personal fans for each of the test takers—and me. But would the test takers' performance have been affected by having small personal fans?

Artificial Threats

When researchers attempt to constrain the threat of naturally occurring variables by manipulating features of an environment, as I would have if I'd given every test taker a battery-operated fan, they may create artificial threats to a study's validity. I wonder how test takers' performance on a test would be affected if the people on both sides of them were using small, battery-operated personal fans. Would the test takers' performance have been affected if the test administrator, me, had been using a little battery-operated fan while they were taking the test? Maybe requesting an air-conditioned room would have been a better solution. However, an artificially introduced threat could have occurred if the new room became too cold and the performance of some of the participants was adversely impacted because they were shivering.

It's impossible to remove all of the possible threats to the validity of a study because in attempting to do so, new ones are created. Threats to research study validity are unavoidable; all research studies have confounding variables. In the Discussion section of a research study, the researcher should note the threats that were recognized before the study was conducted and the measures that were taken to reduce them. The researcher should also comment on additional threats and shortcomings that arose so readers can judge for themselves and their own purposes how they might incorporate the findings into their own knowledge base. However, a researcher can minimize many threats through careful and appropriate design.

Research Design

Four features of research distinguish the main types of research design. The first is the presence or absence of an *experimental treatment*. The second is the presence or absence of *legitimate comparison groups*. The third is how the participants are identified (*random selection and assignment* or not). The fourth is the presence or absence of a *pretest* to verify whether there are pre-existing differences among groups. These features can be used to sort research designs into four categories: *pre-experimental, quasi-experimental, true experimental*, and *ex post facto* designs. Before describing these types of research design, I discuss each of the features that distinguish them: experimental treatment, legitimate comparison groups, random selection and assignment of participants, and pretest.

Important Distinguishing Features of Research Designs

The design of a study is critical when considering its soundness, usefulness, and generalizability. Additionally, the design of a study has an impact on how the results of a study can be interpreted. For example, a researcher who conducts a well-designed true experiment may have the basis for making causal statements about the findings—the researcher may be able to assert that the experimental treatment caused the results that were observed. In contrast, no matter how well designed an ex post facto study is, no causal statements can be made about the findings because the necessary experimental conditions aren't met. Some researchers fail to indicate the type of design for their studies, so readers of research must be familiar with the characterizing features of different types of research design so they can figure out the design of a study for themselves.

Experimental Treatment

An *experimental treatment* is an innovation or modification that the researcher introduces into the research setting to allow investigation of whether the change has an impact on the interaction of the independent and dependent variables. The experimental treatment or treatments are represented in the levels of the independent variable; in most experimental studies the unmodified condition is included as one of the levels of the independent variable. This unmodified level of the independent variable is referred to as the *non-experimental group*, or the *control group*. Take, for example, a French teacher in a school where all students of French listen to authentic radio broadcasts for 10 minutes during each class meeting (because previous research indicated that learners' pronunciation improved from listening to radio broadcasts). One teacher believes that listening to radio broadcasts 20 minutes a day might lead to even greater improvement, so he enlists the aid of one of his colleagues to investigate this possibility. The independent variable in this study is *amount of listening to authentic broadcasts in French*. His class continues to listen to authentic broadcasts for 10 minutes a day, but his colleague requires 20 minutes of exposure to authentic broadcasts for his students. One level of the independent variable is the existing condition in the classes where the students listen to authentic materials for 10 minutes each day. This is the non-experimental group. The second level of the independent variable, the experimental treatment, is reflected by the change to the existing practice: The group that experiences 20 minutes of listening to radio broadcasts during each class meeting is the experimental group. To investigate whether amount of listening to authentic radio broadcasts has an impact on accuracy of pronunciation, the researcher has to collect data in each of the two conditions—*with 10 minutes exposure to authentic spoken language* and *with 20 minutes exposure to authentic spoken language*.

The presence of an experimental treatment indicates that the researcher has chosen to use one of the three experimental designs—pre-experimental, quasi-experimental, or true experimental—rather than the fourth type of research design, ex post facto, which doesn't have an experimental treatment. Whether the study is pre-experimental, quasi-experimental, or true experimental is determined by the presence or absence of *legitimate comparison groups* and how the legitimate comparison groups are formed, through *random selection and assignment of participants to the levels of the independent variable* or through the use of a *pretest*. The discussion of these important concepts begins with legitimate comparison groups.

Legitimate Comparison Groups

The presence of legitimate comparison groups allows the researcher to investigate systematically whether an experimental treatment (represented by one of the levels of the independent variable) has an impact on the dependent variable or variables. A study has legitimate comparison groups when a procedure is followed at the outset of the study to establish the comparability of the participants in the experimental group(s) and the non-experimental group.

Establishing legitimate comparison groups can be done in two different ways. Random selection and random assignment of the participants to the levels of the independent variable is one way to ensure that the non-experimental and experimental groups are comparable to one another, though it's usually not possible—or desirable—in small-scale language education research. Instead many researchers establish legitimate comparison groups through pretesting all of the participants. They then use the pretest scores to verify that existing groups are comparable, to create comparable groups, or to statistically equate the groups.

Experimental studies that have a comparison group but involve neither random selection and assignment of participants nor a pretest don't have legitimate comparison groups. These studies are considered pre-experimental; pre-experimental studies are useful for exploratory purposes but don't allow researchers to make causal interpretations. Researchers who want to make causal interpretations of their findings need to have random selection and random assignment of participants to the levels of the independent variable or a pretest to form legitimate comparison groups.

Random Selection and Assignment of Participants

Random selection of participants and their random assignment to the levels of the independent variable result in the strongest type of experimental design, the true experiment, because the participants are considered representative of the population of interest, *and* the groups representing the levels of the independent variable are comparable.

Random selection refers to how participants in a research study are identified or selected. First, a population of possible participants is defined. According to Sprinthall (1994), a *population* is "the entire number of persons, things, or events (observations) having at least one trait in common" (p. 495). Shavelson (1996) notes that populations are "so large that all possible observations cannot be made, so a subset of observations must be drawn" (p. 214). *Ninth-graders studying Spanish in public schools in California* might be considered a population—the ninth-graders have at least one trait in common and there are many of them, more than could be included in a single study. A sample of the population, "a subset of observations," would have to be identified as participants.

When participants are selected from a population so that "every element or individual in the entire population has an equal chance of being chosen" (Sprinthall, 1994, p. 496), a *random sample* is formed. Random sampling of a population is very rare in small-scale language education research because much of the research is done in existing classrooms with the learners who are present in those classrooms. However, random selection *is* one of the defining characteristics of the strongest type of research design, the true experimental design. The other defining feature of a true experimental design is that the randomly selected participants are randomly assigned to the levels of the independent variable. Random assignment implies that every individual has an equal chance of being assigned to a particular level of the independent variable—there's no pattern to how people are assigned to the non-experimental and experimental conditions in the study. Random selection of participants and their random assignment to the experimental and non-experimental conditions ensure that (1) the participants are representative of the population and (2) the groups representing the levels of the independent variable are comparable. Random selection and assignment is considered the strongest approach to creating legitimate comparison groups because the groups are comparable and the participants are representative of the population from which they're drawn, allowing generalization of research findings to the population.

Pretest

Researchers in small-scale language education research usually can't carry out random selection and assignment of their participants because they don't have access to all members of the population of interest and can't randomly select and assign participants to the levels of the independent variable in their study. They're probably not even interested in achieving random selection and assignment because the focus of their research is typically the researchers' local setting. However, if the researchers wish to make causal interpretations of their research results, they need to establish legitimate comparison groups for their studies. Legitimate comparison groups are established through pretesting. Shavelson (1996) describes the critical features of a pretest. First, the pretest "should be the same as or parallel to the posttest," and second, the pretest "should be related to the dependent variable" (p. 22).

The French teachers mentioned above, who are interested in investigating whether learners develop more accurate pronunciation when they listen to 20 minutes of authentic radio broadcasts versus 10 minutes, certainly can't randomly select participants for their study. They teach in a particular school and the students enroll in a particular section of French according to their schedule and choice—but the researchers *can* use a pretest to check that the two classes are comparable at the outset of the study. As noted by Shavelson, the pretest must measure the dependent variable, pronunciation accuracy in this study. Additionally, to be considered a pretest the measure of pronunciation accuracy has to be the same as, or an equivalent form of, the test of pronunciation accuracy that's given at the conclusion of the study, the *posttest*.

Legitimate comparison groups can be established in one of three different ways using pretesting and posttesting. First, the performance of existing groups can be compared to verify that there are no differences among them, as was done by these French teachers. Second, taking individuals' performance on the pretest into account, participants can be assigned to the non-experimental and experimental conditions to *create* groups that have a comparable degree of pronunciation accuracy. Third, performance on the pretest can be used to statistically equate the groups.[5]

Using pretesting to establish legitimate comparison groups creates what's known as a quasi-experimental design. Quasi-experimental designs aren't as powerful as true experimental designs because the participants aren't necessarily representative of a population of interest; however, because the groups are comparable, quasi-experimental designs do allow causal interpretation of the findings. For example, when the French teachers use the pretest-posttest technique to establish that the two classes are comparable at the outset, if they find that the students

who listened to 20 minutes of authentic broadcasts develop more accurate pronunciation than those who listened to only 10, they can assume that listening to
authentic broadcasts caused the difference in accuracy.

In summary, these three features of experimental studies—the presence or
absence of an experimental treatment, the presence or absence of legitimate comparison groups, and the manner in which the legitimate comparison groups are
formed—determine whether an experimental study is pre-experimental, quasi-
experimental, or true experimental. The fourth type of research design, *ex post
facto,* is characterized by *not* having an experimental treatment. In ex post facto
research, there is no innovation or modification of existing practice. Data are
simply collected, typically from existing groups, to investigate whether there is a
relationship between the variables with assigned roles. Ex post facto research, like
pre-experimental research, is useful for exploratory purposes but doesn't allow
causal interpretation of the findings.

The type of research design determines how the results of a study can be
interpreted. Researchers don't always tell their readers the type of design they've
used (though they should), so it's important for readers to be able to determine a

---

1. **Is there an experimental treatment?**

    YES   **NO**
    The study is   The study is ex post facto.
        pre-experimental,
    OR   quasi-experimental,
    OR   true experimental.

2. **Are there legitimate comparison groups (formed through random
    selection and assignment <u>or</u> through using a pretest to establish
    that there are no pre-existing differences between groups)?**

    YES   **NO**
    The study is   The study is pre-experimental.
        quasi-experimental
    OR   true experimental.

3. **Are the groups defined by the levels of the independent variable
    established through random selection and assignment?**

    YES   **NO**
    The study is true experimental.   The study is quasi-experimental.

FIGURE 3.1 Questions to Guide Identification of Research Design

study's design from the information that's given. Readers can ask themselves three ordered questions to discover the design of a study:

1. Is there an experimental treatment?
2. Are there legitimate comparison groups? (Legitimate comparison groups are formed through random selection and assignment of participants or through using a pretest to establish that there are no pre-existing differences between the groups.)
3. Are the groups defined by the levels of the independent variable established through random selection and assignment?

The questions work as a flow chart as shown in Figure 3.1; when they are addressed in a specific order, the three yes/no questions guide the identification of a study's design as one of the four major types of statistical research: ex post facto, pre-experimental, quasi-experimental, or true experimental.

Characteristics of each of the four categories of research design and example studies are presented in the final section of this chapter.

Characteristics of the Four Main Categories of Research Design

Of the four categories of research design, three involve some type of experimental treatment (pre-experimental, quasi-experimental, and true experimental), and one has no experimental treatment (ex post facto).

In the research designs for the example studies that I describe below, each uppercase G refers to a *group,* one of the levels of the independent variable. The superscript *random* added to G indicates that the groups were formed by random selection and assignment; the superscript *intact* means that the groups were not formed by random selection and assignment. The uppercase O refers to an observation or test—a data collection event. The subscript number on O indicates a pretest (O_1) or a posttest (O_2); in studies that have repeated testing, the subscript number indicates the order of the repeated testing. The uppercase T refers to the presence of a treatment, an experimental level of the independent variable; Ø symbol in the T position means *no treatment* and refers to the non-experimental level of the independent variable.

Pre-experimental Designs

Pre-experimental designs are appropriate for exploratory research. They lack legitimate comparison groups, so they don't provide the basis for causal interpretation of the results. Neither do they support generalization of the findings—but they are useful for gaining a deeper understanding of a particular environment or forming ideas or hypotheses that may serve as a foundation for subsequent quasi-experimental or true experimental research. Two important defining characteristics of a pre-experimental design are (1) presence of an experimental treatment, and (2) lack of legitimate comparison groups. Example A illustrates these two features of a pre-experimental design.

Example A

A teacher is investigating whether having her students create vocabulary logs has an impact on their rate of vocabulary development. After giving her students a pretest to measure their vocabulary knowledge, she asks them to begin keeping a vocabulary log. In the logs, the students note the most interesting or useful new words they've heard, the definition of each entry, the translation of each entry into the students' first language, and an example sentence or phrase in which the word is used. The students share their vocabulary entries with their classmates once a week. At the end of 8 weeks the teacher gives the vocabulary test again as a posttest. She calculates the improvement of each of the students to determine whether the learners showed any improvement in the breadth of their vocabulary.

Comments: Notice that there's only one group of participants. There's data collection before the treatment in the form of a pretest, O_1, and there's data collection at the conclusion of the research project, represented by O_2. The teacher introduces an innovation in practice to the learning environment, a treatment (use of vocabulary logs, represented by T), and gives a pretest, but the participants in the study all experience the same experimental condition, so there are no legitimate points of comparison. The pre-experimental design for this study can be characterized as *one group pretest-posttest*.

The design can be represented as:

$$G^{intact} \qquad O_1 \qquad T \qquad O_2$$

Below is a second pre-experimental design.

Example B

A teacher and one of her colleagues are investigating whether having learners create vocabulary logs has an impact on their rate of vocabulary development. The teachers want to do a study in which they compare the rate of development among learners who create logs and learners who don't, so one of the teachers asks her students to begin keeping vocabulary logs. In the logs, the students note the most interesting or useful new words they've heard, the definition of each entry, the translation of each entry in the students' first language, and an example sentence or phrase in which the word is used. The students share their vocabulary entries with their classmates once a week. The students in the other class engage in the usual vocabulary development activities. At the end of 8 weeks both teachers give a vocabulary test to measure the vocabulary development of the students in the two classes. The teachers compare the vocabulary development of the learners who created vocabulary logs and the learners who didn't create logs.

Comments: Notice that although there are two groups of participants in this study, no attempt was made at the outset of the study to verify their comparability. Because the groups' initial comparability wasn't established, a causal interpretation can't be made at the conclusion of the study of any difference in their vocabulary development. Like Example A, this study has a pre-experimental design; in this case the design can be characterized as *intact group comparison*.

The graphic representation is:

G_1^{intact} T O_1
G_2^{intact} $\emptyset$ O_1

Quasi-experimental Designs

Quasi-experimental designs are common in small-scale language education research and allow causal interpretations when the studies are carefully designed and executed. Cautious generalization is possible, limited by the specific and unique features of the participants and research setting. Quasi-experimental designs have two distinguishing characteristics. The first is the presence of an experimental treatment. The second is the use of a pretest to verify that existing groups are comparable, to form comparable groups, or to statistically equate groups. Regardless of which of the three approaches is used to verify or create comparable groups, a quasi-experimental design has legitimate comparison groups.

Example C

As in Example B, two teachers are investigating the possible impact of having learners create vocabulary logs on their rate of vocabulary development. These teachers, too, want to compare the rate of development among learners who create logs and learners who do not. The teachers give all the students the same vocabulary test at the beginning of the study. They then check the means and standard deviations of the scores for the two classes to verify that the classes are similar to one another in terms of their vocabulary knowledge. One of the teachers then asks her students to keep vocabulary logs. The other teacher simply presents new vocabulary in class and has the students practice using the vocabulary. At the end of 8 weeks the teachers give the same vocabulary test to their students again. The teachers compare the vocabulary development of the learners who created vocabulary logs and the learners who did not.

Comments: There is an experimental treatment, T, which one of the two groups receives; the other group receives the usual instruction ($\emptyset$). A pretest (O_1) is used to verify that the two groups are similar at the outset of the study in terms of vocabulary development. A posttest is administered at the conclusion of the study (O_2). This study employs a quasi-experimental design that can be characterized as *intact groups, pretest-posttest*.

The graphic representation is:

$$G_1^{\text{intact}} \quad O_1 \quad T \quad O_2$$
$$G_2^{\text{intact}} \quad O_1 \quad \emptyset \quad O_2$$

Note that Example C, if carefully conducted, allows causal interpretation of any difference in the vocabulary development of the two classes because the teachers used the pretest results to confirm that the two classes were similar in this regard at the outset of the study. Example D also allows cautious causal interpretation.

Example D

Believe it or not, there's another teacher who's investigating the possible impact of having learners create vocabulary logs on their rate of vocabulary development. She works alone but wants to compare the rate of vocabulary development for her students when they make logs and when they don't. During the first six weeks of the term, the students encounter and discuss new vocabulary and the teacher gives a vocabulary test every two weeks to establish a baseline level of vocabulary knowledge. After the third vocabulary test, she asks her students to begin keeping vocabulary logs. As in Examples A and B, the students note the most interesting or useful new words they hear, the definition of each entry, the translation of each entry in the students' first language, and an example sentence or phrase in which the word is used. The students share their vocabulary entries with their classmates once a week. The teacher continues to give vocabulary tests every two weeks for the next six weeks. She compares the test performance of the students before they started keeping vocabulary logs to their test performance after they began keeping vocabulary logs to determine whether keeping logs had a positive impact on their vocabulary development.

Comments: The design of this study can be characterized as quasi-experimental and *time series* because the pretesting, O_1, O_2, and O_3, serves to establish a baseline to which the students' performance on the post-tests, O_4, O_5, and O_6, can be compared.

The design can be represented like this:

$$G^{\text{intact}} \quad O_1 \quad O_2 \quad O_3 \quad T \quad O_4 \quad O_5 \quad O_6$$

True Experimental Designs

True experimental designs are rare in small-scale language education research, although when well executed they allow causal interpretation of the findings and generalization of the findings to the population from which the participants were drawn. Even if the researchers are interested in the generalizability of their findings, language education researchers don't often have the possibility of randomly selecting their participants and randomly assigning them to the levels of the independent variable. True experimental designs have (1) an experimental treatment, and (2) legitimate comparison groups formed through random selection *and* random assignment.

Example E

The teachers who work for a group of large international language schools have decided to investigate whether supplementing the schools' instructional programs with music will have an impact on learners' accuracy of pronunciation. From among the 5,000 students registering for high beginning-level classes, 200 are randomly selected to participate in the study. Half of these, 100 students, are randomly assigned to the usual instruction. The other 100 students are randomly assigned to the treatment of studying lyrics and singing; the lyrics lessons and singing are incorporated into the class activities. At the beginning of the term, all of the students take a test to measure the accuracy of their pronunciation. At the end of the term, an equivalent form of the same test is given to the students so they can see how much they've improved. The teachers compare the posttest scores for the group of 100 who didn't receive the lyrics and singing lessons to the posttest scores for the group of 100 students who did receive the lyrics and singing lessons.

Comments: The participants in this study are selected randomly from a population and assigned randomly to either the experimental or non-experimental group. Though the participants take a pretest, it isn't necessary for creating legitimate comparison groups—random selection and random assignment of the participants ensure comparable groups. This study employs a true experimental design that can be characterized as *control group pretest-posttest*.

The design is represented like this:

$$G_1^{random} \quad O_1 \quad T \quad O_2$$
$$G_2^{random} \quad O_1 \quad \emptyset \quad O_2$$

Study F is also a true experimental design.

Example F

This example study is set up very similarly to Example E—the only difference is that there's no pretest. The teachers who work for a group of large international language schools have decided to investigate whether supplementing the school's instructional programs with music will have an impact on learners' accuracy of pronunciation. From among the 5,000 students registering for beginning-level classes, 200 are randomly selected to participate in the study. Half of these, 100 students, are randomly assigned to the usual instruction. The other 100 students are randomly assigned to receive the treatment of studying lyrics and singing. The lyrics lessons and singing are incorporated into the class activities. At the end of the term, all 200 students take a test of their pronunciation accuracy. The scores for the 100 students who didn't receive the lyrics and singing lessons are compared to the scores for the 100 students who did receive the lyrics and singing lessons.

Comments: This study employs a true experimental design too. This one can be characterized as *control group posttest only.*

The design can be represented like this:

$$G_1 \text{ random} \quad T \quad O_1$$
$$G_2 \text{ random} \quad \emptyset \quad O_1$$

Ex Post Facto Designs

Ex post facto designs, the fourth type of research design, don't have an experimental treatment. Studies of this type are often used to investigate the strength of relationships among variables, though some allow comparison of different existing groups. Ex post facto designs are characterized by one feature, the lack of experimental treatment. How the participants are selected is not relevant for categorizing ex post facto designs.

Example G

A researcher is interested in whether there is a relationship between graduate students' analytic scores on the GRE and their grades in statistics classes. She has permission to collect the GRE data for all of the graduate students studying at state universities in the state. She also has access to their grades in their required introductory statistics class. She calculates the correlation between the scores on the GRE and the grade in the statistics class.

Comments: There's no experimental treatment, so this is an ex post facto design. It's *correlational* in nature—the researcher explores whether the scores on one variable (O_1) are related statistically to the scores on another (O_2).

The design can be represented graphically as:

G O_1 O_2

Another type of ex post facto design is represented by Example H.

Example H

This researcher is interested in exploring whether learner style (visual, auditory, kinesthetic) is related to learners' ultimate success in their study of a second/foreign language. He works at a large school so he's able to identify 300 newcomers to the school who have studied language for two to three years. He asks each to complete a questionnaire that identifies his or her learner style. He then contacts the admissions office and receives the newcomers' scores on the school's admission test. He compares the three types of learners to see if there is a difference among them in terms of language ability.

Comments: There is no experimental treatment, so this is an ex post facto design too. It can be characterized as a *criterion group* study.

G_1 O_1
G_2 O_1
G_3 O_1

Practice Problems 8 and 9 allow you to try applying the information you've just read about research designs and threats to validity.

Practice Problems

An answer key is available on the companion website (www.routledge.com/cw/turner).

Practicing the Concepts—Variable Roles

Take another look at the list you made when completing Practice Problem 1 from Chapter Two. Here's the list:

Variable name	Type of scale
Native language of learner	_____
Language learning aptitude	_____

Language ability	_____
Learner's age	_____
Learner's sex	_____
Learner's personality	_____
Teacher's experience	_____
Teacher's education	_____
Teacher's personality	_____
Class meeting time	_____
Frequency of class	_____
Duration of class	_____
Configuration of seats	_____

You may also have a list of variables that you identified, including:

Two nominal variables:
Two ordinal variables:
Two interval variables:

For each of the brief problems that follow, identify the variables and indicate which have been assigned the role of independent variable and which have been assigned the role of dependent variable.

1. Researcher plans to investigate whether a teacher's amount of experience has an impact on the students' success in learning a foreign language.

    Independent variable(s): _____
    Dependent variable(s): _____

2. Jean (that's me) plans to do a research project to investigate whether students who are enrolled in morning classes have the same degree of success in learning as students who are enrolled in late afternoon classes.

    Independent variable(s): _____
    Dependent variable(s): _____

3. I wonder whether learners whose first language is Spanish or French find learning Japanese more challenging than learners whose first language is Thai or Vietnamese.

    Independent variable(s): _____
    Dependent variable(s): _____

4. Do you think that extroverts are more likely to develop a high degree of oral fluency than introverts?

    Independent variable(s): _____
    Dependent variable(s): _____

5. Can you think of any moderator variables that might play a role in studies 1–4?

6. Can you think of any control variables that might play a role in studies 1–4?

7. Referring to the lists above (if you'd like), write two brief research problems of your own.

    a.

    b.

8. A school district supervisor was concerned about the reading scores of children in her district because they were lower than the state average, so she bought a new curriculum for developing reading skills. The supervisor arranged to have 60 first-graders randomly selected from among all of the first-graders in the district. The sample included both native and non-native speakers of English. These 60 students were then randomly assigned to two different conditions for reading instruction, 30 to each condition. The new curriculum was used in condition A; the existing curriculum was used in condition B. At the end of the academic year, *all* of the first-graders, including the 60 in the study, took the state's standardized reading test. The supervisor compared the average scores of the students who were in condition A (the new curriculum) with those in condition B.

    a. What is the independent variable and how many levels does it have?

    b. What is the dependent variable?

    c. What type of scale do you think "measures" the dependent variable?

    d. Is there an explicit control variable?

    e. Is there an explicit moderator variable?

    f. Identify two major threats to the internal validity of the study *and* what might be done to attempt to reduce each.

    g. Identify two major threats to the external validity of the study *and* what might be done to attempt to reduce each.

    h. Into which of the four categories of research design does this study best fit?

9. A college Spanish teacher wanted to get a grant from the college to take her students to Mexico during spring break. When she made her request to the dean, she was told that the school would need evidence of the academic value of the trip before investing any money in the project. Unfortunately, the teacher could find no research on the benefits of short-term immersion experiences (although she was motivated to search very thoroughly!). However, she had kept very careful records of her Spanish students over the last five years. She went back through her files and compared the Modern Language Association Spanish Achievement Test scores of students who traveled in Spanish-speaking countries with the scores of students who had not traveled in Spanish-speaking countries. As the teacher entered her former students' test scores into the computer to analyze the data, she wondered whether among the students who had traveled in Spanish-speaking countries (or not), the men or the women had tended to do better. She decided to analyze the data for this possibility too.

a. What is the independent variable and how many levels does it have?

b. What is the dependent variable?

c. What type of scale do you think "measures" the dependent variable?

d. Is there an explicit control variable?

e. Is there an explicit moderator variable?

f. Identify two major threats to the internal validity of the study *and* what might be done to attempt to reduce each.

g. Identify two major threats to the external validity of the study *and* what might be done to attempt to reduce each.

h. Into which of the four categories of research design does this study best fit?

Notes

1 The 1-way chi-squared statistic is the exception; it's used to analyze one nominal-scale independent variable to determine whether there is a statistically significant pattern within the data. Details on the 1-way chi-squared statistic are presented in Chapter Twelve.

2 My use of the terms *test reliability* and *test validity* here refer to features of data collection tools and procedures. These features of the tools and procedures have an impact on a study's internal and external validity.

3 Internal consistency is calculated using a correlation formula and ranges from 0 to 1; the internal consistency of a norm-referenced test can be considered good if it's around .80 or higher. Chapters Ten and Eleven address Pearson's product moment correlation coefficient, Spearman's rho, and Kendall's tau, three commonly used correlation formulas.

4 There is much more to be explored regarding test validity—consider consulting one of these sources:

Bailey, K.B. (1998). *Learning about language assessment: Dilemmas, decisions, and directions.* Boston: Heinle/Cengage Learning.
Douglas, D. (2010). *Understanding language testing.* London, UK: Hodder Education.
Fulcher, G. (2010). *Practical language testing.* London, UK: Hodder Education.

5 The third technique will be discussed in Chapter Eight in the discussion of the parametric statistic known as analysis of covariance (ANCOVA).

4

HOW ARE RESEARCH QUESTIONS FORMED AND WHAT ARE THE PARTS OF WELL-WRITTEN RESEARCH REPORTS?

I believe that good research questions, those that broaden or deepen the knowledge of the researcher and others in the researcher's communities, are formed through reading, discussions with colleagues, observation, experience, and careful reflection.

Hatch and Lazaraton (1991, pp. 9–12) make a number of suggestions for researchers to look for "good questions," with which I concur based on my experiences training researchers and doing research myself. These suggestions include:

1. Reflect on your language teaching and/or language learning experiences as a potential source for research questions.
2. Talk with colleagues, classmates, and students about language teaching and language learning as possible sources of research questions and to refine your ideas.
3. Identify journals that are relevant to your field and interests and read (or scan) articles that are interesting to you, focusing on the questions that were addressed by these researchers and their suggestions for further research.
4. Keep a research journal—write down issues you think are interesting and worth exploring. (And start your journal today!)

I'm convinced that one of the most important considerations for a researcher when forming a research question is that the topic is personally and professionally interesting. Identifying a research topic and forming a research question is an iterative process that requires the researcher to reflect on his or her reading, experience, and observations as a learner and teacher. New researchers tell me they find discussing their ideas about learning or teaching language useful, particularly ideas that are intriguing or even a little mysterious. They tell me that talking about possible research designs for the study they have in mind is useful, including how they envision the variables and how the research might actually be conducted. Explaining their ideas to someone else helps them identify important concerns and clarify details. An iterative process of reflection and discussion provides a venue for them to refine their research ideas and allows them to gain a sense of their audience's interests and background knowledge. The chapter activity is designed to engage the new researcher in the first steps of this iterative process.

Given that research is conducted to contribute to the knowledge of researchers and their communities, research results are often shared in writing or formal oral presentations. Guidelines exist for the structure of research reports, and readers who are aware of these guidelines find reports that follow them to be more understandable than reports that don't. The discussion of the structure of a statistical research report that follows is based on the guidelines presented in the fifth and sixth editions of the *Publication Manual of the American Psychological Association* (APA, 2001, 2010) but don't vary greatly from other published guidelines for research reports.

Nataliya Borkovska gave me permission to include as an example her research report, *The Effect of Specialized Vocabulary Presentation Technique on Non-native Speakers' Vocabulary Retention*. You'll find it in its entirety on the companion website for this book (www.routledge.com/cw/turner).

The Parts of a Research Proposal/Research Study

According to the *Publication Manual of the American Psychological Association* (APA, 2001), the principal sections of a statistical research proposal or report are:

- abstract
- introduction
- method
- analysis
- results
- discussion
- references
- appendices

In the discussion that follows, I note the type of information each section typically includes. All of the information that I mention should be included in a proposal or report, though some authors choose not to use the eight terms listed above as headings for their sections; some authors choose headings that reflect the content of their studies instead of the structure. Note that for some sections there are differences in what is included depending on whether the document is a proposal or a final research report. Though some novice researchers initially resist writing a comprehensive proposal, being able to write an informative and readable proposal is a very important professional skill. A well-written proposal is often necessary to convince people to participate in a study, to receive permission to conduct a study, to satisfy institutions' research participant requirements, and to apply for grants or awards to support research.

Abstract

An abstract is a short summary of a proposal or a completed study. The abstract should be concise, informative, and well written. The word limit varies among different publications—I've seen abstracts as brief as 100 words and as long as 400 words. Nataliya's has 318 words. Regardless of the length, abstracts should be informative and well written, because they introduce readers to the critical features of a study and may also serve to entice readers into reading beyond the abstract. The information that should be included in an abstract includes:

- the rationale or foundation for the study
- a clear statement of the topic and purpose or research question
- a description of the participants
- a description of the materials
- a description of the procedures
- a description of how the data will be analyzed (proposal) *or* a description of how the data were analyzed (research report)
- a summary of the potential value of the proposed study despite whatever limitations it may have (proposal) *or* a summary of the results and their implications (research report).

Nataliya included information on all of these points in her abstract. The rationale and purpose are clearly and succinctly provided in the first two sentences. In the third sentence, Nataliya provides information about the 14 participants—they're all non-native speakers of English and they're from seven different countries. Some readers might feel the need for more information on the participants—their age, for example—information that Nataliya does provide in the more detailed description of the participants in the study itself.

Nataliya outlines the procedures, including mention of the materials used, in the fourth through tenth sentences. The statistic Nataliya used to analyze the data is presented in the eleventh sentence. In the final sentence in the abstract, Nataliya interprets the findings and gives an indication of their potential usefulness.

Introduction

The introduction to a research proposal or research report presents the background, rationale, and framework for the study. The research purpose or research question is also explicitly stated. Authors don't need to entitle this section "Introduction" because the location and content of the section indicate its purpose, but they should include the following information in this section:

- background and rationale for the study
- the empirical or theoretical framework for the study in the form of a description of the situation, problem, or issue *and* a review of related research or discussion of relevant theory
- a statement of purpose, usually presented in two ways, and by some researchers, in a third manner as well:

    1. a prose description
    2. an explicit research question
    3. optionally, as formal research hypotheses.

Nataliya entitles the introduction of her research report euphoniously. In the first section, she explains why the teaching of specialized vocabulary is a relevant and interesting topic and provides some background for her study. The section in which she discusses the published literature on the nature of vocabulary knowledge and research on different approaches to teaching vocabulary is entitled "Literature Review." Some researchers don't include an explicit heading for the introduction or the literature review, relying on their readers' knowledge of the typical structure of a research report to understand that these sections appear first; however, Nataliya included these explicit headings to facilitate even novice researchers' understanding of the report's organization. In the section entitled "The Current Study," she provides an explicit prose statement of the specific research issue as well as a focused research question. Finally, she presents the formal research hypotheses, both the null hypothesis and the two-tailed alternative hypothesis.[1]

Method

The next section of a research proposal or research report is the Method(s) section, in which the author describes the plan for conducting the study. Included in this section are definitions of the variables and description of the participants, data collection tools, materials, and (for an experimental study) the experimental and non-experimental conditions. Some authors choose not to use the heading "Method" and make separate sections for each of the components listed below.

- Participants—relevant information about the participants is provided (number, how selected, important characteristics, etc.).
- Materials—the development and critical features of the data collection tools (questionnaires, tests, interview questions) are described, as are critical features of instructional materials, etc., that might be part of the experimental or non-experimental conditions. The data collection tools and other materials are included in appendices when possible.[2]

• Procedures—a description of how the proposed or completed study is conducted; that is, the manner in which the experimental and non-experimental conditions (if any) were presented and how the materials, etc., were used. The researcher should also indicate the type of research design. The explanation of the procedures should include enough detail for a reader to understand exactly how the study was done, including data collection.

In the Methods component of her report, Nataliya has three separate sections, Participants, Materials, and Procedures. In the Participants section, she restates their number and the fact that they're all non-native speakers of English. She includes more details than found in the abstract about their nationality and explains that they are adults studying or preparing to study for graduate degrees. She includes the important fact that only one has a background in a business-related field, the technical area of concern in the study.

In the Materials section of her report, Nataliya describes the development and features of the pretest she used to establish the comparability of the non-experimental and experimental groups in her study. She explains that she used a published learning styles survey to balance the two groups in terms of this characteristic as well and directs her readers to the appendix, where the survey is included. She also identifies the specific reading text that she chose and the source for the definitions of key terms. Finally, she describes the vocabulary test that she used to measure the participants' retention of the vocabulary they encountered in the reading text.

Nataliya describes in detail how the study was actually conducted in the Procedures section of her report and includes a discussion of what the participants in both the experimental and the non-experimental groups were asked to do.

Analysis

Some researchers include the description of the analysis in the Method(s) component of the study; some include this discussion as a separate component. Very sadly, some simply fail to describe how they analyzed their data! Regardless of the type of research, the report should include a detailed description of how the data were collected, organized, and analyzed. How a researcher analyzed his or her data shouldn't be a mystery—if a researcher can't explain how he or she did the analysis, it's possible that the analysis wasn't done systematically, and if data were not collected, organized, and analyzed systematically, the study can't be considered sound.

In the Analysis section of a research *proposal*, the researcher describes how data are to be arranged or organized and the analysis plan. In the Analysis section of a research *report* the researcher describes how the data were actually arranged or organized and how they were analyzed. For statistical research, the researcher should indicate the specific statistical formula[3] used and why it is appropriate. Important details include mention of how the assumptions for the statistic are to be checked (proposal) or were checked and met (study). When the researcher sets in advance the level of probability (*alpha*) used to interpret the statistical results,[4] the alpha level is stated in this section. The formal research hypotheses, the *null hypothesis* and *alternative hypotheses*, are presented as well if they aren't mentioned in the Introduction.

Nataliya combines the Analysis and Results sections of her report, as some researchers choose to do. My comments on the Analysis section of her report are therefore included below.

Results

There is no Results section in a research *proposal* because the research hasn't actually been conducted; however, a research *report* includes a section in which the author presents and summarizes the results of the analysis. The value of the inferential statistic that was used in the analysis should be reported along with the degrees of freedom and the exact probability of the statistic.[5] The effect size should also be reported when it can be calculated. Raw, unanalyzed data are not included except, perhaps, to illustrate a particular point; charts and graphs are often used to concisely display the analysis outcomes.

Under the "Results and Discussion" heading, Nataliya first presents a section entitled "Analysis and Results." In this section, she indicates the research design and the features of the study that allow her to characterize the design as quasi-experimental. She presents the descriptive statistics for the vocabulary test used to measure the dependent variable, vocabulary retention, and then indicates the statistic she used to determine whether there was a statistically significant difference in the vocabulary retention of the experimental group and the non-experimental group. She states the reasons for choosing this particular statistic and gives the level of probability at which she interprets the results. Finally, she reports the outcome of her analysis; she provides the observed value of the inferential statistic she used in her analysis and the exact probability of that value. She also notes that there is no statistically significant difference between the experimental and non-experimental groups.

Some authors combine the Analysis and Results sections, as Nataliya did, although the *Publication Manual of the American Psychological Association* (APA, 2001) indicates that the analysis should not be interpreted in the Results section. Nataliya follows APA format, including a separate section after Analysis and Results entitled "Discussion and Implications," where she interprets her results.

Discussion/Conclusions

In the Discussion section of a research *proposal,* the author describes the potential value of the proposed study despite its limitations. In the Discussion section of a research *report*, sometimes entitled "Conclusions" or "Implications," or

"Discussion and Implications," as Nataliya entitles this section of her study, the author addresses the value and implications of the study, with direct reference to the research question(s). Limitations of the research are typically addressed here and suggestions for further research are often indicated.

In the Discussion and Implications section of her report, Nataliya comments thoughtfully on the outcome of her study and offers possible explanations for the unanticipated lack of difference in the vocabulary retention of the non-experimental and experimental groups. She notes several limitations to the study despite her careful planning and implementation and provides some direction for future research on the effect of type of vocabulary presentation on the retention of specialized vocabulary.

References

All sources cited in a study are included in the References section; the References list includes only works cited in the study. When submitting a manuscript for publication, authors are typically responsible for formatting the manuscript according to the style manual used by the specific publication.

Nataliya includes all of the sources she cites in her reference list as well as the sources for the reading text and definitions encountered by the participants. The reference list is appropriately included before the appendices, as indicated in the APA manual.

Appendices

The APA manual (2001) notes that "an appendix is helpful if the detailed description of certain material is distracting in, or inappropriate to, the body of the paper" (p. 28). The types of material that might be presented in appendices include, but are not limited to, data collection instruments, example lessons, and descriptions of equipment or software that are not published elsewhere.

In the nine appendices Nataliya attaches to her study, she presents the vocabulary review and background questions she developed to be used as a pretest, the learning style preferences questionnaire she used, the reading text she chose, the definitions, and the separate materials used by the experimental group and by the non-experimental group. She also includes information from the development of the vocabulary retention test and the participant consent form. This complete set of appendices would almost certainly be shortened for publication in a journal because journals constrain the length of articles, but I've included all of the appendices because I appreciate (and admire) Nataliya's thoroughness, and I think you will too.

To help you get started on thinking about your own research project, take a look at the Chapter Activity.

Chapter Four Activity

1. Draft a research question that you think would be interesting to investigate. Phrase it as a question or a statement. (For example, "What is the effect of the type of media used in a language class on students' comprehension of the class material?" or "I'd like to investigate how using audio recordings versus video recordings might influence how much students understand of what is presented in a class session.")

2. Define the independent and dependent variables for your idea. For example:

   Independent variable: type of media (a nominal-scale variable with two levels—audio and video)
   Dependent variable: student comprehension (an interval-scale variable that will be measured by a test of how much students understood from particular lessons)

Note: It's very likely that you'll decide to modify your research question before writing your research proposal or carrying out the study. Please don't think that the question you pose now is the big question that you must pursue. You can modify or even start over with a new idea later as you engage in the process of reading, reflection, observation, and discussion that leads to the development of a sound research proposal.

Notes

1 In the discussion of statistical logic in Chapter Five, the concepts of the null hypothesis and alternative hypotheses are explained.
2 When secure tests are used for data collection, actual test items or tasks should not be disclosed; however, sample items/tasks should be provided.
3 If the research has several research questions and several different analyses are performed, justification for each statistic used should be provided.
4 Details on setting a level of probability for interpreting the findings of a study are presented in Chapter Five.
5 The phrase "value of the statistic" and the concepts represented by degrees of freedom, exact probability, and effect size will be explained in Chapter Five.

5

WHAT IS LOGICAL ABOUT STATISTICAL LOGIC AND WHAT PURPOSES DOES IT SERVE?

Up to this point in the book, you've been dealing with variables, variable roles, research design, threats to research validity, and descriptive statistics. This chapter introduces statistical logic and *inferential statistics.* Unlike descriptive statistics, which characterize the central tendency and dispersion of a set of data, inferential statistics are formulas used in the context of statistical logic to reduce quantitative data to a single number or a small set of numbers. Statistical logic serves as the platform for interpreting the single number or set of numbers; the interpretation is typically presented as a probability statement.

Inferential statistics allow researchers to test formal research hypotheses about data by comparing the outcome of their analyses to statistical models. Inferential statistics don't provide proof, they simply provide evidence to support probability statements about formal hypotheses. Researchers use statistical logic and inferential statistics to test a *null hypothesis*—a formal assertion that whatever patterns the researchers are investigating are probably not present. Researchers also propose an *alternative hypothesis.* As part of statistical logic, researchers set the level of probability they'll use when comparing their outcomes with the models. Probability is traditionally expressed as 95%, 99%, or 99.9% certainty, though some language education researchers doing small-scale studies might interpret their studies at 90% certainty. When researchers compare their data with a model, they decide whether the null hypothesis is likely to be true or whether the null hypothesis is not likely to be true. If it's not likely to be true, the null hypothesis is rejected and the alternative hypothesis is accepted as probably being true.

You might have wondered when you were reading Chapter Two why I asked you to spend so much time examining the normal distribution model, particularly since I explained that the normal distribution model is the reference point for interpreting parametric statistics and the focus of this text is on non-parametric statistics. Why do we need to consider a model to make a probability statement? And why examine the normal distribution model?

Building Models for Interpreting Patterns in Data

Models allow us to estimate the likelihood of some particular outcome or event. To illustrate how a model can work as the foundation for estimating the likelihood of something, I'll use an example from a dance lesson. My older brother, Steve, is a very good West Coast Swing dancer, as is his wife, Peggy. Steve offered to teach me a few West Coast moves, including a right spin. Peggy assured me that Steve leads very clearly, with consistent signals, and all I have to do is understand the signals he gives me through my right hand. As she explained, when he wants his dance partner to take a spin to the right, he raises her right hand slightly, connects his arm to hers from the wrist to the elbow, and initiates the turn by pulling her slightly toward him with his left arm, which is across her back. (Got that?) What's a little tricky about learning the right spin is that there are several different moves signaled through the right hand, so it's a good idea to have a sense of the proportion of these moves that become right spins.

Imagine that I decide to collect a little data to help me develop this sense. I systematically observe Steve while he dances, focusing only on identifying what move follows when Steve raises his partner's right hand. With some help from a video camera crew (my nieces), I collect 4 hours of dance videotape. With Steve and Peggy supplying the names of the moves, I compile the data presented in the bar chart in Figure 5.1. (I wish the chart were turquoise instead of grey; use your imagination to color our world, ok?) Steve raises his dance partner's right hand a total of 67 times, leading to 6 dips, 7 double spins, 31 right spins, 10 tuck send outs, and 13 whips.

I can use the data in the chart as a model for anticipating what type of move will come after a dance partner raises my right hand. It's easy to see that the most likely move is a right spin—31 of the 67 moves in the dataset, about 46% of them, were right spins. Based on this model, I can expect 46% of the moves after my right hand is raised to be right spins. A much less likely move is a dip—only 6 of the 67 moves were dips—about 9% of them. I wouldn't expect very many dips to be initiated by my partner at all. Okay, honestly, I don't think this model would really help me much in learning how and when to do a right spin—and I didn't really try. In fact I didn't really even collect these data—I made them up—but I hope you can see how a model *could* be built to provide the basis for determining the probability of some outcome or event. The normal distribution model can be used to make probability statements too. To our advantage, statisticians defined its characteristics so we don't have to build the model ourselves. You're already familiar with the characteristics of the normal distribution model, so I'll use it in my explanation of statistical logic.

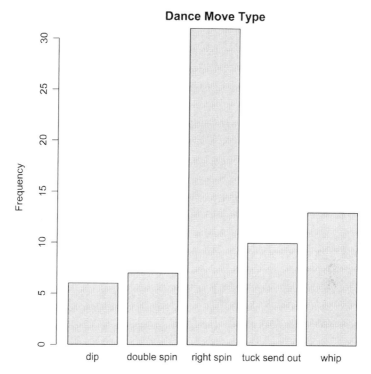

FIGURE 5.1 Distribution of Dance Moves Initiated by Raising Partner's Right Hand

Using the Normal Distribution Model for Interpreting Patterns in Data

Do you recall the characteristics of a distribution of z-scores from Chapter Two? The z-distribution is a normally distributed population of scores with the mean, mode, and median set at zero and a standard deviation of one point. Another defining characteristic of the z-distribution shape is the percentage of values that falls within each standard deviation unit, so the z-score distribution looks like Figure 5.2.

Additionally, as shown in Figure 5.3, in the population of z-scores 95% are between −1.96 and +1.96, as shown by the two grey, inward-pointing arrows. The two tails of the distribution represent 5% of the z-values, 2.5% on each end, as shown by the double-headed arrows.

As shown in Figure 5.4, 99.9% of the z-scores values are between −3.29 and +3.29 and .1% of the scores are on the tails. A similar model could be made with 99% of the z-scores in the middle and 1% of them divided across the two tails; the boundaries for this model are −2.58 and +2.58.

There are sets of models similar to these z-models for each of the different parametric statistics, and sets of different types of models for non-parametric statistics.

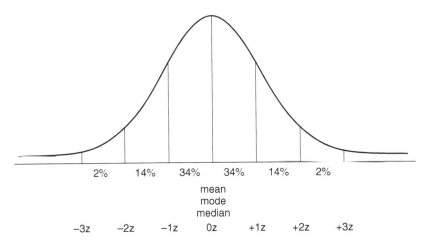

FIGURE 5.2 The *z*-Score Distribution

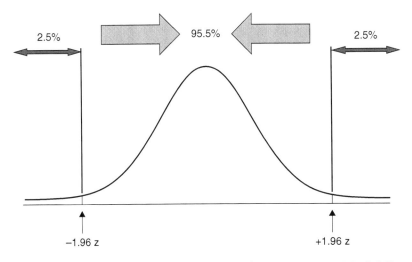

FIGURE 5.3 The Distribution of *z*-Scores for Hypothesis Testing at 95% Probability

As I'll explain later in this chapter, when using one of these models to interpret a statistic, if the value that's calculated falls in the center part of the model, one accepts that the null hypothesis is probably true. If the value that's calculated falls in one of the tails, the null hypothesis is probably not true and is rejected. When the null hypothesis is rejected, the alternative hypothesis is accepted, and the probability of the alternative hypothesis being true is reported at 95%, 99%, or 99.9%. One of the first steps in statistical logic is establishing the level of probability for making this interpretation.

In the next section, I explain each of the 10 steps that form statistical logic. You can think of statistical logic as a sort of rule book for joining in the game

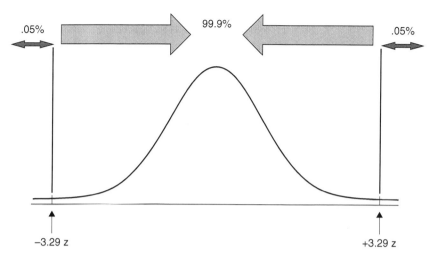

.05%   99.9%   .05%

−3.29 z   +3.29 z

FIGURE 5.4 The Distribution of *z*-Scores for Hypothesis Testing at 99.9% Probability

of reading, conducting, and reporting the results of statistical research. The rules are fairly straightforward, though like the rules for some sports they may seem counterintuitive. I think the rules of baseball are a good example. In baseball, to score a *run* (what baseball players must do to earn a point), the player standing at the home position has to hit a ball and run from the home position to first base, then to second base, then to third base, and then back to the home position. An uninformed observer of baseball might wonder why the hitter doesn't stay at the home position after hitting the ball; the home position is where the hitter has to be to score a point, so why not just stay there? (By the way, that uninformed observer might be a good friend of mine from France who went with me on a cross-cultural adventure to a Dodgers game.) The answer is simply that the rules of baseball require the hitter to go to first, second, and third and return to home before being awarded the point. People who play or watch the game of baseball need to know the rules to understand the action. So it is with statistical logic. People who want to play the research game—read statistical research with thorough understanding and write statistical research that's understandable to others—must follow the rules of statistical logic, which are summarized in Figure 5.5.

Explanation of Statistical Logic and Its 10 Steps

I think it's best to illustrate the steps in statistical logic with an example study. The example study I'll use is an investigation of the possible difference between two sets of data, though there are other types of studies. The null hypothesis is: "There's no statistically significant difference between the two sets of data." The alternative hypothesis is: "There is a statistically significant difference between the two sets of data." The researchers are investigating whether having English language students

---

The 10 Steps in Statistical Logic

1. State the formal research hypotheses, the null hypothesis and the alternative hypothesis or hypotheses.
2. Set alpha, the level of probability for interpreting the analysis.
3. Select the appropriate statistic for analysis of the data.
4. Collect the data.
5. Verify that the conditions for appropriate use of the statistic, the assumptions, are met.
6. Calculate the observed value of the appropriate statistic.
7. Determine the degrees of freedom for the statistic and use degrees of freedom and alpha to find the critical value of the statistic <u>OR</u> calculate the exact probability for the observed statistic calculated in Step 6.
8. To interpret the outcome of the analysis, compare observed value and the critical value <u>OR</u> compare the exact probability to alpha.
9. Interpret the findings as a probability statement using the hypothesis accepted in Step 8.
10. Interpret the meaningfulness of the findings and calculate effect size if possible.

FIGURE 5.5 The 10 Steps in Statistical Logic

engage in chat room discussions with their classmates for 10 minutes, four times a week, results in their attaining a higher degree of accuracy in the use of articles than if they simply email their classmates for 10 minutes, four times a week. The research question is: "Is there a difference in the accuracy of article usage by learners who engage in synchronous student-to-student interaction and learners who engage in non-synchronous student-to-student interaction?" The independent variable is *type of student-to-student interaction*, with two levels, learners' engagement in synchronous chat and learners' engagement in non-synchronous email. The dependent variable is learners' *accuracy of article usage*. The researchers collected the dependent variable data using an interval-scale test of the accurate use of articles.

Statistical logic has the same 10 steps regardless of the type of inferential statistic used. Though the emphasis in this text is on non-parametric statistics, I chose to use a parametric statistic, the Case II Independent Samples *t*-test, to introduce statistical logic because this *t*-test formula has components that are familiar from the first chapters. Additionally, its interpretation is rather transparent and based on a familiar model, the normal distribution. Here's a reminder of relevant points from the previous chapters before I set the conceptual scene for statistical reasoning.

First, remember from Chapter Three that reliability and validity are essential characteristics of a test. When we give a reliable, valid language test to a group of people, we can expect their scores to be fairly stable, useful indicators of their ability and knowledge. However, test scores aren't perfect indicators of learners' knowledge and abilities; even the best of tests don't measure perfectly and completely and people don't perform perfectly consistently. Because tests don't measure perfectly and people don't perform perfectly consistently, if we gave the same test to the same person 100 times (erasing the person's brain each time of any memory of having taken the test, of course!), the individual's 100 scores would vary a bit. In fact, the 100 scores would form a normal distribution.

Now imagine that instead of inflicting this strange imaginary testing on a single individual, we gave the test to an entire class and calculated the mean score for the class. Then imagine we administered the test to the class 99 more times, each time calculating the mean. These means would form a normal distribution too; a few times everyone in the class would perform well and a few times everyone would perform poorly, but 68% of the means would fall within one standard deviation of the center of the distribution and 96% would fall within two standard deviations of the center of the distribution. A normal distribution would be generated for any class that we imagined testing 100 times under these conditions.

Now imagine that we give a test to one class and calculate the mean for that class. Then we give the test to another class and calculate the mean for the second class too. Then we find the difference between the two means. Let's call that difference between the two means *t*. (Why call it *t*? Let's say it's called *t* because the phrase *the difference between the two means* starts with the letter *t*.) If we did this 100 times, can you imagine that the differences would vary? In fact, there would be a normal distribution of *t*-values, "the differences between the means." The distribution would look something like Figure 5.6. (I think I've got the right number of *t*-values; care to count them?)

Now back to the example study. The researchers wanted to know whether English language learners who engage in chat room discussions with their classmates for 10 minutes, four times a week attain a higher degree of accuracy in the use of articles than learners who use email for 10 minutes, four times a week. The researchers wanted to be able to make a statement about learners in general, so they randomly selected participants from a population of learners and then assigned each one (randomly!) to one of the two conditions. As noted above, the independent variable has two levels, synchronous chat room interaction and

```
                    t
                  t t t t t
                 t t t t t t t
               t t t t t t t t t t t
             t t t t t t t t t t t t t t
           t t t t t t t t t t t t t t t t t
         t t t t t t t t t t t t t t t t t t t t
       t t t t t t t t t t t t t t t t t t t t t t t
```

FIGURE 5.6 Distribution of *t*-Values Representing the 100 Differences Between Two Means

non-synchronous email interaction. Class 1 participated in synchronous chat interactions and Class 2 participated in non-synchronous email interactions. The dependent variable is learners' accuracy of article usage, as measured by an interval scale test of the accurate use of articles that's designed to yield normally distributed scores when it's given to its intended audience. The study has a true experimental design—the results of a pretest are used to confirm the equivalency of the two randomly created classes at the outset of the study—and a posttest is administered at the end of the study. The posttest scores, the means, and standard deviations for the two classes are presented in Table 5.1 (please note that the data are fabricated).

Now think about what's behind the scenes here. We have a mean score for each of the two classes, but recall that these means are not perfect indicators of the groups' abilities because even well-designed, reliable, valid tests don't measure perfectly (and humans don't perform perfectly). If we gave the test 100 times and

TABLE 5.1 Accuracy of Articles Posttest Scores, Means, and Standard Deviations (fabricated data)

Student	Class One: Chat	Class Two: Email
1	15	15
2	19	17
3	19	17
4	22	20
5	23	21
6	23	22
7	25	22
8	25	23
9	25	23
10	26	24
11	27	25
12	27	26
13	28	26
14	30	26
15	33	28
n	15	15
Mean	24.46667	22.33333
Median	25	23
Mode	25	26
Standard deviation	4.56488	3.79222
Range	18 points	13 points

calculated the difference between the groups each time, we'd find that the differences between the groups would fall in a normal distribution. When we examine the means for the two groups, it *looks* like the chat class has a higher mean than the email class, but how certain can we be that there truly is a difference? What looks like a difference—24.4667 *is* a larger number than 22.3333—may be due to chance. Following the 10 steps in statistical logic allows us to make a probability statement about whether the pattern we think we see in the data is simply due to chance or is strong enough to be due to something other than chance—in this case, due to the different types of student-to-student interaction.

I'll now illustrate the steps in statistical logic, the set of rules that allows researchers to make probability statements.

Step 1: State the Formal Research Hypotheses, the Null Hypothesis, and the Alternative Hypothesis or Hypotheses

A generic null hypothesis for the study described above states that there is no difference between the means of the two classes; that is, any apparent difference between the two means is due to chance. In words, the generic null hypothesis is:

There is no statistically significant difference between the two means.

In symbols, the null hypothesis looks like this:

$$\mathbf{H_0:}\ \overline{X}_1 = \overline{X}_2$$

The generic alternative hypothesis is:

There is a statistically significant difference between the two means.

In symbols, the alternative hypothesis looks like this:

$$\mathbf{H_1:}\ \overline{X}_1 \neq \overline{X}_2$$

Whether presented in words or in symbols, one of the hypotheses stated in Step 1, either the null or the alternative hypothesis, is used later in the steps in statistical logic as the foundation for a probability statement.

I'll put more information in the generic null and alternative hypotheses to make hypotheses for the example study that reflect the example study's variables.

> **Null hypothesis: There is no statistically significant difference between the mean accuracy of article usage of the class that engages in synchronous student-to-student interaction and the mean of the class that engages in non-synchronous student-to-student interaction.**

Alternative hypothesis: There is a statistically significant difference between the mean accuracy of article usage of the class that engages in synchronous student-to-student interaction and the mean of the class that engages in non-synchronous student-to-student interaction.

Step 2: Set Alpha, the Level of Probability for Interpreting the Analysis

The level of probability used to interpret the formal research hypotheses is set by the researcher. The researcher's action of stating the level of probability is referred to as *setting alpha*. After being set, alpha is referred to as the *probability level, p-level*, or simply *p*. Traditionally, alpha is set at .05, .01, or .001.[1] Setting alpha at .05 allows the researcher to make statements of 95% likelihood; setting alpha at .01 allows probability statements of 99% likelihood; and setting alpha at .001 allows probability statements of 99.9% likelihood. The researcher's choice depends on the type of research, the consequences of the research, the audience for the research, and the researcher's personality. (Some researchers can't handle much ambiguity regardless of the type of research they do and always set alpha at a very rigorous, high level.) For example, alpha might be set at .05 when a researcher's goal is simply to explore a question or issue. In contrast, alpha might be set at a stricter level, .01 or .001, if decisions affecting the allocation of resources or even people's lives might be made on the basis of the findings. I decided to set alpha at .05 for the example study because no critical decisions about people or resources will be made on its basis—it's exploratory research.

Step 3: Select the Appropriate Statistic for Analysis of the Data

To select the appropriate inferential statistic, the researcher needs to consider the nature of the research question, the type and number of variables, and how the participants were selected. In Chapters Six through Twelve, you'll study several different types of inferential statistics. One family of statistics, the three *t*-test formulas, is suitable when the researcher wants to investigate whether there's a statistically significant difference between the normally distributed scores of two groups (samples) drawn from a population.

The appropriate statistic formula for analyzing the data in this study is the Case II Independent Samples *t*-test. This particular parametric statistic is appropriate for several reasons: (1) the participants were randomly selected from a normally distributed population, (2) the independent variable has two levels, (3) the two groups involved in the study comprise different students, (4) the dependent variable is interval in nature and probably normally distributed in the population and the groups, and (5) the researcher wants to determine whether there is (probably) a difference between the two classes. (The detailed discussion in Chapters

Six and Seven will address these points as well as other information about the parametric and non-parametric statistics used to examine the difference between two groups.)

Step 4: Collect the Data

When a researcher follows the steps in statistical logic strictly and traditionally, the null and alternative hypotheses are formed, alpha is set, and the particular inferential statistic that the researcher plans to use to analyze the data is proposed *before* the data are collected. Performing the first three steps before collecting the data reflects the careful thinking that must go into defining the variables, articulating the precise research questions, planning how to identify and recruit the participants, considering the implications and uses of the research, and determining the degree of rigor needed when reporting the results. Following the steps in the proper order also helps the researcher remain focused on his or her question, ensuring that the data can be analyzed and will inform the research question.

Step 5: Verify That the Assumptions for the Statistic Are Met

Once the data are collected, the researcher *must* check the data to verify that the conditions for appropriate use of the statistic identified in Step 3 are actually satisfied in the data that were collected. The *t*-test formulas, like all parametric inferential statistics, require that the data be interval scale and normally distributed in each group. After collecting data, a researcher who plans to use a parametric inferential statistic must make and check a frequency distribution (a histogram) of the data to verify that the scores are normally distributed and that there are no outliers. The Shapiro–Wilk statistic or the kurtosis and skewness statistics described in Chapter Two should also be calculated and interpreted. If the researcher discovers that the conditions are not met for use of the statistic proposed in Step 3, the researcher should revise the analysis plan, choosing a statistic that's appropriate for the data. (In Chapter Four, you read a study by Nataliya Borkovska. In her proposal, Nataliya had indicated she would use one of the *t*-test formulas in her analysis, but when she collected and reviewed her data, she discovered that she didn't meet the assumptions for use of the *t*-test—the data weren't normally distributed. Through reviewing the data, she determined that the non-parametric Mann–Whitney *U*-test[2] was the appropriate statistic to use in her analysis despite the fact that she had originally proposed to use a *t*-test formula.)

To keep this initial explanation of the steps in statistical logic clear and simple, general information about the conditions for use of the Case II Independent Samples *t*-test is presented; the detailed discussion is in Chapter Six. In addition to random selection of participants from a population and random assignment to the groups that represent the levels of the independent variable, the three conditions that must be met for appropriate use of the Independent Samples *t*-test formula are:

(1) The independent variable has two levels.
(2) The dependent variable is measured on an interval or interval-like scale and the scores for each of the two groups are normally distributed.
(3) The two groups are either exactly the same size *or* the variance in the scores of the first group is approximately equal to the variance of the scores in the second group.

To check that these *assumptions* about the conditions are met, the first point is verification that there are really only two levels to the independent variable. This seems to be true; there are two groups of students participating in the study, one that's engaged in synchronous student-to-student interaction and one that's engaged in non-synchronous student-to-student interaction.

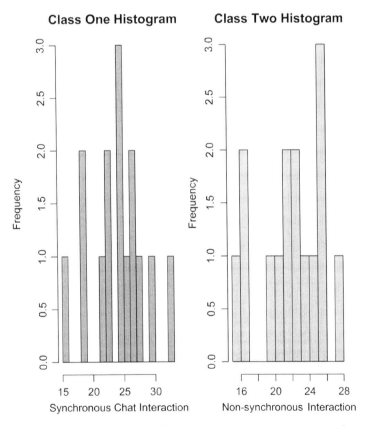

FIGURE 5.7 Frequency Distribution of Accuracy of Articles Posttest Scores for Class 1 and Class 2

To check the second assumption, I made a frequency histogram for each of the two sets of scores (see Figure 5.7)[3] and looked at the shapes to see whether the scores seemed normally distributed and whether there were any outliers, scores a lot higher or lower than the others in the set. The histogram for Class 1, the class that engaged in synchronous chat interactions, resembles a normal distribution. Using R, I also calculated the Shapiro–Wilk statistic for the data from Class 1. Because the exact p-value for W, the Shapiro–Wilk statistic, is greater than .05, I can be reasonably certain that the data are normally distributed; the Shapiro–Wilk statistic confirms that the chat group data approximate a normal distribution ($W = -0.9786, p = .9586$). The histogram for Class 2, the class that did email interactions, seems to approximate a normal distribution too. The Shapiro–Wilk statistic for the Class 2 data confirms that the scores approximate a normal distribution ($W = 0.9462, p = .4673$). Though the distributions of the data for the two classes are not perfectly normal in shape, examination of the histograms and interpretation of the Shapiro–Wilk statistic confirm that the two sets of data satisfy the assumption of normality.

The third condition to be met is that the two groups are exactly the same size or the variances of the two groups are approximately equal. In the example study, the two classes are exactly the same size, so I don't need to be concerned about the approximate equivalence of the variances.[4] Having completed these checks, I've verified that the use of the Case II Independent Samples t-test formula to analyze the data is justified, so I now use the formula to calculate the observed t-value.

Step 6: Calculate the Observed Value of the Appropriate Statistic

In Step 6, the researcher actually carries out the calculations to determine the *observed value* of the statistic that was proposed in Step 3.

I proposed to use the Case II Independent Samples t-test formula. This formula takes into account the means of the two groups, the size of the two groups, and the standard deviations of the two groups. The formula looks like this:

$$t_{observed} = \frac{\bar{X}_1 - \bar{X}_2}{\sqrt{\dfrac{S_1^2}{n_1} + \dfrac{S_2^2}{n_2}}}$$

The means, standard deviations, and n sizes are presented in Table 5.1. When I insert this information into the formula, it looks like this:

$$t_{observed} = \frac{24.46667 - 22.33333}{\sqrt{\dfrac{4.56488^2}{15} + \dfrac{3.79222^2}{15}}}$$

First, in the upper part of the equation (the numerator), I find the difference between the mean of the first group and the mean of the second group; in the lower part of the equation (the denominator), I square the standard deviations:

$$t_{observed} = \frac{2.13334}{\sqrt{\dfrac{20.83813}{15} + \dfrac{14.38093}{15}}}$$

Then for each part of the denominator, each group, I calculate the value of the standard deviation squared divided by the number of people in the group:

$$t_{observed} = \frac{2.13334}{\sqrt{1.38921 + .95873}}$$

Then I add these two values in the denominator:

$$t_{observed} = \frac{2.13334}{\sqrt{2.34794}}$$

Then I use a calculator to determine the square root of the value in the denominator:

$$t_{observed} = \frac{2.13334}{1.53230}$$

Then I divide the number on top (the numerator) by the number on the bottom (the denominator):

$$t_{observed} = \frac{2.13334}{1.53230} = 1.39225, \text{ rounded to } 1.39$$

The goal, $t_{observed}$, is 1.39. In calculating $t_{observed}$, I took into account the size of each group, the performance of each individual in the group (as subsumed in the calculation of the mean score for each class), and the standard deviation of each group. All of this information is reduced to one number, $t_{observed}$, according to the mathematical rules expressed in the Case II Independent Samples t-test formula.

Note that when I follow the steps in statistical logic, it's in Step 6 that the observed value is calculated. In the first five steps, the researcher states the hypotheses, sets the level of probability for interpreting the findings, states the specific inferential formula to be used to analyze the data, collects the data, and checks to see that the data meet the conditions for use of the statistical formula the researcher proposed in Step 3. In the final four steps, the researcher interprets the observed value of the statistic, makes an appropriate probability statement, and determines the meaningfulness of the outcome.

Step 7: Determine the Degrees of Freedom for the Statistic and Use Degrees of Freedom and Alpha to Find the Critical Value of the Observed Statistic <u>OR</u> Calculate the Exact Probability for the Observed Statistic

Step 7 can be accomplished in two different ways. The first, comparing the *critical value* for a statistic to the *observed value* (the value that was calculated in Step 6), is done using charts of these critical values. The second approach requires calculating the exact level of probability for the observed statistic determined in Step 6; however, most statistical software programs, including *R*, calculate and report exact probability within seconds, allowing interpretation of statistical significance without referring to a chart of critical values. I believe most researchers who use *R* or some other statistical software program will prefer the second option, but I explain the critical chart approach and several very important concepts first.

Using the Critical Value Approach

When using the critical value approach in Step 7, an understanding of two new concepts, *degrees of freedom* and *critical value*, is needed. I explain these concepts before illustrating how to carry out the critical value approach.

The term *degrees of freedom* refers to the number of independent values in a calculation. Consider this equation, A + B = C, which can be converted to C − B = A or C − A = B. Only two of the values in each of the three equations can vary; if you set two of the values, you can calculate the third. So if you know that A is 12 and C is 83, you know that B has to be 71 (C − A = B; 83 − 12 = 71). B can't vary once A and C are known; only two of the three numbers in these equations can vary. Because two of the three are free to vary, these equations have two degrees of freedom. For each inferential statistic formula, information about how to calculate the degrees of freedom is provided. For the Case II Independent Samples *t*-test formula, the degrees of freedom formula is $[(n_1 - 1) + (n_2 - 1)]$. So, for the example study the degrees of freedom can be worked out like this: $[(15 - 1) + (15 - 1)]$ is $(14 + 14)$, so the degrees of freedom are 28. The degrees of freedom are needed when a researcher follows the critical value approach to interpreting the analysis because degrees of freedom allow the researcher to find the right critical value for a particular study from a chart of critical values.

The second new concept is *critical value*. I need to digress again to explain what lies behind the notion of critical value. For the example study, alpha was set at .05, which means that the findings will be interpreted with 95% certainty, so take a look at the *t*-distribution in Figure 5.8. When $t_{observed}$ is in the middle 95% of the possible *t*-values, the null hypothesis must be accepted. The vertical bars show the boundaries between the 95% of possible $t_{observed}$ values in the middle of the distribution and the 2.5% of them on each tail. These boundaries can be calculated for

```
                            t
                          t t t t t
                        t t t t t t t
                      t t t t t t t t t t t
                    t t t t t t t t t t t t t t t
                    t t t t t t t t t t t t t t t
          t t | t t t t t t t t t t t t t t t t | t t
          t t | t t t t t t t t t t t t t t t t | t t

        2.5%              95%              2.5%
```

FIGURE 5.8 A Model Distribution of *t*-Values for Interpreting 95% Probability

t-distributions with different numbers of participants, and a chart of critical values can be created, like Figure 5.9.

In Figure 5.9, the chart of critical values for *t*, the degrees of freedom indicate which line to use. The column headings show the boundaries of the *t*-distribution for alpha set at .05, .01, and .001. Charts of critical values for $t_{observed}$ are usually organized somewhat similarly to Figure 5.9, though different chart assemblers structure their charts a bit differently.[5]

The $t_{observed}$ value that I calculated was 1.392. Fundamentally, what I need to know is where this $t_{observed}$ value falls in a model distribution of *t*-values when degrees of freedom are 28. I want to know whether $t_{observed}$ falls in the middle of the distribution or in one of the tails. When $t_{observed}$ is in the middle, the null hypothesis must be accepted—it's in the middle 95% of the distribution. (I think of this area in the middle of the distribution as Null Hypothesis Land.) When $t_{observed}$ is in one of the tails (Alternative Hypothesis Land), the null hypothesis is rejected and the alternative hypothesis is accepted.

I used the level of alpha that I set in Step 2 and the degrees of freedom that I determined in this step, Step 7, to find the critical value of *t* when the degrees of freedom are 28. I need this information to move to Step 8. When the degrees of freedom are 28 and alpha is set at .05, the $t_{critical}$ value is 2.0484.

Using the Exact Probability Approach

R and other statistical software programs are programmed to calculate the exact level of probability for a specific $t_{observed}$. In Chapter Six, I illustrate how to calculate $t_{observed}$ values using *R* but here I simply provide some of the *R* output; $t_{observed}$ = 1.3922, the degrees of freedom are 28, and the exact level of probability for the $t_{observed}$ value is .1748. Instead of using alpha and degrees of freedom to find the $t_{critical}$, the exact probability can be used to interpret the outcome. All I need to proceed to Step 8 is the exact *p*-value, which for this study is .1748.

Degrees of freedom	α = .05	α = .01	α = .001
1	12.7060	63.6551	636.0450
2	4.3026	9.9247	31.5989
3	3.1824	5.8408	12.9242
4	2.7764	4.6041	8.6103
5	2.5706	4.0322	6.8688
6	2.4469	3.7074	5.9589
7	2.3646	3.4995	5.4079
8	2.3060	3.3554	5.0414
9	2.2621	3.2498	4.7809
10	2.2282	3.1693	4.5869
11	2.2010	3.1058	4.4369
12	2.1788	3.0545	4.3178
13	2.1604	3.0123	4.2208
14	2.1448	2.9768	4.1404
15	2.1314	2.9467	4.0728
16	2.1199	2.9208	4.0150
17	2.1098	2.8983	3.9651
18	2.1009	2.8784	3.9216
19	2.0930	2.8609	3.8834
20	2.0860	2.8454	3.8495
21	2.0796	2.8314	3.8193
22	2.0739	2.8188	3.7921
23	2.0686	2.8073	3.7676
24	2.0639	2.7970	3.7454
25	2.0596	2.7874	3.7251
26	2.0555	2.7787	3.7067
27	2.0518	2.7707	3.6896
28	2.0484	2.7633	3.6739
29	2.0452	2.7564	3.6594
30	2.0423	2.7500	3.6459
35	2.0301	2.7238	3.5912
40	2.0211	2.7045	3.5510
45	2.0141	2.6896	3.5202
50	2.0086	2.6778	3.4960
60	2.0003	2.6603	3.4602
70	1.9944	2.6479	3.4350
80	1.9901	2.6387	3.4164
90	1.9867	2.6316	3.4020
100	1.9840	2.6259	3.3905

FIGURE 5.9 A Chart of Critical Values for t

Step 8: To Interpret the Outcome of the Analysis, Compare the Observed Value and the Critical Value <u>OR</u> Compare the Exact Probability to Alpha

So now I've reached the point in statistical logic where I accomplish my primary goal; I use the information I collected in the first seven steps to identify which of the formal research hypotheses from Step 1 I'll accept. Then I make an appropriate probability statement. First, I explain how this is done using the critical value approach, then I explain how it's done when interpreting exact probability. Using either approach is fine, but most researchers who do their calculations using statistical software use the exact probability approach because the software calculates exact probability and a chart of critical values isn't needed.

Using the Critical Value Approach

If the observed value of the statistic (the value that was calculated) is *less* than the critical value (from the chart), the null hypothesis is accepted. If the observed value of the statistic (the value that was calculated) is *greater* than the critical value (from the chart), the null hypothesis is rejected and the alternative hypothesis is accepted. The general rules for interpreting the outcome of an inferential analysis when using the critical value approach are:

> **If the observed value of the statistic ≤ the critical value of the statistic → accept the null hypothesis.**
>
> **If the observed value of the statistic > the critical value of the statistic → reject the null hypothesis.**

For the example study, $t_{observed}$ is 1.392. Using the chart of critical values for t in Figure 5.9, I find the proper row of information for degrees of freedom = 28 and discover that the critical value for t is 2.048. Because 1.392 (the observed t-value) is less than 2.048 (the critical t-value), I accept the null hypothesis.

The observed t-value falls in the middle 95% of the distribution of possible t-values, so I conclude that the apparent difference between the two groups is probably due to chance. For this study, I conclude that there's probably no difference between the two groups' accuracy of article usage due to the type of student interaction, chat or email. If $t_{observed}$ had fallen *outside* the middle 95% of the distribution, in one of the tails with 2.5% of the distribution of possible t-values, I would have concluded that the difference is probably, with 95% certainty, due to whether the participants engaged in synchronous or nonsynchronous student interaction.

Using the Exact Probability Approach

In Step 2, I set alpha at .05, establishing that I plan to interpret the outcome of the analysis at 95% likelihood. The rules for comparing the exact probability with alpha are:

> **If the exact probability ≥ alpha → accept the null hypothesis.**
> **If the exact probability < alpha → reject the null hypothesis.**

The R output (retrieved in Step 7) indicates that the exact level of probability for the observed value of t is .1748. The exact probability is greater than alpha, .05. Following the rules for interpreting exact probability, I accept the null hypothesis. The difference between the two groups didn't reach the 95% level of certainty for rejecting the null hypothesis. I have only approximately 82.82% certainty, so I accept the null hypothesis.

Step 9: Interpret the Findings as a Probability Statement

In this step, I actually make the probability statement that's the expected outcome of an inferential analysis. The formal research hypothesis that I accepted is recast as a probability statement. I accepted the null hypothesis, so the probability statement looks something like this:

> **We can be 95% certain that there is no statistically significant difference between the mean accuracy of article usage of the class that engages in synchronous student-to-student interaction and the mean of the class that engages in non-synchronous student-to-student interaction.**

Step 10: Interpret the Meaningfulness of the Finding

In the last step in statistical logic, the meaningfulness of the outcome is interpreted from two perspectives. First, regardless of whether the null hypothesis was accepted or rejected, the findings are interpreted with reference to the research question. In the example study, the research question was: "Is there a difference in the accuracy of article usage by learners who engage in synchronous student-to-student interaction and learners who engage in non-synchronous student-to-student interaction?" In Step 9, I stated that I could be 95% certain that there is no statistically significant difference between the two groups' accurate use of articles. When the findings are reported, as indicated in the *Publication Manual of the American Psychological Association* (APA, 2010, p. 34), the hypothesis is recast as a probability statement and the observed value of the statistic, the degrees of freedom, and the exact probability of the observed value as indicated. Effect size is also reported when possible.

The *effect size* of the observed statistic is generally calculated and reported because though inferential statistics allow us to make probability statements, they don't indicate anything about the relative size or importance of the outcome. Inferential statistics indicate only whether the outcome is due to chance (when the null hypothesis is accepted) or due to something other than chance (when the null hypothesis is rejected and an alternative hypothesis is accepted). As Field, Miles, and Field (2012) note, an effect statistic is "an objective and (usually) standard measure of the magnitude of the observed effect" (p. 57). Because effect size is an objective standardized measure, effect size allows the results of one study to be compared to those of another. Field and colleagues (p. 58) provide these general guidelines for interpreting effect size when a standardized effect statistic is used:

.10 is a small effect.
.30 is a medium effect.
.50 is a large effect.

Effect size can be calculated for $t_{observed}$ values, but there are a lot of new concepts in this chapter, so I don't calculate and report effect size here. (You'll find a detailed explanation of the calculation and interpretation of effect size for the *t*-test formulas in Chapter Six.) Consequently, my written report might look something like this:

> **The results of the analysis indicate with 95% certainty that the type of student-to-student interaction, synchronous or non-synchronous, has no significant effect on the learners' accurate use of articles ($t = 1.3922$, degrees of freedom = 28, $p = .1748$).**

Practice Problem

A teacher of Spanish at a very large language school wanted to know if the amount of exposure students have to authentic spoken Spanish would have an impact on their accuracy of pronunciation. He decided to include only beginning-level learners in his study, although there are intermediate- and advanced-level students at the school. From among the very large number of beginning students (think *population*, okay?), he randomly selected 40 participants and assigned each to one of two classes. The two classes were taught in the same way and using the same instructional materials, with one exception: As a weekly homework assignment, the students in Class 1 watched or listened to two hours of Spanish TV and radio and read Spanish for four hours, while Class 2 watched or listened to six hours of

Spanish TV and radio. All of the students kept a weekly log of their homework hours. At the end of the course, the teacher had each student take the computer-delivered *Versant for Spanish* test (Pearson Education, 2011), a test of speaking ability that gives a pronunciation accuracy score (among other components). The *Versant for Spanish* test yields scores between 20 and 80 and provides descriptions of examinees' pronunciation accuracy. (Check the companion website for the answers.)

1. Identify the independent variable.
2. What type of scale defines the independent variable?
3. Identify the levels of the independent variable.
4. Identify the dependent variable.
5. What type of scale defines the dependent variable?
6. Identify any explicit control variables.
7. Identify any explicit moderator variables.
8. What is the research design for this study?
9. The (fabricated) data are presented in the chart—follow the steps in statistical logic to determine whether there is a statistically significant difference in the groups' performance on the *Versant for Spanish* test.

Class 1	Class 2
62	63
60	68
60	63
55	58
58	57
57	59
55	54
47	57
36	40
47	45
48	42
44	47
44	49
49	49
42	39
44	47
39	37
39	34
38	36
36	39

Notes

1 If you're curious, check Field, Miles, and Field (2012, pp. 52–53) for an interesting discussion of and speculation on how .05, .01, and .001 came to be the probability levels researchers use for interpreting their findings.

2 Nataliya used the term Mann–Whitney U-test, though the statistic is also known as the Wilcoxon Rank Sum test. I use the term Wilcoxon Rank Sum statistic in this text because the R command for the statistic is **wilcox.test**.

3. The histogram for Class 1 was made in R using this command: **hist (Class.One, xlab = "Synchronous Chat Interaction", ylab = "Frequency", col = "lime green", breaks = 18, main = "Class One Histogram")**. The histogram for Class 2 was made in R using this command: **Class.Two, xlab = "Asynchronous Interaction", ylab = "Frequency", col = "light blue", breaks = 12, mean = "Class Two Histogram")**.

4. In Chapter Six, I introduce a statistic, Levene's Test, that allows the assumption of equal variances to be checked, but because the two classes in the example study are exactly the same size, it isn't necessary to calculate and interpret the Levene's Test statistic.

5. The values presented in this chart were calculated using the tool found at easycalculation. com, retrieved June 17, 2013, from http://easycalculation.com/statistics/critical-t-test. php. The code used for calculating these values is:<iframe src=http://easycalculation. com/statistics/embedded_critical-t-test.php? width="400"height="500"frameborder= "0"></iframe>.

SECTION II
Analyzing Differences Between Two Sets of Data

6

THE PARAMETRIC *t*-TEST STATISTICS

In Chapter Six, I address the small family of parametric inferential statistics known as *t-tests*. A *t*-test formula can be used when the participants in a study are randomly selected from a normally distributed population and these additional conditions are met: (1) The independent variable is nominal and has two levels, and (2) the dependent variable is interval scale and the data are normally distributed in each of the groups defined by the levels of the independent variable. The *t*-test formulas are used when a researcher wants to know whether the difference between two sets of normally distributed data is statistically significant.

There are three different *t*-test formulas. The Case II Independent Samples *t*-test formula, the formula I used in the explanation of statistical logic in Chapter Five, is appropriate when comparing the performance of two distinct groups of participants on the same dependent variable. The Case II Paired Samples *t*-test formula is appropriate when comparing the performance of the same people on the same dependent variable, as in a pretest–posttest design; it can also be used when comparing the dependent variable performance of carefully matched pairs of people. The third *t*-test formula, Case I *t*-test, is appropriate when comparing the dependent variable performance of a sample of participants with the performance of the population from which the sample was drawn.

All three *t*-test formulas yield a $t_{observed}$ value. A $t_{observed}$ value may be either positive or negative, though it's the absolute value of $t_{observed}$ that's interpreted. In the discussion that follows, I explain and illustrate the use of each of the three *t*-test formulas, beginning with the Case II Independent Samples *t*-test. I recommend you review the explanation of statistical logic in Chapter Five before working through this discussion.

The explanation of the Case II Independent Samples *t*-test is illustrated using a study inspired by Jennifer Grode's (2011) research on learners' perceptions of their enjoyment and the usefulness of different types of instructional material. In the example study, the researcher adapts Jennifer's survey instrument to collect data on learners' perceptions of their enjoyment of an age-specific textbook versus a textbook designed for younger learners (fabricated data). The Case II Paired Samples *t*-test statistic is illustrated using data collected by Jennifer Grode herself (2011) in her own survey research on learners' opinions regarding learning through authentic versus textbook-based instructional materials.[1]

Case II Independent Samples *t*-Test

The Case II Independent Samples *t*-test is used to compare the dependent variable performance of two distinct groups of people, as in the study in Chapter Five on the impact of type of student-to-student interaction (synchronous versus non-synchronous) on the development of accuracy of article usage.

Researchers in language education typically don't have access to populations of language learners from which they can draw a random sample for their study—nor is generalization of research outcomes to a population the primary goal of much of the small-scale research done by teachers and others in language education. I don't have access to a population of language learners and neither do any of my colleagues or students who are willing to share their data, so I use a fabricated study to illustrate this discussion of the Case II Independent Samples *t*-test statistic.

Example Study

Because the example study is fabricated, I don't work out all of its procedural details. Please simply imagine that a teacher of Spanish wrote a new textbook based on her careful analysis of the needs and interests of beginning-level learners of Spanish who are over the age of 25. She believed that the textbook would be perceived by these learners as being more enjoyable than other textbooks because it reflects the needs and interests of that population, adult learners of Spanish over the age of 25. She received a grant for her research and had access to a very large number of learners with these characteristics through her professional associations. She randomly identified 120 to participate in her study, which took place at the school where she works. The 120 participants received one term of study tuition free and were reimbursed for housing and travel expenses. Half of the participants used the teacher's textbook in their studies and half used her textbook's main competitor, a beginning-level Spanish textbook that was designed for college-age students. The classes were taught by experienced teachers familiar with the textbook they were assigned to use. The teacher/author investigated whether learners' perceived level of enjoyment of their textbook differed depending on whether their textbook was designed for their age and interests or for younger students. The research question was: Does learners' perceived enjoyment of their beginning-level Spanish textbook differ depending on whether the text is designed for their age group or designed for younger adult learners?

The independent variable for the investigation, type of Spanish textbook, had two levels, *age-specific* design (AS) and design for *young adult learners* (YAL). At the end of the participants' first term of Spanish language study, the teacher administered her data collection tool, a questionnaire that she adapted from Grode's (2011) study on learners' perceptions of their enjoyment and the usefulness of different types of learning materials. The researcher received 39 questionnaires from the AS group and 58 from the YAL group. The data for the dependent variable in the study, *degree of perceived enjoyment of the textbook*, were collected through two of the questionnaire items: (1) perceived enjoyment of the readings in the textbook, and (2) perceived enjoyment in completing the activities in the textbook. Each Likert-scale item yielded a score between 1 (not at all enjoyable) and 9 (extremely enjoyable). To determine each participant's score on perceived enjoyment of the textbook, the scores from the two questionnaire items were summed, so the possible range for the dependent variable was 2 to 18 points. Though the tool yields ordinal data, the scale is continuous[2] and the researcher assumed that the data would be normally distributed in the population.[3] She thought that the relatively large number of participants and the type of data (interval-like data with a possible range of scores from 2 to 18) suggested that the data would be normally distributed. (The data for the two groups can be found in the resources section of the companion website (www.routledge.com/cw/turner).

She can consider using one of the three *t*-test statistics to analyze the data because the participants were randomly selected from a population and randomly assigned to the two levels of the independent variable. In addition, the dependent variable is interval scale (or interval-like), and the data are likely to be normally distributed in the two groups. From among the three *t*-test statistics, the Case II Independent Samples *t*-test formula is the best choice for the analysis because the participants in the two groups are different individuals.

The 10 steps in statistical logic are followed to conduct the analysis. In Steps 7 and 8, I describe both the critical value approach and the exact probability approach to interpreting the outcome. As a reminder, here are the 10 steps.

1. State the formal research hypotheses, the null hypothesis and the alternative hypothesis/hypotheses.
2. Set alpha, the level of probability for the analysis.
3. Select the appropriate statistic for analysis of the data.
4. Collect the data.
5. Verify that the assumptions for the statistic are met.
6. Calculate the observed value of the appropriate statistic.

7. Determine the degrees of freedom for the statistic and use degrees of freedom and alpha to find the critical value of the statistic OR calculate the exact probability for the observed statistic calculated in Step 6.
8. To interpret the outcome of the analysis, compare the observed value and the critical value OR compare the exact probability to alpha. Apply one of the appropriate sets of rules to the comparison.

    Critical value approach:
    > If $t_{observed} \leq t_{critical} \rightarrow$ accept the null hypothesis.
    > If $t_{observed} > t_{critical} \rightarrow$ reject the null hypothesis.

    Exact probability approach:
    > If exact probability $\geq$ alpha $\rightarrow$ accept the null hypothesis.
    > If exact probability $<$ alpha $\rightarrow$ reject the null hypothesis.

9. Interpret the findings as a probability statement using the hypothesis accepted in Step 8.
10. Interpret the meaningfulness of the findings and calculate the effect size if possible.

I follow these steps to investigate whether there's a statistically significant difference in the Spanish learners' perceived enjoyment of their textbook depending on whether the text is age specific or not.

Step 1: State the Formal Research Hypotheses

As you read in Chapter Five, when strictly following the rules of statistical logic, the null hypothesis is stated explicitly. For this study, the null hypothesis is:

> **There is no statistically significant difference in learners' perceived enjoyment of an age-specific textbook versus a textbook for younger learners. (These words can be represented by the symbols $H_O : \overline{X}_1 = \overline{X}_2$.)**

If the researcher were only interested in whether there was a difference in the learners' perception of enjoyment between the two learner groups, not whether one group had a higher degree of enjoyment than the other, then a two-tailed, non-directional alternative hypothesis would be stated.[4] However, she wanted to be able to make a statement about the direction of the difference; she was seeking support for her idea that her textbook would be perceived as more valuable than other textbooks, due to the care she took it making it relevant and interesting. She proposed two one-tailed, directional alternative hypotheses, like these:

Alternative hypothesis 1: There is a statistically significant difference in learners' perceived enjoyment of an age-specific textbook and a textbook for younger learners, with learners using an age-specific textbook reporting more enjoyment than learners using a textbook for younger learners. (These words can be represented by the symbols $H_1 : \overline{X}_1 > \overline{X}_2$.)

Alternative hypothesis 2: There is a statistically significant difference in learners' perceived enjoyment of an age-specific textbook and a textbook for younger learners, with learners using an age-specific textbook reporting less enjoyment than learners using a textbook for younger learners. (These words can be represented by the symbols $H_2 : \overline{X}_1 < \overline{X}_2$.)

Step 2: Set Alpha

This research is exploratory in nature, so the researcher set alpha at .05. This means that she'll report the outcome of her statistical analysis as having 95% certainty.

Step 3: Select the Appropriate Statistic for Analysis of the Data

The researcher's primary purpose for conducting this study was to get a sense of whether beginning-level adult learners of Spanish prefer an age-specific textbook to one that's designed for younger learners. She investigated whether her participants had a different perception of their enjoyment in using a text depending on the text design—some of the participants in the study used an age-specific text and some used a text that was designed for younger learners. The independent variable had two levels, AS and YAL. The participants in the two levels of the independent variable were distinct from one another; none of the participants used both textbooks. The dependent variable, *perceived enjoyment of the textbook*, was defined using an interval-like scale, and the researcher believed that the scores for each of the two groups defined by the independent variable would be normally distributed. She therefore proposed to use the Case II Independent Samples *t*-test statistic to analyze her data because in addition to the participants being randomly selected from a normal distribution, (1) the independent variable has two levels, (2) there are different participants in the two groups, (3) the dependent variable is interval or interval-like and the data for both groups may approximate a normal distribution, and (4) she wanted to determine whether the two groups differed in their perceived enjoyment of their textbook.

Step 4: Collect the Data

In performing Step 4, she collected and organized her data.[5]

Step 5: Verify That the Assumptions Are Met

In addition to the participants being randomly selected from a normally distributed population, there are three assumptions for using the Independent Samples t-test formula:

1. The independent variable is nominal and has only two levels; the two levels are represented by different participants.
2. The dependent variable is interval scale or interval-like, and the data for both groups defined by the independent variable approximate a normal distribution.
3. When calculation of $t_{observed}$ is done with a handheld calculator, the two groups defined by the levels of the independent variable must be exactly equal in size or the variances of the groups must be approximately equal. When using R to calculate $t_{observed}$, this assumption is irrelevant because R uses Welch's t-test formula for calculating the Case II Independent Samples t-test. Welch's t-test formula corrects for violation of this assumption.[6]

The first assumption is met because the independent variable has only two levels, the users of the AS textbook and the users of the YAL textbook, and none of the participants is in both groups. To determine whether the second assumption is met, the researcher must examine the normality of the AS user data and the YAL user data. For each set of data, the researcher should examine the histogram and calculate and interpret the Shapiro–Wilk statistic.

As for the third assumption, when the calculations are done with a calculator, the researcher must check the variances of the two groups to be sure that they're approximately equal because there are 39 AS users and 58 YAL users (the groups aren't exactly the same size). In Box 6.1, I introduce a statistic that may be new to you, the Levene's Test statistic, to check the equality of the variances. When the two groups aren't the same size, R uses the Welch t-test formula to calculate the observed value of the Case II Independent Samples test; the formula corrects for violation of the assumption of equal variances; however, checking the equality of the variances remains an important step for researchers who want to have a thorough understanding of important features of their data.

In Box 6.1, I show how to import a dataset into R, make a histogram and calculate the Shapiro–Wilk statistic for each group, and calculate the Levene's Test statistic.

Box 6.1 Importing a Dataset Into *R* and Checking the Assumption of Normality for the AS Textbook User and YAL Textbook User Data

A researcher can create and import an Excel spreadsheet rather than enter the data directly into *R*. The spreadsheet should have two columns, one for the independent variable and one for the dependent variable. In the independent variable column, enter a 1 for people in the first group and a 2 for people in the second group. In the dependent variable column, simply enter the dependent variable value for each participant. In the first row of each column, give the variable a simple (memorable and easy to type) label.

R creates a heading for each column if there isn't one; be sure to view the dataset after importing it to verify the names of the columns—the names are needed in the commands.

Save the Excel spreadsheet in the MS-DOS comma separated values (csv) format (for PC users) and in the equivalent csv format for Mac users. The spreadsheet can be imported using the **read.csv = (file.choose(), header = T)** command.

The **read.csv(file.choose(), header = T)** command gives you access to documents you've saved on your computer and allows you to select the appropriate document to import.

First enter the name you want to give to the dataset, then type the complete command. I import the dataset for the example study, which I gave the name **enjoy.data.**

The dataset includes the data for the two questionnaire items I'll compile to form the dependent variable and a column of information that indicates whether an individual is an AS user or a YAL user. (Before you attempt to import the dataset, retrieve it from the companion website and save it somewhere on your computer—and remember where you put it!)

```
> enjoy.data = read.csv (file.
  choose(), header = T)
```

(Continued)

Box 6.1 (*Continued*)

The **header** = **T** component of the command tells *R* that the first row of information in the Excel file is a header (**header** = **T** is the shortened form of **header** = **TRUE**). When you enter the command, find the document where you saved it on your computer. Click on it and open it to import it into *R*.	
R won't give any indication that the dataset was imported, but it's available if you followed the steps correctly. Use the **View** command (with an uppercase **V**) to review the dataset in a separate pop-up window. I recommend that you develop a habit of reviewing any dataset you import to verify that you've got what you meant to import! When you review the *enjoy.data* dataset, you'll see three columns of information, each with a heading that indicates the name of the variable. The dataset has scores for 97 people. The first column in the dataset is labeled *text*; in this column of data, 1 indicates AS textbook users and 2 indicates YAL textbook users. This variable is recognized by *R* as *enjoy.data$text*. The second column, *readenj*, includes the participants' scores on the item measuring perceived enjoyment of textbook readings; the set of scores is recognized by *R* as *enjoy.data$readenj*. The third column, *pracenj*, includes the participants' scores on the item measuring perceived enjoyment of completing exercises in a textbook; this set of scores is recognized as *enjoy.data$pracenj*.	**> View (enjoy.data)** The data for the first four people are shown below. 	*text*	*readenj*	*pracenj*	 |---|---|---| | 2 | 7 | 7 | | 2 | 5 | 5 | | 2 | 7 | 7 | | 2 | 2 | 3 |
Create a new dependent variable, *totenjoy*, by summing the values for *readenj* and *pracenj*. To place the new dependent variable in the *enjoy.data* dataset, the name you assign to the new variable must include the name of the dataset **enjoy.data**, the dollar sign, and the name of the new variable (**totenjoy** in this case). The new variable is recognized by *R* as *enjoy.data$totenjoy*.	**> enjoy.data$totenjoy = enjoy.data$readenj + enjoy.data$pracenj**

(Continued)

Box 6.1 (*Continued*)

View the dataset to check that the new variable has been added.	> View (enjoy.data) The data for the first four people are shown below. | text	readenj	pracenj	totenjoy
---	---	---	---
2	7	7	14
2	5	5	10
2	7	7	14
2	2	3	5	
To check that the *totenjoy* data are normally distributed for both the AS users and the YAL users, create two separate datasets, one for each group, using the **subset** command. Enter the name for the first new subset of the data (I used **AS.user. dataset**), then enter the **subset** command. Then, in parentheses, give the name of the dataset to be split (*enjoy.data*) followed by a comma. Then type the name of the independent variable—the variable used to split the dependent variable dataset (*text*). This should be followed by two equal signs and, in double quotation marks, the value of the independent variable for the subset group, 1 in this case.	> AS.user.dataset = subset (enjoy.data, enjoy. data$text == "1")
View the new dataset to verify that it contains only the participants coded 1.	> View (AS.user.dataset)
Create the dataset for the YAL users.	> YAL.user.dataset = subset(enjoy.data, enjoy. data$text == "2")
View the new dataset to verify that it contains only the participants coded 2.	> View (YAL.user.dataset)
Calculate the mean and standard deviation for the AS users.	> mean (AS.user. dataset$totenjoy) Output: [1] 9.846154 > sd (AS.user. dataset$totenjoy) [1] 4.782305
Calculate the mean and standard deviation for the YAL users.	> mean (YAL.user. dataset$totenjoy) Output: [1] 9.724138

(*Continued*)

Box 6.1 (Continued)

	> sd (YAL.user. dataset$totenjoy) Output: [1] 4.068678
To create a space for side-by-side histograms of the scores for the AS group and the scores for the YAL group, use the command **par (mfrow = c (1,2))**	> **par (mfrow = c (1,2))**
Create a frequency distribution of the *totenjoy* scores for the AS textbook users. Label the x-axis and give the distribution a main title. Indicate a color for the distribution using the **col** command (I envision green here) and indicate 10 breaks using the **breaks** command.	> **hist (AS.user. dataset$totenjoy, col = "green", breaks = 10, xlab = "Perceived Enjoyment", main = "Age-specific Text")**
Create a frequency distribution of the *totenjoy* scores for the YAL textbook learners. Label the x-axis and give the distribution a main title. Indicate a color for the distribution using the **col** command (envision light blue) and indicate 10 breaks using the **breaks** command (see Figure 6.1).	> **hist(YAL.user. dataset$totenjoy, col = "light blue", breaks = 10, xlab = "Perceived Enjoyment", main = "YAL Text")**
Use the **shapiro.test** command to verify that the data for the AS textbook users are normally distributed.	> **shapiro.test (AS.user. dataset$totenjoy)** The output looks like this: Shapiro–Wilk normality test data: AS.user.dataset$totenjoy $W = 0.9504$, $p = .085$
And finally, use the **shapiro.test** command to verify that the data for the YAL textbook users are normally distributed.	> **shapiro.test (YAL.user.dataset$totenjoy)** The output looks like this: Shapiro–Wilk normality test data: YAL.user.dataset$totenjoy $W = 0.9697$, $p = .1553$

Now I interpret the histograms and the Shapiro–Wilk outcomes for the two sets of data.

Both the AS and the YAL histograms are presented in Figure 6.1. The histogram of the AS textbook user data is on the left. There are a few more people than expected with scores below 4 for a normal distribution; however, the data approximate a normal distribution. The histogram of the YAL textbook user data (on the right) seems to approximate the normal distribution model too, although it appears somewhat skewed due to there being a few more cases at the left end of the distribution than at the right.

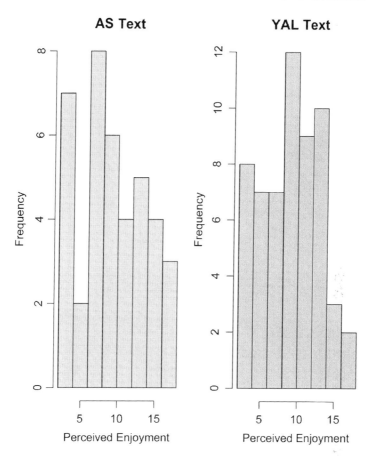

FIGURE 6.1 Distribution of Enjoyment Scores for Users of Age-Specific and Young Adult Textbooks

Now I interpret the Shapiro–Wilk values. Recall that the Shapiro–Wilk statistic is interpreted by examining its *p*-value. The null hypothesis for the Shapiro–Wilk statistic is H_0: *The data are normally distributed.* When the *p*-value is greater than .05, we must accept the null hypothesis; when the *p*-value is less than .05, we reject the null hypothesis and accept the alternative hypothesis, H_1: *The data are not normally distributed.*

For the AS textbook user data, the *p*-value for the Shapiro–Wilk statistic is 0.085 (the Shapiro–Wilk value itself is 0.9504). The *p*-value, 0.085, is greater than the alpha level set in Step 2 (α = .05), so we accept the null hypothesis. There's 95% certainty that the scores for users of the AS textbook are normally distributed. For the YAL textbook user data, the *p*-value for the Shapiro–Wilk statistic is 0.155 (the Shapiro–Wilk value is 0.9697). The *p*-value for these data is also greater than .05, so we can be reasonably confident that the scores for the YAL users are normally distributed too.

To check the third assumption, that the two groups defined by the levels of the independent variable are exactly equal in size or the variances are approximately equal, the first step is to verify whether the two groups are the same size. We know that they aren't, but for some other dataset we might have to check the number of participants in each group. In Box 6.2, I remind you of the **length** command, whose output is the number of cases.

Box 6.2 Using *R* to Verify the Number of Participants in a Group

Enter the **length** command to verify the number of participants.	**> length (AS.user.dataset$totenjoy)** Output: [1] 39
Enter the **length** command to verify the number of participants.	**length (YAL.user.dataset$totenjoy)** Output: [1] 58

Because the groups aren't the same size—there are 39 AS textbook users and 58 YAL textbook users—I need to verify whether the variances for the groups are approximately equal. Eyeballing the squared standard deviations can give a sense of whether the variances might be approximately equal. However, the Levene's Test statistic, which can be calculated using *R*, allows an objective view. At this point in time, the command for carrying out the Levene's Test statistic resides in a package called "car" that can be added to *R*. In Box 6.3, I show how to add the package and how to carry out the Levene's Test statistic. After that explanation, I explain how to interpret the outcome of the Levene's Test formula.

Box 6.3 Using *R* to Check the Assumption of Equality of Variances With the Levene's Test Statistic

The one-word command for executing the Levene's Test statistic is in the downloadable package named *car*. Download the package using the **install.packages** command.	**> install.packages ("car")**
Import the package into *R*'s library using the **library** command.	**library (car)**

Use the **leveneTest** command to calculate the Levene's Test statistic. I use the dataset that includes both the users of the AS textbook and the users of the YAL textbooks (*enjoy.data*). I give the name of the dependent variable first, then a comma, then the name of the independent variable.	**leveneTest (enjoy.data$totenjoy, enjoy.data$text)**
	The output looks like this:
	Levene's Test for Homogeneity of Variance
	(center = median)
	         Df F value Pr(>F)
	Group 1 1.419 0.2365
	         95

The Levene's Test statistic is reported as an *F*-value (*F* = 1.419, single under-scored in the output); the exact probability of the *F*-value is interpreted [Pr(>F) = .2365, double underscored in the output] (Field, Miles, & Field, 2012, p. 188). The null hypothesis for the Levene's Test statistic is H_0: *The variances of the groups are equal.* The alternative hypothesis is H_1: *The variances of the groups are not equal.* When the exact probability of the Levene Test *F*-value is greater than .05, the null hypothesis is accepted and there's 95% certainty that the variances are equal. When the exact probability of the Levene's Test *F*-value is less than 0.05, the null hypothesis is rejected and the alternative hypothesis is accepted. There's 95% cer-tainty that the variances are not equal. For the analysis of the *totenjoy* data, because the exact *p*-value (*p* = 0.2365) is greater than .05, the null hypothesis is accepted. There's 95% certainty that the variances are equal. (Remember that R uses Welch's *t*-test to calculate the observed value of the Case II Independent Samples *t*-test statistic; Welch's *t*-test compensates for any violation of the assumption of equal variances, so when using R the assumption of equal variances is irrelevant.)

In summary, both the second and third assumptions are met; the data for the users of the AS textbook and the users of the YAL textbook approximate a normal distribution, and although the groups aren't exactly the same size, the Levene's Test statistic shows that the variances are sufficiently similar. If I weren't satisfied that the data for both groups approximated the normal distribution model and the variances were approximately equal, I'd use a non-parametric statistic to ana-lyze the data, the Wilcoxon Rank Sum statistic (see Chapter Seven).

Step 6: Calculate the Observed Value of the Appropriate Statistic

In Step 6, I calculate the observed value of the Case II Independent Samples *t*-test. First, I show the calculations step by step, then I illustrate how to use R to calculate the $t_{observed}$ value. Keep in mind that the Case II Independent Samples *t*-test is a parametric statistic; the model for determining statistical significance is the normal distribution.

The formula for a Case II Independent Samples *t*-test is:

$$t_{observed} = \frac{\overline{X}_1 - \overline{X}_2}{\sqrt{\dfrac{s_1^2}{n_1} + \dfrac{s_2^2}{n_2}}}$$

In this formula, $\overline{X}_1$ is the mean of the first group, $\overline{X}_2$ is the mean of the second group, s_1^2 is the standard deviation squared of the first group, and s_2^2 is the stan-dard deviation squared of the second group. The formula also includes the size of the first group, n_1, and the size of the second group, n_2. To calculate the value of $t_{observed}$, the first step is to determine the mean and standard deviation of each group.

Here are the descriptive statistics for the two classes—they're needed to cal-culate $t_{observed}$.

Users of the AS textbook	Users of the YAL textbook
n = 39	n = 58
Mean = 9.84615	Mean = 9.72414
Standard deviation = 4.78231	Standard deviation = 4.06868

Here, I entered the values into the formula:

$$t_{observed} = \frac{9.84615 - 9.72414}{\sqrt{\dfrac{4.78231^2}{39} + \dfrac{4.06868^2}{58}}}$$

Next I find the difference between the mean of the first group and the mean of the second group and square the standard deviations.

$$t_{observed} = \frac{.12201}{\sqrt{\dfrac{22.87049}{39} + \dfrac{16.55416}{58}}}$$

For each group, I divide the standard deviation squared by the number of people in the group:

$$t_{observed} = \frac{.12201}{\sqrt{.58642 + .28542}}$$

I add the two values in the denominator:

$$t_{observed} = \frac{.12201}{\sqrt{.87184}}$$

I use a calculator to determine the square root of that value:

$$t_{observed} = \frac{.12201}{.93372}$$

Then I divide the numerator by the denominator:

$$t_{observed} = \frac{.12201}{.93372} = .13067 = \mathbf{.1307}$$

The $t_{observed}$ value is .1307.[7]
  I now illustrate how to carry out these calculations using R. The first step is a reminder of how to import an Excel file (in the comma separated values [csv] format).

Box 6.4 Using *R* to Calculate the Observed Value for a Case II Independent Samples *t*-Test

Import the *enjoy.data* dataset using the **read.csv** command (see Box 6.1 for details on this command).	**> enjoy.data = read.csv(file. choose(), header = TRUE)**
I didn't calculate the descriptive statistics for the data in the two separate datasets created in Box 6.1,[8] but the descriptive statistics should be reported. The **sapply** command is another way to create separate datasets for the AS and YAL textbook users so that the descriptive statistics can be calculated (and side-by-side histograms can be created). To calculate the mean, I embed the **split** command inside the **sapply** command and add **mean** after a comma.	**> sapply (split (enjoy. data$totenjoy, enjoy. data$text), mean)** Here are the means: 1 2 9.846154 9.724138
Use the **par(mfrow = c(1,2)) command** to create a space for side-by-side histograms. The **hist** command embedded in the **sapply** command generates the histograms. Note that using this set of commands, the charts are the same color and they don't have separate titles.	**> par(mfrow = c(1,2))** **> sapply (split (enjoy. data$totenjoy, enjoy. data$text), hist, col = "purple")** 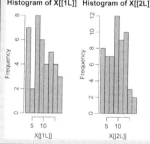
The standard deviation for each of the two sets of data can be calculated using the **sd** command embedded in the **sapply** command.	**> sapply (split (enjoy. data$totenjoy, enjoy. data$text), sd)** Here are the standard deviations: 1 2 4.782305 4.068678
To calculate $t_{observed}$, use the **t.test** command. There are several shortcuts embedded in this command. Inside parentheses, the name of the dependent variable is given first (*totenjoy*), then a tilde (~), then the name of the independent variable (*text*). The **data = enjoy.data** part of the command indicates that	**> t.test (totenjoy ~ text, data = enjoy.data)** In the output, the $t_{observed}$ value has a single underscore, the degrees of freedom value is bolded, and the exact level of probability has a double underscore.

(*Continued*)

Box 6.4 (*Continued*)

the dataset called "enjoy.data" should be used.[9] Note that *R* uses the Welch's *t*-test formula for calculating $t_{observed}$. The Welch's *t*-test formula compensates for the different *n* sizes and the fact that the variances are not exactly equal. The reported degrees of freedom (*df*) reflect the compensation, which is why *df* = 72.536 (see the information in the output that's bolded) rather than 95 $[(n-1) + (n-1)]$.	data:totenjoy by text $t = \underline{0.1307}$, *df* = **72.536**, $p = \underline{\underline{0.8964}}$ mean in group 1 mean in group 2 9.846154 9.724138

Step 7: Determine the Degrees of Freedom for $t_{observed}$ and Use Degrees of Freedom and Alpha to Find the Critical Value of the Statistic OR Calculate the Exact Probability of $t_{observed}$

Either of the two approaches described in Step 7 can be used, but the critical value approach is typically used when the calculation of $t_{observed}$ is done with a calculator. The exact probability approach can be used when the calculation of $t_{observed}$ is done using *R* and other statistical software programs, because they report the exact probability.

Using the Critical Value Approach

The formula for degrees of freedom for a Case II Independent Samples *t*-test is $[(n_1 - 1) + (n_2 - 1)]$. For this study, $df = [(39 - 1) + (58 - 1)]$, or 95. Alpha was set at .05.

I now have the information needed to find the correct critical value in the chart of $t_{critical}$ values, Figure 5.9. The chart shows that for 90 degrees of freedom and alpha of .05, $t_{critical} = 1.987$. Note that I used the critical value for *df* = 90, because the chart doesn't have a $t_{critical}$ value for *df* = 95; by tradition, researchers use the slightly more rigorous value of $t_{critical}$ than the slightly more lenient one when the chart use doesn't have the exact degrees of freedom needed. Using *df* = 90 instead of *df* = 95 provides a slightly more rigorous interpretation.

Using the Exact Probability Approach

When using the exact probability approach to interpreting the outcome, I use *R* (or some other statistical program) to calculate $t_{observed}$, and from the output I retrieve the value of $t_{observed}$ (single underscored in the output) and the exact level of probability for $t_{observed}$ (double underscored in the output). When I use *R* to calculate the Independent Samples *t*-test statistic, I also retrieve the degrees of freedom (bolded in the output) because R uses the Welch t-test formula for cal-culating $t_{observed}$, which compensates for differences in the size and variance of the two groups. The degrees of freedom reflect this compensation:

> data: totenjoy by text
> $t = 0.1307$, $df = 72.536$, $p = 0.8964$

Step 8: To Interpret the Outcome of the Analysis, Compare the Observed Value and the Critical Value OR Compare the Exact Probability to Alpha

In Step 8, the outcome of the analysis is determined using either the critical value approach (if calculations were done with a calculator) or the exact probability approach (if calculations were done using R).

Using the Critical Value Approach

The rules for comparing $t_{observed}$ and $t_{critical}$ are:

> If $t_{observed} \leq t_{critical}$ → accept the null hypothesis.
>
> If $t_{observed} > t_{critical}$ → reject the null hypothesis.

When $t_{observed}$ and $t_{critical}$ are compared, we see:

$$.13\ 07 < 1.987.$$

When $t_{observed}$ is less than $t_{critical}$, as is the case here, the null hypothesis is accepted.

Using the Exact Probability Approach

The rules for comparing the exact level of probability for $t_{observed}$ to alpha (α) are:

> If exact probability $\geq$ alpha → accept the null hypothesis.
>
> If exact probability $<$ alpha → reject the null hypothesis.

The output from R indicates that the exact level of probability for $t_{observed}$ is $p = .8964$; alpha was set at .05.

$$.8964 > .05$$

Because the exact probability is greater than alpha, the null hypothesis is accepted. The difference between the means of the two groups isn't large enough to reach the level of certainty needed to reject the null hypothesis. The researcher set alpha at .05 and wanted 95% certainty; the exact probability in this analysis shows only about 11% certainty, so the null hypothesis must be accepted.

Null hypothesis: There is no statistically significant difference in learners' perceived enjoyment of an age-specific textbook and a textbook for younger learners.

Step 9: Interpret the Findings as a Probability Statement

In Step 9, the probability statement is made using alpha and the null hypothesis accepted in the previous step, so:

There's 95% certainty of no statistically significant difference in learners' perceived enjoyment of an age-specific textbook and a textbook for younger learners.

Step 10: Interpret the Meaningfulness of the Findings

As noted in Chapter Five, there are two avenues for interpreting the meaningfulness of an inferential statistic, the first with reference to the research question. Recall that the researcher who conceived this fabricated study wanted to know whether the use of an age-specific textbook had an impact on learners' enjoyment of the text. The research question was: "Does learners' perceived enjoyment of their beginning-level Spanish textbook differ depending on whether the text is designed for their age group or designed for younger adult learners?"

The second avenue for interpreting the meaningfulness of a statistical outcome, the effect size, should be calculated even when the null hypothesis is accepted. According to Field, Miles, and Field (2012, p. 384), the effect size formula for the Case II Independent Samples t-test is:

$$\sqrt{\frac{t^2}{t^2 + df}}$$

In the first set of calculations below, based on my calculation of $t_{observed}$ that I did with a calculator, I use $df = 98$:

$$\sqrt{\frac{.1307^2}{.1307^2 + 95}} = \sqrt{\frac{.01708}{.01708 + 95}} = \sqrt{\frac{.01708}{95.01708}} = \sqrt{.0001797} = .0134052$$

When I use R to calculate $t_{observed}$ and the exact p-value, I use the degrees of freedom from the R output to calculate effect size:

$$\sqrt{\frac{.1307^2}{.1307^2 + 72.536}} = \sqrt{\frac{.01708}{.01708 + 72.536}} = \sqrt{\frac{.01708}{72.55308}} = \sqrt{.0002354} = .0153427$$

The guidelines for interpreting effect size (Field et al., 2012, p. 58) are: 0–.10 is a weak effect; .11–.30 is a moderate effect, and .31 or greater is a strong effect; both of the effect size values are weak.

The researcher reports the $t_{observed}$ value, the degrees of freedom, exact probability (or alpha, when calculations are done with a calculator rather than statistics software), and effect size.[10] The researcher's statement regarding the outcome would look something like this if the critical value approach were used in Step 8:

> **Given that statistical logic led us to accept the null hypothesis, I feel confident that learners' perception of their enjoyment of a textbook does not depend on whether it is age specific; there is 95% certainty of no statistically significant difference in the perceived enjoyment of learners using an age-specific text and learners using a textbook for younger learners (t = .13, df = 95, α = 0.05). Additionally, I found that the effect size, 0.0133, is quite small (Field et al.).**

The researcher's statement would look something like this when the exact probability approach is used in Step 8:

> **R was used to calculate the observed value of t (t = 0.1307, df = 72.536, p-value = 0.8964). Given that statistical logic led us to accept the null hypothesis, I feel confident that learners' perception of their enjoyment of a textbook does not depend on whether it is age specific; there is 95% certainty no statistically significant difference in the perceived enjoyment of learners using an age-specific text and learners using a textbook for younger learners. Additionally, I found that the effect size, 0.0153, is quite small (Field et al.).**

Case II Paired Samples *t*-Test

I now discuss the second type of *t*-test, the Case II Paired Samples *t*-test. The Case II Paired Samples *t*-test can be used in research that has a pretest and a posttest because the formula is designed to compare two means on *the same* dependent variable for *the same* group of people. It can also be used when a researcher has two sets of dependent variable data from the same participants, as in Jennifer Grode's (2011) study of learners' perceptions of the usefulness of two types of materials. It can also be used in a matched-pair design; that is, when there are different individuals in the two groups to be compared but each individual in one group is matched on all relevant background variables to an individual in the other group. (Matched-pair designs are somewhat rare in language education research because researchers typically don't have access to the large number of potential participants needed to create matched pairs.)

Jennifer used the Case II Paired Samples t-test formula to determine whether learners' perceived usefulness of authentic materials differed from their perceived usefulness of instructional materials. The dependent variable data on perceived usefulness for each of the two types of materials were collected using four 9-point Likert-scale items (eight items in total). To determine each participant's perceived usefulness score, the responses to the four relevant items were summed, so the possible range for the dependent variable is 4 to 36 points. The research question that guided this part of Jennifer's research was: "What are language learners' perceptions of the usefulness of authentic versus instructional materials?" (Grode, 2011). (The data for the 93 participants who gave responses for all eight of the relevant items can be found in the resource section of the companion website (www.routledge.com/cw/turner); they're also presented in Table 6.2.)

I follow the 10 steps in statistical logic to investigate whether there's a statistically significant difference in learners' perception of the usefulness of authentic versus instructional materials.

Step 1: State the Formal Research Hypotheses

For this study, the null hypothesis is:

> **There is no statistically significant difference in the learners' perceptions of the usefulness of authentic versus instructional materials.**

Jennifer proposed two alternative hypotheses because she was interested in making directional interpretations of her findings—two one-tailed, directional alternative hypotheses:

> **Alternative hypothesis 1: There is a statistically significant positive difference in the learners' perceptions of the usefulness of authentic versus instructional materials.**

> **Alternative hypothesis 2: There is a statistically significant negative difference in the learners' perceptions of the usefulness of authentic versus instructional materials.**

Step 2: Set Alpha

I'll set alpha for our analysis here at .01; the researcher and other teachers may make decisions about resources on the basis of the findings.

Step 3: Select the Appropriate Statistic for Analysis of the Data

Jennifer was interested in determining whether there's a statistically significant difference in learners' perceptions of the usefulness of authentic versus instructional materials. She was interested in this question in a general sense, so she did her best to collect data from a sample of participants from a population of learners by using an online survey to collect her data. The independent variable, *type of material*, has two levels, authentic and instructional. The dependent variable scores, *overall perceived usefulness*, are the interval-scale outcomes for the four authentic-materials items and the four instructional-materials items. Each of the 231 participants who responded to Jennifer's survey had an overall usefulness score for authentic materials and for instructional materials, though only 93 responded to all of the questions she analyzed in this part of her research. She used the Case II Paired Samples *t*-test formula because (1) she wanted to determine whether there was a difference in overall perceived usefulness, (2) the independent variable has two levels and participants have two dependent variable scores, and (3) the dependent variable is interval or interval-like and the data may approximate a normal distribution.

Step 4: Collect the Data

In performing Step 4, the data are collected and organized. The descriptive statistics for the 93 participants who responded to all eight items are presented in Table 6.1. The histograms are in Box 6.5. (The dataset can be found in the resources section of the companion website (www.routledge.com/cw/turner).

Step 5: Verify That the Assumptions Are Met

In addition to the participants being drawn randomly from a normally distributed population, there are two assumptions for using the Case II Paired Samples *t*-test formula:

1. The independent variable is nominal and has only two levels; the two levels are represented by the same participants.
2. The dependent variable is interval scale or interval-like and the dependent variable data for both levels of the independent variable approximate a normal distribution.

The first assumption for this analysis is met because the independent variable has only two levels, the learners' perception of the usefulness of authentic and

TABLE 6.1 Mean and Standard Deviation for Overall Usefulness of Two Types of Materials

n = 93	*Mean*	*Standard deviation*
Overall usefulness of instructional materials	24.7634	6.13861
Overall usefulness of authentic materials	26.8817	7.47438

instructional materials. Additionally, each of the 93 participants who responded to all of the items relevant to this part of her research has a score for the dependent variable, *perceived overall usefulness*, for both authentic and instructional materials.

To determine whether the second assumption was met, calculating and interpreting the Shapiro–Wilk statistic would have served as an objective measure of the normality of the distributions. However, at the time Jennifer did the research, she wasn't aware of the Shapiro–Wilk statistic and verified the normality of the two datasets by creating and examining histograms (see Box 6.5), one for the scores for the learners' perception of the usefulness of authentic materials and one for the learners' perception of the usefulness of textbook-based instructional materials. However, when the Shapiro–Wilk statistic *is* calculated for each of the two datasets, the objective view they allow indicates that neither of the two sets of data meets the condition of normality. The Shapiro–Wilk value for the usefulness of authentic materials level of the variable is W = 0.9519 and the exact *p* = .001797; for the usefulness of textbook-based instructional level of the variable, the Shapiro–Wilk value is W = 0.9195 and the exact $p = 2.542^{e-05}$. (The notation $p = 2.542^{e-05}$ means "move the decimal place 5 places to the left," so 2.542^{e-05} is really .00002542.) As I noted above, the null hypothesis for the Shapiro–Wilk statistic is H_0: *The data are normally distributed,* so when the *p*-value is greater than .05, the null hypothesis is accepted; and when the *p*-value is less than .05, the null hypothesis is rejected and the alternative hypothesis is accepted. The *p*-value for both datasets indicates that we must reject the null hypothesis and accept the alternative hypothesis, that the data are probably not normally distributed. In fact, because the assumption that the data are normally distributed is not met, a non-parametric statistic would be a better choice for the analysis. As one of the practice problems for Chapter Seven, you can reanalyze the data using an appropriate non-parametric statistic. In this chapter, I proceed with the parametric analysis, as Jennifer did.

Step 6: Calculate the Observed Value of the Appropriate Statistic

Like the Case II Independent Samples *t*-test formula, the Paired Samples *t*-test formula is a parametric statistic, and the model for determining statistical significance is the normal distribution. The calculations are not difficult but the steps are a bit tedious—at least I think they are. Table 6.2 shows the steps and reduces the possibility of my making mathematical mistakes. After demonstrating how to carry out the steps with a calculator, I illustrate how to use R to do the calculations.

The formula for the Case II Paired Samples *t*-test is:

$$t_{observed} = \frac{\overline{X}_1 - \overline{X}_2}{s_{\overline{D}}}$$

where $\overline{X}_1$ is the mean for perceived overall usefulness of instructional materials and $\overline{X}_2$ is the mean for the perceived overall usefulness of authentic materials. The value $s_{\overline{D}}$ is the standard error of the difference between the means. There are two steps in calculating $s_{\overline{D}}$:

First,

$$s_D = \sqrt{\frac{\sum D^2 - \left[(1/n_{pairs})(\sum D)^2\right]}{n_{pairs} - 1}}$$

Second,

$$s_{\overline{D}} = \frac{s_D}{\sqrt{n_{pairs}}}$$

To find the value for s_D using the first of the two formulas, I first need to determine D for each pair of values—the difference between each individual's pair of scores. Table 6.2 displays each individual's scores for the perceived usefulness of the authentic materials and the perceived usefulness of the instructional materials, the difference between the two scores, and the difference squared. At the bottom of the chart, you'll find the total for the values of D and the total for the values of D^2.

TABLE 6.2 Grode's Data and Steps in Calculating $t_{observed}$ for Case II Paired Samples t-Test

Participant	Perceived usefulness of instructional materials	Perceived usefulness of authentic materials	D	D²
1	27	32	−5	25
2	4	4	0	0
3	35	36	−1	1
4	31	36	−5	25
5	20	34	−14	196
6	25	28	−3	9
7	27	34	−7	49
8	26	30	−4	16
9	28	36	−8	64
10	20	28	−8	64
11	29	33	−4	16
12	30	29	+1	1
13	29	33	−4	16
14	28	34	−6	36
15	23	24	−1	1

(*Continued*)

TABLE 6.2 (*Continued*)

Participant	Perceived usefulness of instructional materials	Perceived usefulness of authentic materials	D	D²
16	26	33	−7	49
17	34	30	−6	36
18	10	26	−16	256
19	30	34	−4	16
20	29	36	−7	49
21	30	36	−6	36
22	27	35	−8	64
23	26	23	+3	9
24	29	25	+4	16
25	26	20	+6	36
26	25	18	+7	49
27	27	26	+1	1
28	12	12	0	0
29	20	36	−16	256
30	31	29	+2	4
31	36	24	+12	144
32	29	30	−1	1
33	24	24	0	0
34	26	29	−3	9
35	25	19	−6	36
36	15	29	−14	196
37	24	22	+2	4
38	28	36	−8	64
39	16	26	−10	100
40	27	17	+10	100
41	26	26	0	0
42	19	30	−11	121
43	32	20	+12	144
44	12	4	+8	64
45	21	34	−13	169
46	21	23	−2	4
47	28	24	+4	16
48	34	27	+7	49

(*Continued*)

TABLE 6.2 (*Continued*)

Participant	Perceived usefulness of instructional materials	Perceived usefulness of authentic materials	D	D^2
49	27	33	−6	36
50	29	36	−7	49
51	16	31	−15	225
52	20	24	−4	16
53	28	29	−1	1
54	22	36	−14	196
55	25	36	−11	121
56	27	25	+2	4
57	29	30	−1	1
58	22	26	−4	16
59	19	18	+1	1
60	20	35	−15	225
61	27	28	−1	1
62	20	20	0	0
63	26	29	−3	9
64	36	28	+8	64
65	29	11	+18	324
66	17	33	−16	256
67	26	29	−3	9
68	32	19	+13	169
69	21	12	+9	81
70	34	13	+21	441
71	26	28	−2	4
72	18	30	−12	144
73	23	28	−5	25
74	31	30	+1	1
75	20	36	−16	256
76	25	24	+1	1
77	8	13	−5	25
78	26	26	0	0
79	26	29	−3	9
80	12	11	+1	1
81	26	36	−10	100

(*Continued*)

TABLE 6.2 (*Continued*)

Participant	Perceived usefulness of instructional materials	Perceived usefulness of authentic materials	D	D²
82	24	30	−6	36
83	26	26	0	0
84	33	20	13	169
85	21	27	−6	36
86	24	20	+4	16
87	22	32	−10	100
88	32	31	+1	1
89	30	35	−5	25
90	27	22	−5	25
91	22	16	+6	36
92	24	32	−8	64
93	18	23	−5	25
	Total		$\Sigma D = -229$	$\Sigma D^2 = 5961$

Now s_D can be calculated using this formula:

$$s_D = \sqrt{\frac{\sum D^2 - \left[(1/n_{pairs})(\sum D)^2\right]}{n_{pairs} - 1}}$$

After filling in the number of pairs of data and the appropriate sums from Table 6.2, I have:

$$s_D = \sqrt{\frac{5961 - \left[(1/93)(-299)^2\right]}{93 - 1}}$$

Here's the next step in calculating s_D:

$$s_D = \sqrt{\frac{5961 - \left[(.01075)(52441)\right]}{92}}$$

and the next:

$$s_D = \sqrt{\frac{5961 - (563.74075)}{92}}$$

and next:

$$s_D = \sqrt{\frac{5397.2593}{92}}$$

and next:

$$s_D = \sqrt{58.66586}$$

and finally (I did warn you about tedium!):

$$s_D = 7.65936$$

Now I can calculate $s_{\overline{D}}$! (Are you excited?!)

$$s_{\overline{D}} = \frac{s_D}{\sqrt{n_{pairs}}}$$

First, I fill in the values for s_D and n_{pairs}:

$$s_{\overline{D}} = \frac{7.65936}{\sqrt{93}}$$

Then, I find the square root of 93:

$$s_{\overline{D}} = \frac{7.65936}{9.64365}$$

So:

$$s_{\overline{D}} = 0.794239$$

Now, finally, I can calculate $t_{observed}$ by filling in the values for the means and $s_{\overline{D}}$!

$$t_{observed} = \frac{\overline{X}_1 - \overline{X}_2}{s_{\overline{D}}} = \frac{24.7634 - 26.8817}{0.794239} = \frac{-2.1183}{0.794239} = \mathbf{-2.66708}$$

The value of $t_{observed}$ is −2.66708.

In Box 6.5, I explain how to use *R* to calculate $t_{observed}$ for the Case II Paired Samples *t*-test statistic.

Box 6.5 Using *R* to Calculate $t_{observed}$ for the Case II Paired Samples *t*-Test Statistic

Import the data (*useful.data*) for the analysis from the companion website using the **read.csv** command, which allows you to see the documents on your computer. (You'll need to open the *useful.data* file in the website and save it on your computer.) Recall that the **header = T** component indicates that the file being imported has a header.	> **useful.data = read.csv(file.choose (), header = T)**
Use the **View** command to take a look at the raw data.	> **View (useful.data)**
Make a histogram of the *totinst* values using the **hist** command. (See Box 6.1 for details on how to name variables within datasets using a dollar sign.)	> **hist (useful.data$totinst, xlab = "Total Instruction", main = "Distribution of Total Instruction Scores", col = "pink")** Here's the histogram: Distribution of Total Instruction Scores
Then calculate the Shapiro–Wilk statistic to check the normality of the distribution of *totinst* values.	**shapiro.test (useful.data$totinst)** Here's the output: Shapiro–Wilk normality test data: useful.data$totinst W = 0.9519, *p* = .001797
Make a histogram of the *totauth* values.	> **hist (useful.data$totauth, xlab = "Total Authentic", main = "Distribution of Total Authentic Scores", col = "orange")** Here's the output:

(Continued)

Box 6.5 (*Continued*)

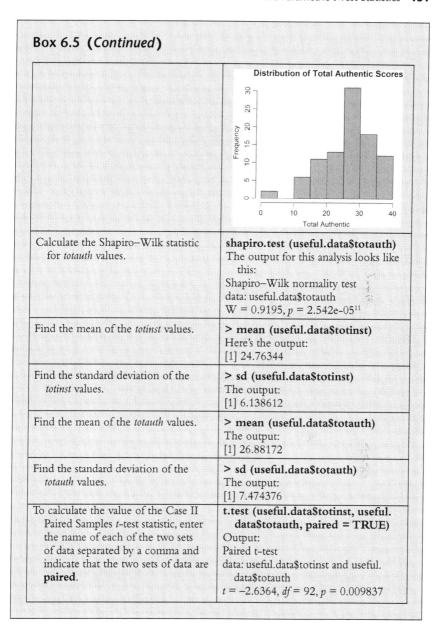

	Distribution of Total Authentic Scores (histogram: Frequency on y-axis 0–30, Total Authentic on x-axis 0–40)
Calculate the Shapiro–Wilk statistic for *totauth* values.	**shapiro.test (useful.data$totauth)** The output for this analysis looks like this: Shapiro–Wilk normality test data: useful.data$totauth $W = 0.9195, p = 2.542e{-}05$[11]
Find the mean of the *totinst* values.	**> mean (useful.data$totinst)** Here's the output: [1] 24.76344
Find the standard deviation of the *totinst* values.	**> sd (useful.data$totinst)** The output: [1] 6.138612
Find the mean of the *totauth* values.	**> mean (useful.data$totauth)** The output: [1] 26.88172
Find the standard deviation of the *totauth* values.	**> sd (useful.data$totauth)** The output: [1] 7.474376
To calculate the value of the Case II Paired Samples *t*-test statistic, enter the name of each of the two sets of data separated by a comma and indicate that the two sets of data are **paired**.	**t.test (useful.data$totinst, useful.data$totauth, paired = TRUE)** Output: Paired t-test data: useful.data$totinst and useful.data$totauth $t = -2.6364, df = 92, p = 0.009837$

Step 7: Determine the Degrees of Freedom for $t_{observed}$ and Use the Degrees of Freedom and Alpha to Find the Critical Value of the Statistic OR Calculate the Exact Probability of $t_{observed}$

The critical value approach is used when the researcher uses a calculator to find the $t_{observed}$ value. When the researcher uses *R*, the exact probability approach can be used.

Using the Critical Value Approach

The formula for the degrees of freedom of a Case II Paired Samples t-test is $(n_{pairs} - 1)$, so $df = 92$ for this study with 93 participants. Alpha was set at .01.

I now have the information needed to find $t_{critical}$ in Figure 5.9, the chart of critical values for t. I use the $t_{critical}$ value for $df = 90$ because the chart doesn't have the $t_{critical}$ value for $df = 92,$[12] so $t_{critical}$ when alpha is .01 is 2.6316.

Using the Exact Probability Approach

The output from R shows that $t_{observed}$ is −2.6364, there are 92 degrees of freedom, and the exact p-value is .009837.

Step 8: Compare the Observed Value and the Critical Value to Interpret the Formal Research Hypotheses

Researchers who use a calculator to calculate $t_{observed}$ use the critical value approach. Researchers who use a software program like R that gives the exact probability can use the exact probability approach, which for this study is a bit more precise than the critical value.

Using the Critical Value Approach

The value of $t_{observed}$ when determined using a calculator is $t = -2.66708$. The $t_{critical}$ value is 2.6316. The absolute value of $t_{observed}$ is compared to $t_{critical}$, so the negative sign must be removed from the $t_{observed}$ value before comparing it with $t_{critical}$. The rules for interpreting the comparison of $t_{observed}$ and $t_{critical}$ are:

If $t_{observed} \leq t_{critical} \rightarrow$ accept the null hypothesis.

If $t_{observed} > t_{critical} \rightarrow$ reject the null hypothesis.

When the sign on $t_{observed}$ is removed, we find that $2.66708 > 2.6316$, so we reject the null hypothesis.

When the null hypothesis is rejected, one of the alternative hypotheses is accepted. The mean for the learners' perception of the usefulness of instructional materials is less than the mean for their perception of the usefulness of authentic materials, so the second alternative hypothesis is accepted.

Using the Exact Probability Approach

The rules for comparing the exact level of probability for $t_{observed}$ to alpha (α) are:

If exact probability $\geq$ alpha $\rightarrow$ accept the null hypothesis.

If exact probability $<$ alpha $\rightarrow$ reject the null hypothesis.

The output from R is: $t = -2.6364$, $df = 92$, $p = 0.009837$.

The exact probability of the $t_{observed}$ value ($t = -2.6364$) is $p = .009837$, which is less than alpha (.01). The rules indicate that the null hypothesis can be rejected. The second alternative hypothesis is accepted, because as I noted immediately above, the instructional-materials mean is lower than the authentic-materials mean.

> **Alternative hypothesis 2: There is a statistically significant difference in the learners' perceptions of the usefulness of authentic versus instructional materials, with the mean for textbook-based instructional materials being lower than the mean for authentic materials.**

Step 9: Interpret the Findings as a Probability Statement

In Step 9, the appropriate probability statement is made using alpha and the hypothesis that was accepted in the previous step, so:

> **We can be 99% certain there's a statistically significant difference in the learners' perceptions of the usefulness of authentic versus instructional materials, with the mean for textbook-based instructional materials being lower than the mean for authentic materials.**

Step 10: Interpret the Meaningfulness of the Findings

Remember that there are two avenues for interpreting the meaningfulness of an inferential statistic. First the researcher refers to the research question, which for this study was: "What are language learners' perceptions of the usefulness of authentic versus instructional materials?" (Grode, 2011). It appears that there is a difference; the researcher found that she could be 99% certain there was a statistically significant difference in the participants' perceptions of the usefulness of these two types of materials; and furthermore, the participants perceived the authentic materials to be more useful than textbook-based instructional materials.

The second avenue is to calculate the effect size. For *t*-tests, the formula for effect size is (Field et al., p. 393):

$$\sqrt{\frac{t^2}{t^2 + df}}$$

I used the $t_{observed}$ value from the R output to calculate effect size; $t_{observed} = -2.6364$. There are 92 degrees of freedom.

$$\sqrt{\frac{-2.6364^2}{-2.6364^2 + 92}}$$

First, I square -2.6364:

$$\sqrt{\frac{6.9506}{6.9506 + 92}}$$

In the next steps, I add the two values in the denominator, then I do the division and find the square root:

$$\sqrt{\frac{6.9506}{98.9506}} = \sqrt{.07024} = .26$$

The effect size is .26. According to the guidelines for interpreting effect size (Field et al., p. 58), .30 indicates a moderate effect, so .26 can be considered a somewhat moderate effect.

Because the design of the study is ex post facto, the researcher has to be extremely cautious in the interpretation of the findings. I believe the results of this study might best be presented in this manner:

> **There is 99% certainty of a statistically significant difference in language learners' perception of the usefulness of instructional materials versus the usefulness of authentic materials, with the learners reporting that authentic materials are more useful ($t_{observed} = -2.6364$, $df = 92$, $p = .009837$). There was a somewhat moderate effect size (0.26). The ex post facto design of the study does not support causal interpretation of the findings but indicate a need for further research on learners' perceptions of the usefulness of these two types of learning materials.**

I'll now discuss and illustrate the third t-test formula, the Case I t-test.

Case I t-Test

The Case I t-test formula is rarely used in small-scale language education research. It allows the researcher to compare the mean of a sample of participants drawn from a population to the mean of the population itself. The results tell us whether the sample is considered part of the general population or distinct from that population. This type of t-test might be used, for example, to determine whether a sample of the sixth-graders from a particular school district in some state performed significantly better (or worse) on an end-of-year test than all of the sixth-graders in that state who took the same standardized test.

The formula for the Case I t-test is:

$$t_{observed} = \frac{\overline{X} - \mu}{\left(s_x / \sqrt{n_x}\right)}$$

In the Case I formula, $\overline{X}$ is the mean of the sample and μ is the mean of the population; s_x is the standard deviation for the sample and n_x is the number of people in
that sample. The formula for degrees of freedom for this type of *t*-test is $(n_x - 1)$,
the number of participants in the sample minus one.

Example Study

In response to educational legislation, near the end of the school year English language learners in public schools in California take a test of their English language
development. A researcher wanted to know whether the sixth-grade students in
his district differed significantly from the sixth-graders in the state of California
in terms of their English language development. The specific research question is:
Is the level of English language development of sixth-graders in the researcher's
district significantly different from the level of English language development of
sixth-graders in the state of California? The researcher identified a random sample
of 20 students from the school district to explore this question. (Fabricated data
are used in this example.)

Now, I follow the steps in statistical logic to address the researcher's question.

Step 1: State the Formal Research Hypotheses

When following the steps in statistical logic very strictly, the null hypothesis and
alternative hypothesis/hypotheses are set before the data are collected.

> **Null hypothesis: There is no statistically significant difference
> between the mean of the sample and the mean of the population
> $(H_0 : \overline{X} = \mu)$.**

> **Alternative hypothesis 1: There is a statistically significant positive
> difference between the mean of the sample and the mean of the
> population $(H_1 : \overline{X} > \mu)$.**

> **Alternative hypothesis 2: There is a statistically significant negative
> difference between the mean of the sample and the mean of the
> population $(H_2 : \overline{X} < \mu)$.**

Step 2: Set Alpha

The proposed research may have important implications for the school, so the
researcher set alpha at .01.

Step 3: Select the Appropriate Statistic for Analysis of the Data

The researcher is interested in knowing whether there's a statistically significant
difference between the mean of a random sample of the students enrolled in the

researcher's district and the mean of all of the students in the state. The dependent variable, *English language development*, is measured by a norm-referenced, interval-scale test that yields normally distributed scores when it's given to its intended population of test takers. Therefore, the researcher proposes to use the Case I *t*-test formula to analyze the data.

Step 4: Collect the Data

Fabricated descriptive statistics for a random sample of 20 students from the City Unified School District and fabricated descriptive statistics for the population are presented below:

Sample mean = 520   Population mean = 508
Standard deviation = 22   Standard deviation = 19
$n = 20$ $n = 150,000$

Step 5: Verify That the Assumptions for the Statistic Are Met

There are two conditions that must be met to use the Case I *t*-test formula:

1. The independent variable is *nominal* and has only two levels. (The two levels are represented by the randomly selected sample and the population itself.)
2. The dependent variable is *interval* in nature and the data are normally distributed in the population.

In the example study, the independent variable does have only two levels: the learners representing the random sample drawn from the school district and the learners representing the population itself. To check that the test used to measure the dependent variable is interval in nature, I'd need to examine the description of the data collection tool, the test, for verification. The technical manual for the test should indicate whether the test yields a normal distribution of scores when it's administered to the intended audience. For this study, review of the technical report indicated that the data should be normally distributed.

Step 6. Calculate the Observed Value of the Appropriate Statistic

Here's the formula for the Case I *t*-test statistic:

$$t_{observed} = \frac{\bar{X} - \mu}{\left(S_x / \sqrt{n_x} \right)}$$

First, I'll enter the descriptive statistics and the *n* size for the sample into the formula:

$$t_{observed} = \frac{520 - 508}{\left(22/\sqrt{20}\right)}$$

In the next calculation, I find the difference between the sample mean and the population mean and also the square root of 20:

$$t_{observed} = \frac{12}{\left(22/4.47\right)}$$

Now I'll simply carry out the math:

$$t_{observed} = \frac{12}{4.92} = \mathbf{2.44}$$

The $t_{observed}$ value is 2.44.

Step 7: Determine the Degrees of Freedom for $t_{observed}$ and Use Degrees of Freedom and Alpha to Find the Critical Value of the Statistic

Because I don't have a set of data from a population to illustrate the Case I *t*-test, I won't use R in the calculation of $t_{observed}$, and I won't be able to calculate the exact probability of $t_{observed}$. For this study, I use only the critical value approach in Step 7.

The formula for the degrees of freedom for a Case I *t*-test is $(n_x - 1)$, so for this study there are 19 degrees of freedom $(20 - 1 = 19)$. Alpha was set at .01. Using this information about degrees of freedom and alpha, I consult Figure 5.9 (the chart of critical values for *t*) and find that $t_{critical} = 2.8609$.

Step 8: To Interpret the Outcome of the Analysis, Compare $t_{observed}$ and $t_{critical}$

The rules for interpreting the comparison of $t_{observed}$ and $t_{critical}$ are:

If $t_{observed} \leq t_{critical} \rightarrow$ accept the null hypothesis.

If $t_{observed} > t_{critical} \rightarrow$ reject the null hypothesis.

When I compare $t_{observed}$ with $t_{critical}$, I have 2.44 < 2.8609. The rules indicate that when the observed value is less than the critical value, the null hypothesis is accepted, so I accept the null hypothesis.

Null hypothesis: There is no statistically significant difference between the mean of the sample and the mean of the population.

Step 9: Interpret the Findings as a Probability Statement

In Step 9, the researcher makes a probability statement using alpha and the hypothesis that was accepted, so:

There's 99% certainty of no statistically significant difference between the mean of the sample and the mean of the population.

Step 10: Interpret the Meaningfulness of the Findings

Remember the two avenues for interpreting the meaningfulness of an inferential statistic when the null hypothesis has been rejected? First is to interpret the findings with reference to the research question. The research question is: "Is the level of English language development of sixth-graders in the researcher's district significantly different from the level of English language development of sixth-graders in the state of California?"

These fabricated data indicate that we can be fairly certain (99%) that sixth-graders in the City Unified School District performed at the same level as sixth-graders in the state of California ($t = 2.44$, $df = 19$, $\alpha = .01$).

Then, we can calculate the effect size using the same formula as for the Case II t-test formulas:

$$\sqrt{\frac{t^2}{t^2 + df}}$$

$$\sqrt{\frac{2.44^2}{2.44^2 + 19}} = \sqrt{\frac{5.9536}{5.9536 + 19}} = \sqrt{\frac{5.9536}{24.9536}} = \sqrt{.2386} = .4885$$

According to the guidelines (Field et al., 2012, p. 58), an effect size of .30 or higher is strong, so an effect size of .4885 can be characterized as very strong. The findings based on the fabricated data might be interpreted and presented in this manner:

The analysis indicates with 99% certainty that there is no statistically significant difference in the English language development of sixth-graders in the City Unified School District and sixth-graders in the state of California ($t = 2.44$, $df = 19$, $\alpha = .01$), though there is a strong effect size (.4885).

R Commands Introduced in Chapter Six

dataset.name = read.csv (file.choose(), header = T) This command takes you to your computer where you can locate a file that you previously saved and import it into *R*.

View (dataset.name) This command displays the dataset in a separate pop-up box. The uppercase V is essential.

new.variable = variable.one + variable.two This command allows you to combine the scores for two variables as a new variable when variables 1 and 2 were entered directly into *R* as separate sets.

dataset.name$new.variable = dataset.name$variable.one.name + dataset.name$variable.two.name This command allows you to combine the scores for two variables as a new variable when a dataset was imported with the values for two variables in separate columns.

install.packages ("name.of.package") This command is the first in a set of two commands that allows you to install a package of *R* commands to supplement *R*'s capability.

library (name of package) This command is the second in a set of two commands that allows you to install a package of *R* commands to supplement *R*'s capability. Note that there are no double quotation marks in this command.

new.subset.data = subset (dataset.name, dataset.name$independent. variable = "level.to.be.new.set") This command creates a separate dataset for one level of the independent variable.

par (mfrow = c(1,2)) This command creates a space for displaying two side-by-side histograms.

shapiro.test (variable.name) This command computes the observed value of the Shapiro–Wilk test of normality and the exact probability of the observed value when the data were entered directly into *R*.

shapiro.test (dataset.name$variable.name) This command computes the observed value of the Shapiro–Wilk test of normality and the exact probability of the observed value when the data were imported into *R* as part of a dataset.

leveneTest (dependent.variable, independent.variable) This command computes the observed value of the Levene's Test statistic when the data were entered directly into *R* as separate sets.

leveneTest (dataset.name$dependent.variable, dataset.name$independent.variable) This command computes the observed value of the Levene's Test statistic when a dataset was imported with the values for the two variables in separate columns.

sapply (split (dataset.name$dependent.variable, dataset.name$independent.variable), mean) This command is one of several that separates the groups defined by the independent variable to calculate the mean for each group when a dataset was imported with the values for the two variables in separate columns.

sapply (split (dataset.name$dependent.variable, dataset.name$independent.variable), sd) This command is one of several that separates the groups defined by the independent variable to calculate the standard deviation for each group when a dataset was imported with the values for the two variables in separate columns.

sapply (split (dataset.name$dependent.variable, dataset.name$independent.variable), hist, col = "color.name") This command is one of several that separates the groups defined by the independent variable to make a histogram for each group when a dataset was imported with the values for the two variables in separate columns. Note that the histograms will be the same color.

t.test (dependent.variable~independent.variable, data = dataset.name) This command calculates the observed value of the Case II Independent Samples t-test statistic when a dataset was imported with the values for the two variables in separate columns.

t.test (group1data, group2data) This command calculates the observed value of the Case II Independent Samples t-test statistic when the data were entered directly into R as separate sets.

t.test (dataset.name$data.for.level.one, dataset.name$data.for.level.two, paired = TRUE) This command calculates the observed value of the Case II Paired Samples t-test statistic when a dataset was imported with the values of the dependent variable in two separate columns.

t.test (group1data, group2data, paired = TRUE) This command calculates the observed value of the Case II Paired Samples t-test statistic when the data were entered directly into R in two separate sets.

Practice Problems

An answer key is available on the companion website (www.routledge.com/cw/turner).

Study A. The coordinator of a private school in Japan that offers a test preparation class for the Test of English for International Communication (TOEIC) was committed to learning how beneficial the school's training course might be. All of the people who attend TOEIC preparation classes at the school complete two practice tests before they take the official TOEIC. In April, 42 people who had completed the test preparation course took the test when it was offered. The coordinator received the official mean for all of the people who took the test in April. The mean and standard deviation for the 42 people who had completed TOEIC preparation and took the test in April are presented below. Did the 42 students who had completed the course perform better on the TOEIC than the population of April test takers? (Descriptive statistics are fabricated.)

All Japanese   People who completed test training + 2 practice tests
Mean = 774   Mean = 820

$$s = 21$$

$$n = 42$$

Follow the steps in statistical reasoning to determine whether people who completed the coordinator's program scored significantly better than test takers who did not. When you report the outcome and make your conclusions in Step 10, please keep in mind the design of the study, which is ex post facto.

Study B. A teacher wanted to know whether students would benefit from completing and discussing a practice final test before taking the final test itself. She designed two equivalent forms of her final test and distributed Form A to her students one week before the date of the final exam so they could complete the practice test as homework. She reviewed the test with the students during the class meeting two days before the final test administration date. The students completed Form B as the final exam. The teacher compared the students' scores on Form A with their scores on Form B to determine whether there was a statistically significant difference in the students' performance on the two test forms. Her students' scores on Form A and Form B are presented in the chart. Fill in the descriptive statistics and follow the steps in statistical logic to determine whether the students performed differently on the two test administrations.

	Score on A	Score on B
Student 1	69	68
Student 2	70	70
Student 3	75	72
Student 4	76	73
Student 5	76	72
Student 6	78	73
Student 7	78	74
Student 8	80	75

(*Continued*)

(*Continued*)

	Score on A	Score on B
Student 9	81	74
Student 10	81	76
Student 11	90	80
Student 12	89	81
Student 13	80	79
Mean		
Median		
Mode		
Standard deviation		
Range		

Follow the steps in statistical reasoning to determine whether there was a statistically significant difference between performance on the two tests. When you report the outcome and make your conclusions in Step 10, keep in mind the design of the study, which is pre-experimental.

Study C. The researcher for a large school district is investigating whether fifth-grade children whose parents receive coaching in how to help their children with homework do better on their homework than children whose parents haven't been coached. The researchers randomly selected 80 fifth-grade children to participate in the study. The parents of 40 of the fifth-grade children, randomly selected from the 80 who had been randomly selected, were invited to participate in six hours of coaching on how to help their children do homework assignments. After these sessions, throughout the term, the parents participated in follow-up sessions, during which they received additional tips on how to help their children. The parents also turned in biweekly surveys that helped the researcher verify that the parents had been following the advice they had received. The parents of the other group of 40 children received the usual reports on their children's progress in school. At the end of the term, all of the children took a state test intended to measure students' learning. The test is designed to yield normally distributed scores. The researcher compared the performance of the children whose parents were coached with the performance of children whose parents weren't coached. The (fabricated) data are located in the resource section of the companion website (www.routledge.com/cw/turner).

1. What is the independent variable and what are its levels?
2. What is the dependent variable?
3. Identify the major category of research design and your reasons for your choice.

Now, follow the 10 steps in statistical logic to determine whether the children whose parents were coached performed significantly better on the state test than the children whose parents weren't coached.

The descriptive statistics for the two groups are presented below. You can retrieve the (fabricated) children's scores on the state test from the companion website (www.routledge.com/cw/turner) if you'd like to use *R*.

Parents Coached	Parents Uncoached
Mean = 85.25	Mean = 80.30
s = 5.77	s = 7.85
n = 40	n = 40

Notes

1 Jennifer adopts Larimer and Schleicher's (1999) definition of authentic materials as materials "that occur naturally in the target language environment . . . that have not been created or edited expressly for language learners" (p. v). Instructional materials are those "created for pedagogic purposes" (Grode, 2011, p. 3).

2 Check Chapter Two for discussion of the two types of ordinal scales if you have a question about the continuous nature of the questionnaire data.

3 I'm not entirely comfortable with this imaginary researcher's assumption about the distribution of the data in the population—the questionnaire is not designed to yield normally distributed data, although it might do so. If this were a real study, I'd encourage the researcher to create or locate a data collection tool that's designed to yield normally distributed data, rather than simply assuming that the one she adapted from another researcher will do so.

4 For this study, the two-tailed, non-directional alternative hypothesis is: There is a statistically significant difference in learners' perceived enjoyment of an age-specific textbook versus a textbook for younger learners.

5 The data can be found on the companion website (www.routledge.com/cw/turner).

6 Welch's *t*-test formula for calculating $t_{observed}$ corrects for the extent to which the variances of the two groups are unequal. This factor is reflected in degrees of freedom and the probability, both of which are adjusted to compensate for any inequality in the variances (Field, Miles, & Field, 2012).

7 I rounded $t_{observed}$ to the thousandth place to coincide with *R*'s level of precision in reporting $t_{observed}$.

8 I could have calculated the descriptive statistics using the AS.user.dataset$totenjoy dataset and the YAL.user.dataset$totenjoy dataset that I created. The commands for mean, mode, and median are in Box 2.6, and the command for standard deviation is in Box 2.8.

9 When you enter the data for the two groups defined by the independent variable separately rather than importing them in a dataset, the values for each group are entered separately using the **name.of.data = c(X, X, X . . .)** command. (See Box 2.4 to check how to enter interval-scale data.) Once both sets of values are entered, and the assumptions for using the *t*-test have been verified, the *t*-test command can be used. When the data are in two separate sets, the command is: **t.test (group1name. of.data, group2name.of.data).**

10 The sixth edition of the *Publication Manual of the American Psychological Association* (APA, 2010) recommends reporting effect size for all inferential statistics.

11 The notation $p = 2.542^{e-05}$ means "move the decimal place 5 places to the left," so 2.542^{e-05} is really .00002542.

12 Researchers use the slightly more rigorous value of $t_{critical}$ than the slightly more lenient one when the chart of critical values doesn't have the exact degrees of freedom needed. Using $df = 90$ instead of $df = 92$ provides a slightly more rigorous interpretation than using $df = 100$.

7

THE NON-PARAMETRIC WILCOXON RANK SUM AND WILCOXON SIGNED RANK STATISTICS

In 1956, Siegel wrote "behavioral scientists rarely achieve the sort of measurement which permits the meaningful use of parametric tests" and noted that "nonparametric statistical tests deserve an increasingly prominent role in research in the behavioral sciences" (p. 31). His observation is still true for much of the small-scale research in language education.

According to Corder and Foreman (2009), parametric statistics are appropriate only when participant selection and assignment to the experimental and non-experimental conditions meet these criteria:

- The participants are randomly drawn from a normally distributed population.
- The groups of participants are independent from one another, except for paired values.
- The data are interval scale and normally distributed in the population and the groups.
- The groups have approximately equal variances.
- The groups are adequately large. (p. 2)

In small-scale language education research, the participants are rarely randomly selected from a normally distributed population. The participants are often the students in a teacher/researcher's own classes, as was the case in Professor Borkovska's study, the one you read about in Chapter Four. Teacher/researcher's classes are often of different sizes, and the dependent variable variances[1] may be different because the participants were assigned to or chose their classes; the classes were created to accommodate the students' needs and schedules, not to meet the rigorous assumptions of a parametric statistic. Language classes are also often rather small, perhaps not as small as Professor Borkovska's classes, but not large enough to be considered "adequately large." As Corder and Foreman explain in a footnote, authors of statistics textbooks don't agree on the minimum number of participants for parametric analyses, though "most researchers" recommend more than 30 (p. 2).

Additionally, the data collection tools used by small-scale language education researchers are often designed to measure students' learning and opinions; these tools aren't designed to yield normally distributed scores, though they might do so sometimes by chance. In short, parametric statistics are often not the right tools for the job researchers do in small-scale language education studies. (You could listen to Marcia Ball's *Right Tool for the Job* again, if you'd like.)

In this chapter, I describe two non-parametric statistics that *are* the right tools. These non-parametric formulas, the Wilcoxon Rank Sum statistic and the Wilcoxon Signed Rank statistic, can be used to determine whether there's a statistically significant difference between two sets of data when any or all of the following conditions are true: The participants aren't randomly selected from a normally distributed population, the number of participants is relatively small, or/and the data are rankable but not normally distributed. Additionally, they're also appropriate when the two groups are unequal in size and the Levene's Test[2] statistic shows that the parametric assumption of equal variances isn't met. Both Wilcoxon statistics require that the independent variable have two levels; the dependent variable may be interval scale or ordinal scale but the data must be rankable.

The Wilcoxon Rank Sum statistic is appropriate for analyzing data from two groups of different people. (These two groups represent the levels of the independent variable.) In Chapter Four, you read Nataliya Borkovska's study of two techniques for presenting new technical vocabulary. She wanted to know which of the techniques was more effective for vocabulary retention. The participants in the experimental group received definitions of new vocabulary and concept maps; the participants in the non-experimental group received concept maps with highlighted vocabulary. Nataliya used the Wilcoxon Rank Sum statistic (she referred to it as Mann–Whitney U) to analyze her posttest data because, as is true of many research studies in language education, the number of participants in her study was rather small and her data weren't normally distributed.

The Wilcoxon Signed Rank statistic can be used when comparing data from paired samples, that is, when determining whether there's a statistically significant difference between two sets of data from the same group of people, as in a pretest–posttest design. My colleague, Professor Pablo Oliva, as part of a larger investigation into what type of feedback his learners of Spanish find most motivating, examined whether the learners in his study showed a difference in their level of motivation from the beginning of the term to the end of the term. He used the Wilcoxon Signed Rank statistic to compare the participants' level of motivation at the outset of the study to their level of motivation at the conclusion of the study.

Interpretation of the non-parametric Wilcoxon Rank Sum statistic and the Wilcoxon Signed Rank statistic is a bit complex, particularly when a researcher uses the critical value approach to interpreting and reporting the outcome. For each of these two statistics there are two slightly different formulas; the formula that a researcher uses depends on the number of participants. And unlike the *t*-test statistics, for which there's only one single-page chart of critical values, there are several different charts of critical values for interpreting the outcomes of the Wilcoxon statistics. I recommend using *R* to calculate the observed value of the Wilcoxon Rank Sum statistic and the Wilcoxon Signed Rank statistic, because *R* also reports the exact probability of the observed statistic, making it very easy to use the "exact probability approach"[3] when interpreting statistical significance. In the discussion that follows, I explain how to calculate the Wilcoxon Rank Sum statistic using each of the two formulas; I then illustrate how to use *R* to do the calculations. I next explain how to use the two Wilcoxon Signed Rank formulas and illustrate their calculation using *R*. An example study is the foundation for each explanation.

Non-parametric Statistics for Comparison of Two Independent Samples

In this section, I introduce the two different formulas for calculating the Wilcoxon Rank Sum statistic, one for small samples (fewer than 30 participants) and one for larger samples. The first steps in the two formulas overlap, as you'll see in the discussion below; however, the Wilcoxon Rank Sum statistic for larger samples has several additional steps that involve converting the outcome to a *z*-score.

Wilcoxon Rank Sum Statistic for Small Datasets (N < 30)

Before describing the premise for the Wilcoxon Rank Sum statistic for small datasets ($N < 30$), here's more information about Professor Oliva's research, which I use to illustrate the discussion.

Example Study

Professor Pablo Oliva had several research questions in his study on motivation among learners of Spanish. He conducted the research in two of his own Spanish classes—one had 10 students and the other had 5. He wanted to investigate whether providing feedback he designed to increase student autonomy and motivation would result in a higher degree of motivation than the type of feedback he typically gave his students. The independent variable for this research was *type of feedback* and it had two levels: (1) the non-experimental group, the class of 5 students who received the usual type of feedback, and (2) the experimental group, the class of 10 students who received the specially

TABLE 7.1 Total Posttest Motivation Scores for Oliva's Non-experimental and Experimental Groups

Student	NE	E
1	51	53
2	50	52
3	47	52
4	46	52
5	45	51
6	–	50
7	–	48
8	–	48
9	–	47
10	–	44

designed feedback. Data on the level of motivation, the dependent variable, were collected using a questionnaire administered at the beginning and end of the term. The range of possible scores for the learners' level of motivation was 0 to 55. The research question he used to guide this part of his investigation was: "Is there a statistically significant difference between the posttest level of motivation of students who received feedback designed to promote autonomy and motivation and those who received the usual type of feedback?" (Oliva, 2011). The motivation posttest scores for the non-experimental and experimental groups are presented in Table 7.1.

The Wilcoxon Rank Sum statistic is appropriate for analysis of the data because the independent variable in Professor Oliva's study, *type of feedback,* has two levels: one class received the first type of feedback, and the other class received the second type of feedback. The participants are from the professor's classes—clearly not drawn randomly from a normally distributed population. Additionally, the posttest values for the dependent variable, *level of motivation,* are rankable, although they don't appear to be normally distributed, as shown in the histograms[4] in Figure 7.1.[5] The data for the non-experimental group in particular are clearly not normally distributed—the distribution is flat (though the columns *are* really tall).

I use the 10 steps in statistical logic to carry out and interpret the analysis. Only the exact probability approach to interpreting statistical significance is presented in Steps 7 and 8 because, as I noted previously, I recommend using this approach to interpreting statistical significance due to the length and complexity of the charts of critical values.

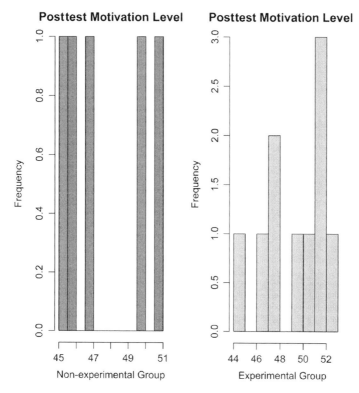

FIGURE 7.1 Histograms of Posttest Motivation Scores for Oliva's Non-experimental and Experimental Groups

1. State the formal research hypotheses, the null hypothesis and the alternative hypothesis/hypotheses.
2. Set alpha, the level of probability for interpreting the analysis.
3. Select the appropriate statistic for analysis of the data.
4. Collect the data.
5. Verify that the conditions for appropriate use of the statistic, the assumptions, are met.
6. Calculate the observed value of the appropriate statistic.
7. Calculate the exact probability for the observed statistic calculated in Step 6.
8. Compare the exact probability to alpha.

> If exact probability $\geq$ alpha $\rightarrow$ accept the null hypothesis.
> If exact probability $<$ alpha $\rightarrow$ reject the null hypothesis.

9. Interpret the outcome of the analysis as a probability statement using the hypothesis accepted in Step 8.
10. Interpret the meaningfulness of the findings and calculate the effect size if possible.

Step 1: State the Formal Research Hypotheses

As noted in Chapter Five, when strictly following the rules in statistical logic, the null hypothesis is always stated first. For this study the null hypothesis is:

> **There is no statistically significant difference between the rankings of the posttest motivation scores for the non-experimental and experimental groups.**

If the researcher simply wanted to know whether there was a difference in the outcomes for the two groups, the researcher would state a single alternative hypothesis. The two-tailed alternative hypothesis doesn't indicate whether the experimental group performed better or worse than the non-experimental group—it simply states that there's a difference.[6] When a researcher is interested in making a probability statement showing that one group performed better than the other, one-tailed, directional alternative hypotheses are needed. Because the hypotheses are set before the data are actually collected, both one-tailed, directional, alternative hypotheses are stated. For this study, the two alternative hypotheses are:

> **Alternative hypothesis 1: The rankings of the posttest motivation scores for the experimental group are systematically higher than those for the non-experimental group.**

> **Alternative hypothesis 2: The rankings of the posttest motivation scores for the experimental group are systematically lower than those for the non-experimental group.**

Step 2: Set Alpha

The research is exploratory in nature, so the researcher decided to set alpha at .05.

Step 3: Select the Appropriate Statistic for Analysis of the Data

The researcher wants to know whether there's a statistically significant difference between the rankings of the motivation scores for participants who received the feedback designed to promote autonomy and motivation and those who received the usual type of feedback. The independent variable, *type of feedback,* has two levels; the two distinct classes represent these two levels. The Wilcoxon Rank Sum statistic can be used to analyze the data because (1) the independent variable has two levels and there are different participants in the two groups, (2) the dependent variable yields rankable outcomes, and (3) the researcher is interested in determining whether there's a difference between the two groups' posttest outcomes.

Step 4: Collect the Data

In this step, the data are collected and organized (see Table 7.1).

Step 5: Verify That the Assumptions for the Statistic Are Met

There are two conditions that must be met to use the Wilcoxon Rank Sum statistic:

1. The independent variable is nominal and has only two levels; the two levels are represented by different participants.
2. The dependent variable yields rankable data.

The first assumption is met by the fact that the independent variable, *type of feedback*, has two levels: feedback designed to promote autonomy and motivation and the usual type of feedback. These two levels represent categories, so they satisfy the requirement that the independent variable be nominal. Additionally, the two levels of the independent variable are represented by Professor Oliva's two classes; none of the students attended both classes, so the two classes have different participants.

The second assumption is met by verifying that the questionnaire used to collect the dependent variable data yields rankable data. Review of the data (Table 7.1) and the histograms (Figure 7.1) shows that the data are rankable. Interpretation of the non-parametric Wilcoxon Rank Sum statistic is based on a model consisting of ranked data—a model to which the data in this study conform.

Though the Wilcoxon Rank Sum statistic is calculated using ranked scores, researchers usually provide descriptive statistics based on the raw scores and make histograms so they can see what the distribution of raw scores looks like. In small-scale language education research, reviewing the histograms may help researchers identify scores that were entered incorrectly or people who perform very differently from the others. In large-scale research, these people may be considered outliers and eliminated from the analysis, but in small-scale research with the goal of gaining a deep understanding of the learners and learning in the local educational environment, identifying these people with extreme scores may allow the researcher to collect additional information to explain why they performed so differently from the others. In some cases, such as if the people with extreme scores entered a class when the other students were already several weeks into their studies, the researcher might decide to omit them from the analysis, but generally they're considered part of the local learning environment and are included. Any additional information the researcher collects about these people with extreme scores should be included in the report.

Some researchers might calculate the Shapiro–Wilk statistic for each group to check whether the data are normally distributed and check for equal variances using the Levene's Test statistic. However, regardless of the outcome for the Shapiro–Wilk and Levene's Test statistics, three factors indicate that a non-parametric statistic rather than a parametric statistic is appropriate: (1) The participants are from intact classes rather than being randomly selected from a population of learners, (2) there are unequal numbers of participants in the two groups and the groups are very small, and (3) the researcher's primary goal is to gain a deep understanding of the local learning environment, not generalization of the findings to a population of learners.

I did calculate the Shapiro–Wilk test value for each of the two datasets and also calculated Levene's Test to check the variances. For the experimental group, the exact probability of the observed value of the Shapiro–Wilk test indicates that the data approximate the normal distribution model ($W = 0.9067$, $p = .2594$); the Shapiro–Wilk test for five scores in the non-experimental group indicates that they could be normally distributed too ($W = 0.9155$, $p = .5012$).[7] Additionally, the Levene's Test statistic indicates that we can assume equal variances ($F = 0.1037$, $p = .7525$).[8] However, the fundamental considerations in using a parametric statistic aren't met—the participants aren't drawn from a normally distributed population, nor do they represent a sample from a normally distributed population. The participants are simply the students in the researcher's language classes, and the researcher's primary interest is to gain a deeper understanding of *these* learners, not of a population of learners.

Step 6: Calculate the Observed Value of the Appropriate Statistic

The Wilcoxon Rank Sum statistic is a non-parametric statistic; the model for determining statistical significance is not the normal distribution. When the two sets of data are combined and ranked, the Wilcoxon Rank Sum statistic allows a researcher to determine whether the rankings are randomly distributed or distributed in such a way that one group tends to rank differently than the other—that one group of participants tends to clump at the top or bottom when the two datasets are combined and ranked.

The first step in calculating the Wilcoxon Rank Sum statistic is to combine the two sets of data and rank them, keeping track of the group for each

TABLE 7.2 Rankings of the Combined Experimental (E) and Non-experimental (NE) Groups

Group (E, NE)	Motivation Score	Rank
E_1	53	15
E_2	52	13
E_3	52	13
E_4	52	13
E_5	51	10.5
NE_1	51	10.5
E_6	50	8.5
NE_2	50	8.5
E_7	48	6.5
E_8	48	6.5
E_9	47	4.5
NE_3	47	4.5
NE_4	46	3
NE_5	45	2
E_{10}	44	1

individual. Table 7.2 presents the 15 participants in order along with their rankings.

To assign the ranks, I ranked the *lowest* score as first and the *highest* as 15th.[9] In the paragraphs that follow, I explain in excruciating detail how to assign ranks.[10] Please note that there's a special formula for calculating a Wilcoxon Sum Rank statistic when there are tied scores in the dataset (the formula and calculations are presented on the companion website (www.routledge.com/cw/turner); I don't use the formula here because it's rather complex and I encourage researchers who plan to use the Wilcoxon Rank Sum statistic to use R, which corrects for tied scores (Verzani, 2005, p. 245).

There's no problem in determining which person is ranked first; the *lowest* ranked person is the one with the score of 44, so I ranked that person first. The second lowest score is 45, so I rank that score second. The third lowest score is 46; that one's ranked third. However, there's a tie for fourth and fifth lowest score; to determine the rank for these two tied scores, I add the ranks (4 + 5); then I divide the total for the ranks by the number of scores tied at that value, $9/2 = 4.5$. Each of the scores of 47 is given a ranking of 4.5.

There are also two scores tied for sixth and seventh place. I add 6 and 7, then I divide the sum of the ranks by the number of scores, 13/2 = 6.5. The rank of 6.5 is assigned to each of the two scores of 48.

There's a tie for eighth and ninth place too, the two scores of 50. I add the ranks for the tied scores, 8 and 9, and divide the sum by the number of tied scores: 8 + 9 = 17 and 17/2 = 8.5. I assign the rank of 8.5 to each of the two scores tied for eighth and ninth place.

There's also a tie for 10th and 11th place (the two scores of 51). I add the ranks (10 + 11 = 21) and divide the sum by 2 (21/2 = 10.5). I assign the rank of 10.5 to the two scores of 51 tied for 10th and 11th place.

Similarly, there is a tie for 12th, 13th and 14th place (the three scores of 52). I add the ranks (12 + 13 + 14 = 39) and divide the sum by 3 (39/3 = 13). I assign the rank of 13 to the three scores of 52. The score of 53 is ranked 15th.

Now I separate the experimental and non-experimental groups and determine the sum of the ranks for the participants in the experimental group (ΣR_E) and the sum of the ranks for the participants in the non-experimental group (ΣR_{NE}) (see Table 7.3).

The next step is to determine the value of W for each group. The general formula for W from Corder and Foreman (2009, p. 61) takes into account the number of people in each of the groups.

TABLE 7.3 Sums of the Ranks for the Separated Non-experimental and Experimental Groups

Non-experimental (NE)	Rank	Experimental (E)	Rank
NE_1	10.5	E_1	15
NE_2	8.5	E_2	13
NE_3	4.5	E_3	13
NE_4	3	E_4	13
NE_5	2	E_5	10.5
		E_6	8.5
		E_7	6.5
		E_8	6.5
		E_9	4.5
		E_{10}	1
Sum of ranks for non-experimental group	$\Sigma R_{NE} = 28.5$	Sum of ranks for experimental group	$\Sigma R_E = 91.5$

$$W = n_1 n_2 + \frac{n_1(n_1+1)}{2} - \sum R_{NE}$$

To calculate W_{NE}, I retrieve the value for $\sum R_{NE}$ from Table 7.3; n_1 refers to the non-experimental group, which has 5 people. The experimental group, n_2, has 10 people.

$$\begin{aligned} W_{NE} &= n_1 n_2 + \frac{n_1(n_1+1)}{2} - \sum R_{NE} \\ &= [(5)(10)] + \frac{5(5+1)}{2} - 28.5 \\ &= 50 + \frac{5(6)}{2} - 28.5 \\ &= 50 + \frac{30}{2} - 28.5 \\ &= 50 + 15 - 28.5 = \mathbf{36.5} \end{aligned}$$

To calculate W_E, I get the value for $\sum R_E$ from Table 7.3. The number of people in the experimental group (n_2) is 10 and the number of people in the non-experimental group (n_1) is 5.

$$\begin{aligned} W_E &= n_1 n_2 + \frac{n_2(n_2+1)}{2} - \sum R_E \\ &= [(5)(10)] + \frac{10(10+1)}{2} - 91.5 \\ &= 50 + \frac{10(11)}{2} - 91.5 \\ &= 50 + \frac{110}{2} - 91.5 \\ &= 50 + 55 - 91.5 = \mathbf{13.5} \end{aligned}$$

The smaller of the two values, W_{NE} and W_E, is the Wilcoxon Rank Sum statistic value; W_{NE} is smaller, so the observed value of the Wilcoxon Rank Sum statistic is 13.5.

In the box below, I show how to calculate the Wilcoxon Rank Sum statistic using R. As noted by Verzani (2005, p. 245), R uses the formula for tied data when it's needed. However, when there are tied scores, the default formula for calculating *probability* shouldn't be used, so I include a command notation, **exact = FALSE**, which tells R to use the appropriate alternate formula.

Box 7.1 Using *R* to Calculate the Wilcoxon Rank Sum Statistic

Enter the data for the non-experimental group; type the name of the level of the variable (I named it *nonexp. feedback*) and the equal sign. Then type a lowercase **c** and within parentheses enter the motivation score for each participant in the non-experimental group. Separate the scores by commas.	> nonexp.feedback = c(51, 50, 47, 46, 45)
View the data, just to make sure they were entered correctly.	**View (nonexp.feedback)**
Enter the data for the experimental group (I named this level of the variable *exp. feedback*).	> exp.feedback = c(53, 52, 52, 52, 51, 50, 48, 48, 47, 44)
View the data.	> View (exp.feedback)
Calculate the descriptive statistics for the non-experimental group.	> summary (nonexp.feedback) Output: Min. 1st Qu. Median Mean 3rd Qu. Max. 45.0　46.0　47.0　47.8　50.0　51.0 > sd (nonexp.feedback) Output: [1] 2.588436
Calculate the descriptive statistics for the experimental group.	> summary (exp.feedback) Output: Min. 1st Qu. Median Mean 3rd Qu. Max. 44.0　48.0　50.5　49.7　52.0　53.0 > sd (exp.feedback) Output: [1] 2.869379
Next enter the **par (mfrow = c(1,2))** command to create a space for side-by-side histograms before entering the commands for the histograms themselves. (The histograms are shown in Figure 7.1.)	> par (mfrow = c(1,2)) > hist(nonexp.feedback, breaks = 10, col = "salmon", main = "Posttest Motivation Level", xlab = "Non-experimental Group")

(Continued)

Box 7.1 (*Continued*)

	> hist (exp.feedback, breaks = 10, col = "pink", main = "Posttest Motivation Level", xlab = "Experimental Group")
Though it isn't necessary, I calculated the Shapiro–Wilk statistic for each group too.	> shapiro.test (nonexp.feedback) Output: data:nonexp.feedback W = 0.9155, p-value = 0.5012 > shapiro.test (exp.feedback) Output: dataa:exp.feedback W = 0.9067, p-value = 0.2594
I use the **wilcox.test**[11] command to calculate the observed value of the Wilcoxon Rank Sum statistic, but tied values in the dataset were a problem when R calculated the exact probability, as shown by the warning (double underscore). Note, too, that I entered the **exp.feedback** group first in the command, and only W_E is reported (single underscore), though it *isn't* the smaller of the two W values. (The lower of the two W values is the one that's reported according to traditional practice.)	> wilcox.test (exp.feedback,nonexp. feedback) Output: data:exp.feedback and nonexp.feedback W = <u>36.5</u>, p-value = 0.1748 alternative hypothesis: true location shift is not equal to 0 <u>Warning message: In wilcox.test.default (exp.feedback, nonexp.feedback):</u> <u>cannot compute exact *p*-value with ties</u>
I change the method used for calculating probability from the default in the appropriate alternative in the new command. There's now no warning!	> wilcox.test (exp.feedback, nonexp. feedback, exact = FALSE)
	Output: data:exp.feedback and nonexp.feedback W = 36.5, p-value = 0.1748 alternative hypothesis: true location shift is not equal to 0

(*Continued*)

Box 7.1 (Continued)

Now I calculate W_{NE} by changing the order in which I enter the levels of the variable. W_{NE} has a single underscore. It's *this* value of W, the lower of the two, that's reported as the observed value of the Wilcoxon Rank Sum statistic. Note, too, that the exact probability of the analysis, p-value = 0.1748 (double underscore), is the same for both W_E and W_{NE}.	**wilcox.test (nonexp.feedback, exp. feedback, exact = FALSE)** Output: data:nonexp.feedback and exp.feedback W = <u>13.5</u>, p-value = <u>0.1748</u> alternative hypothesis: true location shift is not equal to 0

The observed value of the Wilcoxon Rank Sum statistic is $W = 13.5$ (I report the lower of the two W values), and the exact probability of that value is $p = .1748$.

Step 7: Calculate the Exact Probability for the Observed Value

The exact level of probability for the observed value of the Wilcoxon Rank Sum statistic, 13.5, as reported in the R output, is $p = .1748$.

Step 8: Compare the Exact Probability to Alpha

Here are the rules for interpreting the exact level of probability:

If exact probability ≥ alpha → accept the null hypothesis.

If exact probability < alpha → reject the null hypothesis.

Alpha was set at .05. The exact probability, $p = .1748$, is greater than alpha, so the null hypothesis is accepted:

There is no statistically significant difference between the rankings of the posttest motivation scores for the experimental and non-experimental groups.

Step 9: Interpret the Findings as a Probability Statement

In Step 9, the researcher makes the appropriate probability statement using alpha and the hypothesis that was accepted in Step 8:

There's 95% certainty of no statistically significant difference between the rankings of the posttest motivation scores for the experimental and non-experimental groups.

Step 10: Interpret the Meaningfulness of the Findings

There are two avenues for interpreting the meaningfulness of an inferential statistic. The first is with reference to the research question(s). The second is to calculate the effect size; however, the effect size formula for the Wilcoxon Rank Sum statistic requires that the observed value (W) be converted to a z-score for interpretation. When there are 30 or fewer participants, the observed value of the Wilcoxon Rank Sum statistic is *not* converted to a z-score for interpretation, so effect size can't be calculated and reported. The fact that effect size can't be calculated should be included in the interpretation of the outcome, so for this study the researcher could report something like this:

On the basis of the outcome of this small study, there is 95% certainty that the type of feedback these learners receive does not have an impact on their level of motivation ($W = 13.5$, $p = 0.1748$). (Effect size cannot be calculated due to the small number of participants.)

Wilcoxon Rank Sum for Larger Datasets (N ≥ 30)

There's overlap in the two approaches to calculating the Wilcoxon Rank Sum statistic; there are a few extra steps when there are 30 or more participants because the observed value of the statistic is converted to a z-score for interpretation. If calculations are done with a calculator and there are tied scores within the dataset, a formula that compensates for tied ranks should be used[12] before converting the outcome to a z-score. Note, though, that when it's needed, R uses the formula that compensates for tied scores. In the next pages, I use a fabricated expansion of Pablo's study to illustrate how to calculate the Wilcoxon Rank Sum statistic for larger datasets (≥30 cases).

Example Study

The year after Professor Oliva conducted the study described above, a colleague of his had the opportunity to conduct similar research at the school where she teaches; however, her classes were larger than Professor Oliva's. The independent variable for her study remained *type of feedback* and the dependent variable was *level of motivation*. The research question was the same as Professor Oliva's: "Is there a statistically significant difference in the posttest level of motivation of students who received feedback designed to promote autonomy and motivation versus those who received the usual type of feedback?" Her non-experimental class had 17 students and her experimental class had 14. Because she was replicating Professor Oliva's study, she followed the same procedures and required her students to complete the motivation questionnaire at the beginning and end of the term. The posttest motivation scores are presented in Table 7.4.

The Wilcoxon Rank Sum statistic is appropriate for analysis of the data because the independent variable in the study, *type of feedback,* is nominal and has two levels, and the dependent variable, *level of motivation*, yields rankable scores.

Step 1: State the Formal Research Hypotheses

As for the study above, the null hypothesis is:

> **There is no statistically significant difference between the rankings of the posttest motivation scores for the non-experimental and experimental groups.**

The researcher wants to make a statement about the direction of the possible difference in the performance of the two groups, so she sets two one-tailed, directional, alternative hypotheses:

> **Alternative hypothesis 1: The rankings of the posttest motivation scores for the experimental group are systematically higher than those for the non-experimental group.**

> **Alternative hypothesis 2: The rankings of the posttest motivation scores for the experimental group are systematically lower than those for the non-experimental group.**

Step 2: Set Alpha

This researcher set alpha at .05.

Step 3: Select the Appropriate Statistic for Analysis of the Data

The researcher wants to know whether there's a statistically significant difference between the rankings of the posttest motivation scores for participants who received the feedback designed to promote autonomy and motivation and those who received the usual type of feedback. The independent variable, *type of feedback,* is nominal and has two levels. The dependent variable, *participants' degree of motivation*, yields rankable data, although the actual values are not normally distributed. She proposed to use the Wilcoxon Rank Sum statistic and convert it to a z-score for interpretation because (1) she's interested in determining whether there is a difference in the posttest outcomes, (2) the nominal-scale independent variable has two levels and the participants in the two levels are distinct from one another, (3) the number of participants is greater than 30, and (4) the dependent variable yields rankable outcomes.

Step 4: Collect the Data

The motivation scores for the researcher's two classes are presented in Table 7.4.

Step 5: Verify That the Assumptions for the Statistic Are Met

There are three conditions that must be met when using the Wilcoxon Rank Sum statistic and converting the observed value to a z-score for interpretation:

1. The independent variable is *nominal* and has only two levels; the two levels are represented by different participants.
2. There are 30 or more participants.
3. The dependent variable yields rankable data.

The first assumption is met by the fact that the independent variable, *type of feedback*, includes two categories: one level is represented by the participants who receive feedback designed to promote autonomy and motivation and the other level is represented by the participants who receive the usual type of feedback. Additionally, none of the students attend both classes, so the two groups are distinct from one another. The second assumption is met by verifying the exact number of participants, 31 in this study. The third assumption is met by verifying that the questionnaire used to collect the dependent variable data yields rankable data. This can be done by reviewing the scores themselves (Table 7.4) and the histograms (in Box 7.2). Additionally, a non-parametric as opposed to a parametric statistic is appropriate because the study involves relatively few participants and they weren't randomly drawn from a normally distributed population.

Step 6: Calculate the Observed Value of the Appropriate Statistic

The Wilcoxon Rank Sum statistic is a non-parametric statistic; the model for determining statistical significance is not the normal distribution. The Wilcoxon Rank Sum statistic allows us to determine whether, when the two sets of data are combined and ranked, the rankings are randomly distributed or distributed in such a way that one group tends to rank differently than the other. The fabricated data for the non-experimental and experimental groups, with the participants in each group numbered, are presented in Table 7.4.

In Table 7.5, the two groups are combined and ranked, with the lowest score ranked first and the highest score ranked 31st.

In Table 7.6, I display the experimental and non-experimental groups separately and determine the sum of the ranks for the participants in the experimental group (ΣR_E) and the sum of the ranks for the participants in the non-experimental group (ΣR_{NE}).

TABLE 7.4 Posttest Motivation Scores for Non-experimental (NE) and Experimental (E) Groups

Student	NE	Student	E
NE_1	56	E_1	54
NE_2	55	E_2	53
NE_3	51	E_3	49
NE_4	50	E_4	46
NE_5	48	E_5	45
NE_6	47	E_6	43
NE_7	44	E_7	40
NE_8	42	E_8	37
NE_9	41	E_9	36
NE_{10}	39	E_{10}	35
NE_{11}	38	E_{11}	34
NE_{12}	32	E_{12}	33
NE_{13}	30	E_{13}	31
NE_{14}	28	E_{14}	29
NE_{15}	27		
NE_{16}	26		
NE_{17}	25		

TABLE 7.5 Ranking of Total Posttest Motivation Scores for Non-experimental and Experimental Groups

Experimental vs. Non-experimental	Total Motivation Score	Ranking
NE_1	56	31
NE_2	55	30
E_1	54	29
E_2	53	28
NE_3	51	27
NE_4	50	26
E_3	49	25
NE_5	48	24
NE_6	47	23
E_4	46	22
E_5	45	21
NE_7	44	20
E_6	43	19
NE_8	42	18
NE_9	41	17
E_7	40	16
NE_{10}	39	15
NE_{11}	38	14
E_8	37	13
E_9	36	12
E_{10}	35	11
E_{11}	34	10
E_{12}	33	9
NE_{12}	32	8
E_{13}	31	7
NE_{13}	30	6
E_{14}	29	5
NE_{14}	28	4
NE_{15}	27	3
NE_{16}	26	2
NE_{17}	25	1

TABLE 7.6 Ranking of Total Posttest Motivation Scores for Non-experimental and Experimental Groups With Total Rank

Student	Ranks for NE group	Student	Ranks for E group
NE_1	31	E_1	29
NE_2	30	E_2	28
NE_3	27	E_3	25
NE_4	26	E_4	22
NE_5	24	E_5	21
NE_6	23	E_6	19
NE_7	20	E_7	16
NE_8	18	E_8	13
NE_9	17	E_9	12
NE_{10}	15	E_{10}	11
NE_{11}	14	E_{11}	10
NE_{12}	8	E_{12}	9
NE_{13}	6	E_{13}	7
NE_{14}	4	E_{14}	5
NE_{15}	3		
NE_{16}	2		
NE_{17}	1		
Sum of ranks for NE group	$\Sigma R_{NE} = 269$	Sum of ranks for E group	$\Sigma R_E = 227$

Next I calculate the value for W for each group, just as I did for Professor Oliva's smaller study. First I calculate the W for the non-experimental group. The formula is:

$$W_{NE} = n_1 n_2 + \frac{n_1(n_1+1)}{2} - \sum R_{NE}$$

The value for $\Sigma\,R_{NE}$ is retrieved from Table 7.6; the number of people in the non-experimental group (n_2) is 17 and the number of people in the experimental group (n_1) is 14.

$$W_{NE} = \left[(17)(14)\right] + \frac{17(17+1)}{2} - 269$$

$$= 238 + \frac{17(18)}{2} - 269$$

$$= 238 + \frac{306}{2} - 269$$

$$= 238 + 153 - 269 = \mathbf{122.}$$

Next I calculate W_E. The formula for W_E is:

$$W_E = n_1 n_2 + \frac{n_2(n_2+1)}{2} - \sum R_E$$

The value for ΣR_E is retrieved from Table 7.6, the number of people in the experimental group (n_1) is 14 and the number of people in the non-experimental group (n_2) is 17.

$$W_E = \left[(17)(14)\right] + \frac{14(14+1)}{2} - 227$$

$$= 238 + \frac{14(15)}{2} - 227$$

$$= 238 + \frac{210}{2} - 227$$

$$= 238 + 105 - 227 = \mathbf{116.}$$

The smaller of these two W values is the observed value of the Wilcoxon Rank Sum statistic, $W_{observed}$; in this case, $W_{observed} = 116$. This is the observed value of W, but when there are more than 30 participants, $W_{observed}$ is converted to a z-score for interpretation (Corder & Foreman, 2009; Shavelson, 1996). The formula for converting W to a z-score from Corder and Foreman (p. 59) is:

$$z = \frac{W_{observed} - \bar{X}_W}{S_W}$$

In this formula, $\overline{X}_W$ represents the mean of W and s_W represents the standard deviation of W.

(1) The formula for $\overline{X}_W$ is:

$$\overline{X}_W = \frac{n_1 n_2}{2}$$

(2) The formula for s_W is:

$$S_W = \sqrt{\frac{n_1 n_2 (n_1 + n_2 + 1)}{12}}$$

First, I calculate the value of $\overline{X}_W$:

$$\overline{X}_W = \frac{n_1 n_2}{2} = \frac{(17)(14)}{2} = \frac{238}{2} = 119$$

Then, I calculate the value of s_W:

$$S_W = \sqrt{\frac{n_1 n_2 (n_1 + n_2 + 1)}{12}} = \sqrt{\frac{[(14)(17)](14 + 17 + 1)}{12}}$$

$$= \sqrt{\frac{(238)(32)}{12}} = \sqrt{\frac{7616}{12}} = \sqrt{634.6666} = 25.1926$$

Then, I can convert $W_{observed}$ to a z-score:

$$z = \frac{W_{observed} - \overline{X}_W}{S_W} = \frac{116 - 119}{25.1926} = \frac{-3}{25.1926} = -.1191\,^{13}$$

As you saw in Chapter Two, a z-score equal to or exceeding $+1.96$ or -1.96 is statistically significant at $p = .05$. In Step 2, alpha was set at .05. The observed value of z, $-.1191$, does not exceed $+1.96/-1.96$, so the null hypothesis is accepted.

For this larger study, in Box 7.2 I add several steps to those presented in Box 7.1 to use R to calculate the observed value of the Wilcoxon Rank Sum statistic *and* the exact level of probability for the observed value of the Wilcoxon Rank Sum statistic. I also demonstrate how to calculate effect size.

Box 7.2 Using *R* to Calculate Wilcoxon Rank Sum Statistic and Exact Probability for 30 or More Participants

Enter the data for the non-experimental group.	> nonexp.feedback = c(56, 55, 51, 50, 48, 47, 44, 42, 41,39, 38, 32, 30, 28, 27, 26, 25)
View the data.	> View (nonexp.feedback)
Enter the data for the experimental group.	> exp.feedback = c(54, 53, 49, 46, 45, 43, 40, 37, 36, 35, 34, 33, 31, 29)
View the data.	> View (exp.feedback)

Calculate the descriptive statistics for the non-experimental group.	> summary (nonexp.feedback)
	 Output:
	   Min. 1st Qu. Median Mean 3rd Qu. Max.
	   25.00 30.00 41.00 39.94 48.00 56.00
	 > sd (nonexp.feedback)
	 Output:
	 [1] 10.42515

Calculate the descriptive statistics for the experimental group.	> summary (exp.feedback)
	 Output:
	   Min. 1st Qu. Median Mean 3rd Qu. Max.
	   29.00 34.25 38.50 40.36 45.75 54.00
	 > sd (exp.feedback)
	 Output:
	 [1] 8.091849

Next enter the **par (mfrow = c(1,2))** command to create a space for side-by-side histograms before entering the commands for the histograms themselves.	> par (mfrow = c(1,2)) > hist(nonexp.feedback, breaks = 10, col = "orange", main = "Posttest Motivation Level", xlab = "Non-experimental Group") > hist (exp.feedback, breaks = 10, col = "purple", main = "Posttest Motivation Level", xlab = "Experimental Group")

(Continued)

Box 7.2 (*Continued*)

Output[14]:

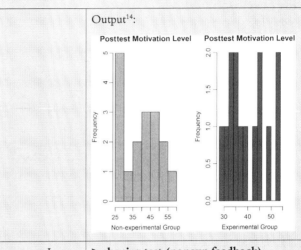

Though it isn't necessary, I calculated the Shapiro–Wilk statistic for each group too.	**> shapiro.test (nonexp.feedback)** Output: W = 0.9344, p-value = 0.2576 **> shapiro.test (exp.feedback)** W = 0.944, p-value = 0.4717
Use the **wilcox.test** command to calculate the observed value of the Wilcoxon Rank Sum statistic. There is no need to use the argument **exact = FALSE)** because there are no tied scores. If there were, **exact = FALSE** must be added so the correct formula for calculating exact probability is used.	**> wilcox.test (nonexp.feedback,exp. feedback)** Output: W = <u>116</u>, p-value = <u>0.9221</u>
I redo the calculation entering the exp. feedback data first so *R* will calculate the *W* for this group too. I need to know which is smaller so I can report the smaller value as $W_{observed}$.	**> wilcox.test (exp.feedback, nonexp. feedback)** Output: W = 122, p-value = <u>0.9221</u>

(*Continued*)

Box 7.2 (*Continued*)

Note, too, that the exact probability of the analysis, $p = 0.9221$ (double underscore), is the same for both W_E and W_{NE}.	
I can calculate effect size for this study because there's a sufficient number of participants to justify calculating a z-score. To calculate effect size, I need to retrieve the z-score from R's calculations. I do that by repeating the command that resulted in the lower W value and requesting a model.	**> study.model = wilcox.test (nonexp. feedback, exp.feedback)**
The command **z=qnorm(study.model)** extracts the z-value for the exact p from this model; the z-value is divided by 2 to focus on just one end of the z-distribution (Field, Miles, & Field, 2012, p. 665).	**> z = qnorm(study.model\$p.value/2)**
To see the z-value, enter **z**.	**> z** Output: -0.0977617[15]
The effect size is calculated using: $$\text{effect size} = \frac{\lvert z \rvert}{\sqrt{N}}$$ Written as an R command, it's **effect.size = abs(z)/ sqrt(N)**	**> effect.size = abs(z)/sqrt (31)**

(*Continued*)

Box 7.2 (*Continued*)

In this formula, the uppercase N indicates the total number of participants.	
To see the effect size, enter **effect.size**.	> **effect.size** Output: 0.01755852

I review the output and report the smaller of the two W values as $W_{observed}$ (single underscored in the R output in Box 7.2).

$$W = 116, p = .9221.$$

Step 7: Calculate the Exact Probability for the Observed Value of the Wilcoxon Rank Sum Statistic

The exact level of probability for the observed value of the Wilcoxon Rank Sum statistic ($W = 116$) is $p = .9221$.

Step 8: Compare the Probability of the Observed Value of the Statistic to Alpha

To interpret the outcome, follow the rules for comparing exact probability to alpha:

If exact probability $\geq$ alpha $\rightarrow$ accept the null hypothesis.

If exact probability $<$ alpha $\rightarrow$ reject the null hypothesis.

Alpha was set at .05. The exact probability, $p = .9221$, is greater than alpha, so the null hypothesis is accepted:

There is no statistically significant difference between the rankings of the posttest motivation scores for the non-experimental and experimental groups.

Step 9: Interpret the Findings as a Probability Statement

In Step 9, the appropriate probability statement is made using alpha and the hypothesis that was accepted in Step 8.

> **There's 95% certainty of no statistically significant difference between the rankings for posttest level of motivation of the non-experimental and the rankings of the experimental group.**

Step 10: Interpret the Meaningfulness of the Findings

Meaningfulness is interpreted with reference to the research question, which is: "Is there a statistically significant different in the posttest outcomes of students who received the feedback designed to promote autonomy and motivation versus those who received the usual type of feedback?" Additionally, effect size should be calculated and reported. The calculation of effect size is shown in Box 7.2, but when the researcher is using a calculator, effect size can still be determined.

The formula for effect size for the Wilcoxon Rank Sum statistic is:

$$\text{effect size} = \frac{|z|}{\sqrt{N}}$$

In this formula, $|z|$ means the absolute value of z. In other words, take the positive or negative sign off the z-value. The z-score I calculated by calculator is $z = -.1191$, so:

$$\text{effect size} = \frac{|-.1191|}{\sqrt{31}} = \frac{.1191}{\sqrt{31}} = \frac{.1191}{5.56776} = .02139$$

The values for the Wilcoxon Rank Sum analyses were slightly different depending on whether I used a calculator or R, reflecting a difference in how many decimal places were carried through the calculations. If the researcher uses R, the report would look something like this:

> **For these 31 students, I conclude that the type of feedback does not have an impact on students' level of motivation; there is 95% certainty of no statistically significant difference between the motivation scores of learners receiving the feedback designed to promote autonomy and motivation and learners who received the usual type of feedback ($W = 116, p = .9211$). The effect size (.01756) is very small.**

If the researcher uses a calculator, the report would look something like this:

> For these 31 students, I conclude that the type of feedback does not have an impact on students' level of motivation; there is 95% certainty of no statistically significant difference between the motivation scores of learners receiving the feedback designed to promote autonomy and motivation and learners who received the usual type of feedback ($W = 116$, W converted to $z = -0.1191$). The effect size is very small (.02139).

Non-parametric Statistics for the Comparison of Two Paired Samples

In this section, I introduce the two different formulas for calculating the Wilcoxon Signed Rank statistic, one for small samples (fewer than 30 participants) and one for larger samples. As is true for the Wilcoxon Rank Sum statistic, the first steps in the two Wilcoxon Signed Rank formulas overlap. When there are more than 30 participants, the outcome is converted to a z-score for interpretation.

Wilcoxon Signed Rank Statistic for Small Datasets (N < 30)

The Wilcoxon Signed Rank statistic for small groups ($N < 30$) is used to determine whether there's a statistically significant difference in the performance of a group of people when they are compared to themselves, as in a study with a pretest–posttest design. This type of study is considered a *paired samples* or *dependent samples* comparison. It's appropriate when (1) the independent variable has two levels and the participants are compared against themselves, as in a pretest–posttest design, or when there are carefully matched pairs of participants, (2) the dependent variable yields rankable outcomes, and (3) the researcher is interested in determining whether there's a difference between the two sets of dependent-variable values. Before describing the premise for the Wilcoxon Signed Rank statistic for small datasets, here's more information on Professor Oliva's research, which I use to illustrate the discussion.

Example Study

Professor Oliva, in his study on factors affecting the motivation of learners of Spanish, collected data on his students' level of motivation both before and after a period of instruction during which they received feedback designed to promote their motivation to study Spanish. He wanted to determine whether there was a statistically significant difference in the level of motivation for the participants who received this special type of feedback, so he compared their pretest level of motivation to their posttest level of motivation. The research question that guided this investigation was: "Is there a statistically significant difference in the pre-feedback and post-feedback level of motivation for students who received feedback designed to promote autonomy and motivation?" To do this analysis, he used the Wilcoxon Signed Rank statistic. The motivation scores for Professor Oliva's participants are presented in Table 7.7.

The Wilcoxon Signed Rank statistic is appropriate for analysis of the data because the independent variable in this study has two levels, which represent the participants' pre-motivational feedback state (no feedback yet) and their post-motivational feedback state (having received the feedback). Data on the *level of motivation*, the dependent variable, were collected using a questionnaire administered at the beginning and end of the term. The range of possible scores for the learners' level of motivation was 0 to 55. The data are rankable, but neither the pre-feedback motivation scores nor the post-feedback motivation scores are normally distributed, as shown in the histograms in Figure 7.2.[16]

In the next pages, I demonstrate how to carry out the calculations for the observed value of the Wilcoxon Signed Rank statistic using a calculator—then I demonstrate how to use R to calculate both the observed value of the Wilcoxon Signed Rank statistic and the exact level of probability for the observed value. Calculating the exact level of probability for the Wilcoxon Signed Rank statistic is necessary because in Steps 7 and 8 I use the exact probability approach to determining statistical significance.

I follow the 10 steps in statistical logic to investigate the research question, "Is there a statistically significant difference in the pre-feedback and post-feedback level of motivation for students who received feedback designed to promote autonomy and motivation?"

Step 1: State the Formal Research Hypotheses

As noted in Chapter Five, when strictly following the rules in statistical logic, the null hypothesis is always stated first. For this study, the null hypothesis is:

There is no statistically significant difference in the rankings of the pre-feedback and post-feedback motivation scores for the participants who received feedback designed to promote autonomy and motivation.

I set two alternative hypotheses, because although I *believe* that if significant difference is found, the posttest level of motivation will be higher than the pretest level, I won't know until I do the analysis. The two one-tailed, directional, alternative hypotheses are:

Alternative hypothesis 1: The rankings of the participants' pre-feedback motivation scores are systematically higher than the rankings of the post-feedback motivation scores.

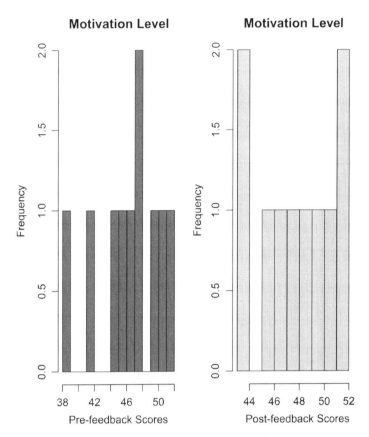

FIGURE 7.2 Histograms of Pretest and Posttest Motivation Scores

> **Alternative hypothesis 2: The rankings of the participants' pre-feedback motivation scores are systematically lower than the rankings of the post-feedback motivation scores.**

Step 2: Set Alpha

This research is exploratory in nature, so I set alpha at .05.

Step 3: Select the Appropriate Statistic for Analysis of the Data

I want to know whether there's a statistically significant difference between the pre-feedback and post-feedback rankings of the motivation scores for participants who received feedback designed to promote autonomy and motivation. The independent variable, represented by the participants' level of motivation before and after the feedback, forms two categories, or levels. The dependent variable, *participants' degree of motivation*, yields rankable data, though the actual values are not normally distributed. I propose to use the Wilcoxon Signed Rank statistic because (1) I'm interested in determining whether there is a difference between the pretest and posttest outcomes, (2) the two sets of data come from exactly the same participants, and (3) the dependent variable yields rankable outcomes. Additionally, a non-parametric statistic is appropriate because the participants are not drawn from a normally distributed population.

Step 4: Collect the Data

The data are presented in Table 7.7.

Step 5: Verify That the Assumptions for the Statistic Are Met

There are three conditions that must be met when using the Wilcoxon Signed Rank statistic:

1. The independent variable is *nominal* and has only two levels.
2. Comparison is of two sets of outcomes for the same participants (or carefully matched pairs of participants).
3. The dependent variable yields rankable data.

The first assumption is met by the fact that the independent variable is represented by the participants' pre-feedback and post-feedback motivation scores. The second is met by verifying that there's exactly the same people in the pre- and post-comparison groups. The third is met by verifying that the questionnaire used to collect the information on the dependent variable yields rankable data and by examining the scores themselves (Table 7.7) and histograms of the scores (Figure 7.2).

Step 6: Calculate the Observed Value of the Appropriate Statistic

The Wilcoxon Signed Rank statistic is a non-parametric statistic; the model for determining statistical significance isn't the normal distribution. The model for determining statistical significance is based on the pattern of differences between the pre and post outcomes for the participants. The outcome for each pair of data is examined to determine whether there is a difference and whether the difference is positive or negative, hence the "signed" part of the statistic's name. The Wilcoxon Signed Rank statistic, like the Wilcoxon Rank Sum statistic, has two versions, one for use with a small number of participants (<30) and another when there are 30 or more participants.[17]

TABLE 7.7 Differences, Ranked Differences, and Signs

Participant	Pretest Total	Posttest Total	Difference	Rank of Difference	Sign
1	48	44	+4	4.5	+
2	52	52	0	exclude	
3	42	46	−4	4.5	−
4	50	50	0	exclude	
5	45	48	−3	3	−
6	46	52	−6	7	−
7	48	47	+1	1	+
8	38	43	−5	6	−
9	47	49	−2	2	−
10	51	51	0	exclude	

The first step in calculating the Wilcoxon Signed Rank statistic is to calculate the difference between each participant's two scores. After calculating the differences, pairs for which there is no difference are excluded from the analysis. In this study, there are three pairs for which there is no difference (see Table 7.7 above).

After excluding the pairs for which there is no difference, I consider the absolute value of each difference and rank the differences from lowest to highest. Participant 7 shows the least difference, 1, so I rank that person first. The next smallest difference is 2; I rank that person second. The next smallest difference is 3, so that person is ranked third. The two differences of 4 are tied for fourth and fifth place, so I add the place values, 4 + 5 = 9, and divide that outcome by 2 (9/2 = 4.5). Each of the differences of 4 is assigned the rank of 4.5. The difference of 5 is ranked sixth, and the difference of 6, which is the largest difference, is ranked seventh. Finally, I identify the sign for each difference. Table 7.7 displays the pretest and posttest scores, the differences, the ranks of the differences, and the signs for the differences.

Next, I find the sum of the ranks for the positive differences and the sum of the ranks for the negative differences (see Table 7.8).

The observed value of the Wilcoxon Signed Rank statistic is the smaller of the two sums of ranks. The sum of ranks for the positive differences is 5.5; the sum of ranks for the negative differences is 22.5; therefore, the observed value of the Wilcoxon Signed Rank statistic is 5.5.

R can be used to calculate both the observed value of the Wilcoxon Signed Rank statistic and its exact probability, as I show in Box 7.3.

TABLE 7.8 Sum of Ranks for Positive and Negative Differences

Rank of Difference	Sign	Positive Signs	Negative Signs
4.5	+	4.5	
exclude	exclude	exclude	exclude
4.5	–		4.5
exclude	exclude	exclude	exclude
3	–		3
7	–		7
1	+	1	
6	–		6
2	–		2
exclude	exclude	exclude	exclude
Total sum of ranks		$\Sigma_{positive} = 5.5$	$\Sigma_{negative} = 22.5$

Box 7.3 Using *R* to Calculate the Wilcoxon Signed Rank Statistic and Exact Probability

Enter the pretest data: type the name of the level of the variable (*pretest* will do) and the equal sign and a lowercase **c.** Then enter each pretest value between parentheses, separated by commas.	> **pretest = c(48, 52, 42, 50, 45, 46, 48, 38, 47, 51)**
View the pretest data.	> **View (pretest)**
Enter the posttest data (I've given the data the name *posttest*).	> **posttest = c(44, 52, 46, 50, 48, 52, 47, 43, 49, 51)**
View the posttest data.	> **View (posttest)**
Calculate the descriptive statistics for the pretest motivation scores.	> **summary (pretest)** Output: Min. 1st Qu. Median Mean 3rd Qu. Max. 38.00 45.25 47.50 46.70 49.50 52.00

(*Continued*)

Box 7.3 (*Continued*)

	> **sd (pretest)** Output: 4.24395
Calculate the descriptive statistics for the posttest motivation scores.	> **summary (posttest)** Output: Min. 1st Qu. Median Mean 3rd Qu. Max. 43.00 46.25 48.50 48.20 50.75 52.00 > **sd (posttest)** Output: [1] 3.190263
Enter the **par (mfrow = c(1,2))** command to create a space for side-by-side histograms before entering the commands for the histograms themselves.	> **par (mfrow =c(1,2))** > **hist(pretest, breaks = 10, xlab = "Pre-feedback Scores", col = "blue", main = "Motivation Level").** > **hist(posttest, breaks = 10, xlab = "Post-feedback Scores", col = "red", main = "Motivation Level")** Output:
Though checking the normality of the distributions isn't necessary, the Shapiro–Wilk statistic[18] can be calculated for each set of scores.	> **shapiro. test (pretest)** Output: $W = 0.9409, p\text{-value} = 0.5635$

(*Continued*)

Box 7.3 (*Continued*)

	> **shapiro.test (posttest)** W = 0.9392, p–value = 0.5444
To calculate the observed value of the Wilcoxon Signed Rank statistic and its exact level of probability, use the **wilcox. test** command, specifying the two levels of the independent variable inside parentheses (separated by a comma) and indicating that the data are paired. The warning (single underscore) indicates that the default formula for calculating exact probability shouldn't be used because of tied scores. In the next command I add **exact = FALSE** so the correct formula for calculating exact probability is used.	> **wilcox.test (pretest, posttest, paired = TRUE)** The output looks like this: data:pretest and posttest V = 5.5, p–value = 0.1755 alternative hypothesis: true location shift is not equal to 0 <u>Warning messages:</u> <u>1: In wilcox.test.default(pretest, posttest, paired =TRUE) :</u> cannot compute exact p-value with ties
Add **exact = FALSE** to indicate that the default formula for calculating exact probability can't be used.	> **wilcox.test (pretest, posttest, paired = TRUE, exact = FALSE)** Output: V = <u>5.5</u>, p–value = <u>0.1755</u> alternative hypothesis: true location shift is not equal to 0
Repeat the command, reversing the order of the two levels of the variable.	> **wilcox.test (posttest, pretest, paired = TRUE, exact = FALSE)** Output: V = 22.5, p–value = <u>0.1755</u> alternative hypothesis: true location shift is not equal to 0

Step 7: Calculate the Exact Probability for the Observed Value of the Wilcoxon Signed Rank Statistic

I review the output from the two analyses and report the smaller of the two W values (single underscore in the R output in Box 7.3) as the observed value of the Wilcoxon Signed Rank statistic, $V_{observed}$. The exact level of probability for the analysis is .1755 (double underscore in the R output).

$$V = 5.5, p\text{-value} = 0.1755.$$

Step 8: Compare the Probability of the Observed Value of the Statistic to Alpha

Here are the rules—again!

> If exact probability $\geq$ alpha → accept the null hypothesis.
>
> If exact probability < alpha → reject the null hypothesis.

Alpha was set at .05, and the exact probability, p = .1755, is greater than alpha, so the null hypothesis is accepted:

> **There is no statistically significant difference in the rankings of the pre-feedback and post-feedback motivation scores for the participants who received feedback designed to promote autonomy and motivation.**

Step 9: Interpret the Findings as a Probability Statement

The probability statement is based on the hypothesis that was accepted in Step 8.

> **There's 95% certainty that there's no statistically significant difference in the rankings of the pre-feedback and post-feedback motivation scores for the participants who received feedback designed to promote autonomy and motivation.**

Step 10: Interpret the Meaningfulness of the Findings

There are two avenues for interpreting the meaningfulness of the outcome. The first is with reference to the research question, "Is there a statistically significant difference in the pre-feedback and post-feedback level of motivation for students who received feedback designed to promote autonomy and motivation?" The second is effect size; however, the formula for effect size for the Wilcoxon Signed Rank statistic requires that the observed value of the statistic be converted to a z-score. When there are fewer than 30 participants, the observed value of the Wilcoxon Signed Rank statistic is *not* converted to a z-score for interpretation, so effect size can't be calculated and reported. The fact that effect size can't be calculated should be included in the interpretation of the outcome, so for this study the researcher could report something like this:

> On the basis of this small study, there's 95% certainty that feedback designed to increase student autonomy and motivation does not have an impact on these students' level of motivation ($V = 5.5$; $p = .1785$). (Effect size cannot be calculated due to the small number of participants.)

Wilcoxon Signed Rank Statistic for the Comparison of Two Paired Samples (N ≥ 30)

Similar to the Wilcoxon Rank Sum statistic, according to various sources (Corder & Foreman, 2009; Hatch & Lazaraton, 1991; Shavelson, 1996), when there's a sufficient number of participants ($N \geq 30$), the observed value of the Wilcoxon Signed Rank statistic is converted to a z-score for interpreting statistical significance.

I illustrate the following explanation of calculating the Wilcoxon Signed Rank statistic by adding fabricated data to Professor Oliva's original data (the fabricated data are presented in Table 7.9) and I follow the 10 steps in statistical logic. I retained the same research question: "Is there a statistically significant difference in the pre-feedback and post-feedback level of motivation for students who received feedback designed to promote autonomy and motivation?"

Step 1: State the Formal Research Hypotheses

For this study, the null hypothesis is:

> There is no statistically significant difference in the rankings of the pre-feedback and post-feedback motivation scores for the participants who received feedback designed to promote autonomy and motivation.

As for the study discussed above, I set two one-tailed, directional, alternative hypotheses.

> Alternative hypothesis 1: The rankings of the participants' pre-feedback motivation scores are systematically higher than the rankings of the post-feedback motivation scores.

> Alternative hypothesis 2: The rankings of the participants' pre-feedback motivation scores are systematically lower than the rankings of the post-feedback motivation scores.

Step 2: Set Alpha

This researcher decided to set alpha at .05.

Step 3: Select the Appropriate Statistic for Analysis of the Data

I want to know whether there's a statistically significant difference in the pre-feedback and post-feedback rankings of the motivation scores for participants who received feedback designed to promote autonomy and motivation. The independent variable, represented by the participants' level of motivation before and after the feedback, has two levels. The dependent variable, *participants' degree of motivation*, yields rankable data, though the actual values are not normally distributed. I propose to use the Wilcoxon Signed Rank statistic and convert the observed value of the Wilcoxon Signed Rank statistic to a z-score for interpreting statistical significance because (1) I am interested in determining whether there is a difference between the pre- and posttest outcomes, (2) the two sets of data are from exactly the same participants, (3) the number of participants is 30 or greater, and (4) the dependent variable yields rankable outcomes.

Step 4: Collect the Data

The data are presented in Table 7.9.

Step 5: Verify That the Assumptions for the Statistic Are Met

There are four conditions that must be met when using the Wilcoxon Signed Rank statistic formula and converting the observed value of the statistic to a z-score for interpreting statistical significance:

1. The independent variable is *nominal* and has only two levels.
2. Comparison is of two sets of outcomes for exactly the same set of participants (or carefully matched pairs).
3. There are 30 or more participants.[19]
4. The dependent variable yields rankable data.

The first assumption is met by the fact that the independent variable is represented by the participants' pre-feedback and post-feedback states; these two states represent two categories. The second is met by verifying that I have exactly the same people in the pre- and post-comparison groups. The third is checked by verifying the number of participants, $N = 31$. The fourth is met by verifying that the questionnaire used to collect the dependent variable yields rankable data, reviewing the scores themselves (in Table 7.9) and examining the histograms for the two sets of scores (in Box 7.4).

Step 6: Calculate the Observed Value of the Appropriate Statistic

The motivation scores for the participants are presented in Table 7.9. This table displays the difference between the pre-feedback and post-feedback outcomes for each pair of scores, the ranking of the scores, and the sign for the difference (positive or negative). At the bottom of the table, I show the sum of the ranks for the positive differences and the sum of the ranks for the negative differences. The outcomes for which there is no difference aren't included in the ranking.

The ranking of the differences is done using the absolute values of the differences; the signs are removed. So, for example, there are two differences of −1 and one difference of +1. These three differences with an absolute value of 1 are tied for first, second, and third place. I add the three places, $1 + 2 + 3 = 6$, and divide the sum by 3 ($6/3 = 2$). The three differences with an absolute value of 1 are assigned the rank of 2.

The two differences with an absolute value of 2 are tied for fourth and fifth place; I add these places and divide by 2 ($4 + 5 = 9/2 = 4.5$). The two differences of two are assigned the rank of 4.5. The three differences with an absolute value of 3 are tied for sixth, seventh, and eighth place. I add these places and divide the sum by 3 ($6 + 7 + 8 = 21/3 = 7$). The differences with an absolute value of 3 are assigned the rank of 7.

The six differences of 4 are tied for ninth through 14th place. These are added and divided by 6: $9 + 10 + 11 + 12 + 13 + 14 = 69/6 = 11.5$. I assign each of the six cases a rank of 11.5.

The two differences of 5 are tied for 15th and 16th place; the sum of the two places is divided by 2 (because there are two scores tied for these places); $31/2 = 15.5$. The two differences with an absolute value of 5 are assigned ranks of 15.5. The three differences of 6 are tied for 17th through 19th place; I add these and divide by 3 ($17 + 18 + 19 = 54/3 = 18$). The absolute differences of 6 are assigned ranks of 18. The single difference of 7 is ranked 20th and the single difference of 8 is assigned the rank of 21. The difference of 10 is assigned the rank of 22 and the difference of 14 is assigned the rank of 23.

There are a lot of tied differences within the data and R does use a formula that corrects for ties. However, here I use the basic formula for several reasons: First, I think it's important to illustrate the basic formula before introducing the more complex formula for tied data. Second, I believe most researchers will use R to do the calculations, and R uses the formula that corrects for tied data when it's needed. Finally, Siegel (1956), the source for the formula for ties for the Wilcoxon Rank Sum statistic, noted that "the practice of giving tied observations the average of the ranks they would otherwise have gotten has a negligible effect on T, the statistic on which the Wilcoxon [Signed Rank] test is based" (p. 77).

Table 7.10 presents the sum of ranks for the positive and negative differences. The participants with no difference are excluded from the analysis. Note that in subsequent calculations, the new, smaller n size is used.

TABLE 7.9 Pre- and Post-motivation Scores, Differences, Ranks of Differences, and Signs
(N = 31)

Participant	Pretest total	Posttest total	Difference	Rank of differences	Sign
1	49	44	+5	15.5	+
2	52	52	0	exclude	exclude
3	37	41	−4	11.5	−
4	37	40	−3	7	−
5	42	46	−4	11.5	−
6	50	50	0	exclude	exclude
7	45	48	−3	7	−
8	35	39	−4	11.5	−
9	46	52	−6	18	−
10	48	47	+1	2	+
11	38	43	−5	15.5	−
12	40	46	−6	18	−
13	43	51	−8	21	−
14	47	49	−2	4.5	−
15	44	47	−3	7	−
16	41	48	−7	20	−
17	35	35	0	exclude	exclude
18	43	43	0	exclude	exclude
19	44	30	+14	23	+
20	35	35	0	exclude	exclude
21	37	33	+4	11.5	+
22	39	49	−10	22	−
23	42	42	0	exclude	exclude
24	48	44	+4	11.5	+
25	48	47	+1	2	+
26	42	42	0	exclude	exclude
27	33	39	−6	18	−
28	51	51	0	exclude	exclude
29	40	38	+2	4.5	+
30	41	45	−4	11.5	−
31	51	52	−1	2	−

TABLE 7.10 Sums of Ranks for Positive and Negative Differences

Rank	Sign	Positive Signs	Negative Signs
15.5	+	15.5	
exclude	exclude		
11.5	–		11.5
7	–		7
11.5	–		11.5
exclude	exclude		
7	–		7
11.5	–		11.5
18	–		18
2	+	2	
15.5	–		15.5
18	–		18
20	–		21
4.5	–		4.5
7	–		7
19	–		20
exclude	exclude		
exclude	exclude		
22	+	23	
exclude	exclude		
11.5	+	11.5	
21	–		22
exclude	exclude		
11.5	+	11.5	
2	+	2	
exclude	exclude		
18	–		18
exclude	exclude		
4.5	+	4.5	
11.5	–		11.5
2	–		2
Total sum of ranks		$\Sigma_{Rpositive} = 70$	$\Sigma_{Rnegative} = 206$

The sum of ranks for the positive differences ($\Sigma_{Rpositive}$) is 70 and the sum of ranks for the negative differences ($\Sigma_{Rnegative}$) is 206. The observed value of the Wilcoxon Signed Rank statistic is the smaller of the two sums of ranks, 70, but as is true for the Wilcoxon Rank Sum statistic, when the number of participants is large, greater than 30, various sources (Corder & Foreman, 2009; Shavelson, 1996) indicate that statistical significance can be interpreted by converting the observed value of the Wilcoxon Signed Rank statistic (referred to as T in the formula below) to a z-score.

Corder and Foreman (2009, p. 39) provide this formula for the conversion:

$$z = \frac{T - \overline{X}_T}{S_T}$$

T is the observed value for the Wilcoxon Signed Rank statistic (70, in this case). The formula for the value of $\overline{X}_T$ is:

$$\overline{X}_T = \frac{n(n+1)}{4}$$

And the formula for the value of s_T is:

$$S_T = \sqrt{\frac{n(n+1)(2n+1)}{24}}$$

First, I calculate the $\overline{X}_T$ value. Note that n is the number of participants who have a positive or negative difference; the participants who showed no difference are excluded from the analysis, so for these calculations, $n = 23$.

$$\overline{X}_T = \frac{n(n+1)}{4} = \frac{23(23+1)}{4} = \frac{23(24)}{4} = \frac{552}{4} = \mathbf{138}$$

Then I calculate S_T:

$$S_T = \sqrt{\frac{23(23+1)[(2)(23)+1]}{24}} = \sqrt{\frac{[23(24)][46+1]}{24}} = \sqrt{\frac{(552)(47)}{24}}$$

$$= \sqrt{\frac{25944}{24}} = \sqrt{1081} = \mathbf{32.88}$$

With these values, I can calculate the z-score for T:

$$z = \frac{T - \overline{X}_T}{S_T} = \frac{70 - 138}{32.88} = \frac{-68}{32.88} = \mathbf{-2.07}$$

Recall that a z-value equal to or exceeding $+1.96$ or -1.96 is statistically significant at $p = .05$; a z-value equal to or exceeding $+2.57$ or -2.57 is statistically significant at $p = .01$. In Step 2, alpha was set at .05. The observed value of z, -2.07, exceeds $+1.96/-1.96$, so the null hypothesis is rejected.

The same steps as presented in Box 7.3 can be used to calculate both the observed value of the Wilcoxon Signed Rank statistic and the exact probability of the observed value so that statistical significance can be determined. As with the Wilcoxon Rank Sum statistic, effect size can be calculated by extracting the value of z from the model R builds to calculate probability.

Box 7.4 Using *R* to Calculate the Wilcoxon Signed Rank Statistic and Exact Probability (*N* ≥ *30*)

Enter the pretest data.[20]	**pretest = c (49, 52, 37, 37, 42, 50, 45, 35, 46, 48, 38, 40, 43, 47, 44, 41, 35, 43, 44, 35, 37, 39, 42, 48, 48, 42, 33, 51, 40, 41, 51)**
View the pretest data.	**> View (pretest)**
Then enter the posttest data.	**> posttest = c(44, 52, 41, 40, 46, 50, 48, 39, 52, 47, 43, 46, 51, 49, 47, 48, 35, 43, 30, 35, 33, 49, 42, 44, 47, 42, 39, 51, 38, 45, 52)**
View the posttest data.	**> View (posttest)**
Calculate the descriptive statistics for the pretest data.	**> summary (pretest)** Output: Min. 1st Qu. Median Mean 3rd Qu. Max. 33.00 38.50 42.00 42.68 47.50 52.00 **> sd (pretest)** Output: [1] 5.375172
Calculate the descriptive statistics for the posttest data.	**> summary (posttest)** Output: Min. 1st Qu. Median Mean 3rd Qu. Max. 30.00 40.50 45.00 44.13 48.50 52.00 **> sd (posttest)** Output: [1] 5.897694

(Continued)

Box 7.4 *(Continued)*

Create a space for side-by-side histograms using the **par (mfrow = c(1,2))** command. Then make a histogram of the pretest data and of the posttest data.	> **par (mfrow = c(1,2))** > **hist (pretest, breaks = 12, main = "Pretest Motivation", xlab = "Pretest Values", col = "chartreuse")** > **hist (posttest, breaks = 12, main = "Posttest Motivation", xlab = "Posttest Values", col = "yellow")** Output: 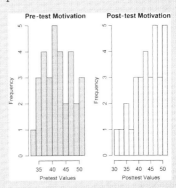
Calculate the Shapiro–Wilk statistic if you're curious—it isn't necessary to check the normality of the datasets for the Wilcoxon Signed Rank statistic, but it's interesting to see the values.	> **shapiro.test (pretest)** Output: W = .965, p-value = .3925 > **shapiro.test (posttest)** Output: W = .9495, p-value = .1511
To calculate the observed value of the Wilcoxon Signed Rank statistic and the exact level of probability for that observed value, use the **wilcox.test** command, specifying the two levels of the independent variable inside parentheses (separated by a comma) and indicating that the data are paired.	> **wilcox.test (pretest, posttest, paired = TRUE)** Output: V = 70, p-value = .03951 alternative hypothesis: true location shift is not equal to 0 Warning messages:

(Continued)

Box 7.4 (*Continued*)

Note the single underscored warning—because there are tied scores, the default formula for calculating probability must be changed using the **exact = FALSE** command.	1: In wilcox.test.default(pretest, posttest, paired = TRUE) : cannot compute exact p-value with ties
This command tells *R* to use the formula for calculating probability that compensates for tied scores.	> **wilcox.test (pretest, posttest, paired = TRUE, exact =FALSE)** Output: V = 70, p-value = .03951 alternative hypothesis: true location shift is not equal to 0
Remember that *R* gives the observed value of the statistic for whichever dataset was entered first in the command, but the smaller of the two possible values of *V* is the one that's reported. To calculate *V* for the posttest data, reverse **pretest** and **posttest** in the command.	> **wilcox.test (posttest, pretest, paired =TRUE, exact =FALSE)** Output: V = 206, p-value = .03951 alternative hypothesis: true location shift is not equal to 0
Effect size for the study can be calculated because there are enough participants to justify converting the $V_{observed}$ to a z-score for interpretation. To calculate effect size, I retrieve the z-score from the model that *R* built to calculate exact probability; I request that *R* make a **study.model**.	> **study.model = wilcox.test(pretest, posttest, paired =TRUE, exact =FALSE)** > **study.model**
The command **z = qnorm(study.model\$p. value/2)** extracts the z-value for the exact *p* for this model; the z-value is divided by 2 to focus on just one end of the z-distribution (Field et al., 2012, p. 665).	> **z = qnorm (study.model\$p.value/2)**
To see the z-value, enter **z**.	> **z** Output: [1] −2.05885

(*Continued*)

Box 7.4 (*Continued*)

Effect size is calculated using this formula: $$\text{effect size} = \frac{|z|}{\sqrt{N}}$$ Written as an *R* command, it's **effect.size = abs(z)/sqrt(N).** In this formula, the uppercase *N* indicates the total number of participants (31 in this case).	> **effect.size = abs(z)/sqrt(31)**
To see the effect size, enter the command **effect.size.**	> **effect.size** Output: .3697804

The observed value of the Wilcoxon Signed Rank statistic is the smaller of the two *V* values, *V* = 70 (the value that has the single underscore in Box 7.4). The exact probability of that observed value is *p* = .03951 (double underscore).

Step 7: Calculate the Exact Probability for the Observed Value of the Statistic

The exact level of probability for the observed value of the Wilcoxon Signed Rank statistic, 70, as reported in the *R* output, is *p* = .03951.

Step 8: Compare the Probability of the Observed Value of the Wilcoxon Signed Ranks Statistic to Alpha

Here are those rules again.

> If exact probability ≥ alpha → accept the null hypothesis.
>
> If exact probability < alpha → reject the null hypothesis.

Alpha was set at .05. The exact probability, *p* =.03951, is less than alpha, so the null hypothesis is rejected and one of the alternative hypotheses is accepted—the one that indicates that the pretest level of motivation is lower than the posttest level of motivation. The high number of negative differences shown in Table 7.9 indicates that the posttest scores are higher than the pretest scores.

> **Alternative hypothesis 2: The rankings of the participants' pre-feedback motivation scores are systematically lower than the rankings of the post-feedback motivation scores.**

Step 9: Interpret the Findings as a Probability Statement

I rejected the null hypothesis, accepted the second alternative hypothesis, and now make a probability statement based on the alternative hypothesis.

> **There's 95% certainty that the rankings of the participants' pre-feedback motivation scores are systematically lower than the rankings of the post-feedback motivation scores.**

Step 10: Interpret the Meaningfulness of the Findings

I first interpret the findings with reference to the research question, which is: "Is there a statistically significant difference in the pre-feedback and post-feedback level of motivation for students who received feedback designed to promote autonomy and motivation?"

I also calculate effect size. According to a 1988 study by Cohen, cited by Corder and Foreman (2009, p. 40) and supported by Field and colleagues (2012), a small effect size is .10, a medium effect size is .30, and a large effect size is .50.

To interpret meaningfulness for the outcome of the calculations done with a calculator, I use the z-value that I calculated, -2.07; the number of participants whose difference is positive or negative is 23, and I use 23 as the N size. The formula for effect size uses the *absolute value* of the z-observed, so the negative or positive sign is removed from the z-score when calculating effect size (Corder & Foreman, 2009):

$$Effect\ size = \frac{|z|}{\sqrt{n}} = \frac{|2.07|}{\sqrt{23}} = \frac{2.07}{4.08} = .43$$

The effect size, .43, can be considered moderately strong. The interpretation might look something like this:

> **For these students, there's 95% certainty that receiving a type of feedback designed to promote autonomy and motivation has a strong, positive impact on their level of motivation (Wilcoxon**

> **Signed Rank value is** $T = 70$, T **converted to a** z**-score** $= -2.07$; **effect size** $= .43$).

If the calculations are done using R, the interpretation is a bit different: We don't know how many people were excluded from the analysis because there was no difference in their pretest and posttest scores (when the calculations are done by calculator, the people with no difference are excluded from the analysis and the N size is reduced.)

The interpretation of the outcomes reported by a person who used R for all of the calculations would look something like this:

> **For these students, there's 95% certainty that receiving a type of feedback designed to promote autonomy and motivation has a strong, positive impact on their level of motivation ($V = 70$, $p = .03951$, effect size $= .3697804$).**

R Commands Introduced in Chapter Seven

wilcox.test (group1.data, group2.data) The command for the Wilcoxon Rank Sum statistic when the data are entered directly into R in separate sets and there are no tied scores.

>wilcox.test (group1.data, group2.data, exact = FALSE) The command for the Wilcoxon Rank Sum statistic when the data are entered directly into R in separate sets and there are tied scores.

study.model = wilcox.test (group1.data, group2.data) This command is the first in a series of three commands used to retrieve the z-value from the model R builds to calculate exact probability for the Wilcoxon Rank Sum statistic (when the number of participants justifies conversion of the outcome to a z-score and there are no tied scores).

z=qnorm(study.model\$p.value/2) This command is the second in a series of three commands used to retrieve the z-value from the model R builds to calculate exact probability for the Wilcoxon Rank Sum statistic.

z This is the third in a series of three commands used to retrieve the z-value from the model R builds to calculate exact probability for the Wilcoxon Rank Sum statistic.

effect.size = abs(z)/sqrt (N) This command is the first in a set of two commands used to calculate the effect size for the Wilcoxon Rank Sum statistic and the Wilcoxon Signed Rank statistic; the value of z is retrieved using the series of three commands that retrieves z from the R model.

effect.size This is the second in a set of two commands used to calculate the effect size for the Wilcoxon Rank Sum statistic and the Wilcoxon Signed Rank statistic (when the number of participants justifies conversion of the outcome to a z-score).

wilcox.test (pretest, posttest, paired = TRUE) The command for the Wilcoxon Signed Rank statistic when the data are entered directly into R in separate sets and there are no tied scores.

wilcox.test (pretest, posttest, paired = TRUE, exact = FALSE) The command for the Wilcoxon Signed Rank statistic when the data are entered directly into R in separate sets and there are tied scores.

study.model = wilcox.test(pretest, posttest, paired = TRUE, exact = FALSE) This command is the first in a series of three commands used to retrieve the z-value from the model R builds to calculate exact probability for the Wilcoxon Signed Rank statistic (when the number of participants justifies conversion of the outcome to a z-score and there are tied scores).

study.model This command is the second in a series of three commands used to retrieve the z-value from the model R builds to calculate exact probability for the Wilcoxon Signed Rank statistic (when the number of participants justifies conversion of the outcome to a z-score.)

qnorm (study.model\$p.value/2) This command is the third in a series of three commands used to retrieve the z-value from the model R builds to calculate exact probability for the Wilcoxon Signed Rank statistic. To retrieve the value of z, type z.

Practice Problems

An answer key is available on the companion website (www.routledge.com/cw/turner).

Study A. Let's first redo the analysis of Jen's data—the study presented in Chapter Six for which we discovered that the assumptions of normal distribution and equal variance were not met! Remember to follow the 10 steps in statistical logic. The data can be retrieved from the companion website (www.routledge.com/cw/turner).

   Study B. Two teachers of English were interested in investigating the effect of explicit instruction in reading strategies on reading comprehension. The two teachers worked together to design the strategy training. So they could compare the outcomes of the usual reading course with those of the new course with the strategy training, one teacher agreed to follow their usual curriculum (the non-experimental group), while the other agreed to try out the new course (the experimental group). They have high-beginner and intermediate-level students in the classes, but they decided to focus their attention on the high beginners. At the beginning of the term, the students in both classes took a pretest that measured their reading comprehension ability. An equivalent form of this test was given at the end of the term as part of the final exam that all the students in the English program take, which has 50 points. (The participants' fabricated scores are presented in the table below.)

1.   Name the independent variable and indicate how many levels it has.
2.   Name the dependent variable.
3.   Identify any control variables and/or moderator variables.
4.   Identify one threat to the internal validity of the study and provide at least one suggestion for how that threat might be reduced.
5.   Identify one threat to the external validity of the study (other than poor internal validity!) and provide at least one suggestion for how that threat might be reduced.
6.   Calculate and report the descriptive statistics for each class.
7.   Follow the 10 steps in statistical logic to determine whether there is a statistically significant difference in the performance of these two classes.

Here are the final exam scores for the two classes.

Student	Non-experimental Class	Experimental Class
1	47	45
2	42	44
3	39	42
4	37	42
5	37	42
6	36	37
7	32	34

Study C. The chair of Arabic Studies at a small, private graduate school wanted to investigate whether students who participated in the intermediate level Summer Intensive Language Program showed a substantial gain in their oral abilities during the 6-week term. She administered the Versant Arabic test at the outset of the term and gave an equivalent form of the test at the end of the term (the possible range for test scores is 0 to 80). Here are the students' fabricated scores on the pretest and posttest.

Student	Pretest	Posttest
1	62	80
2	48	60
3	50	50
4	30	48
5	30	44
6	28	26
7	26	30

8. What is the independent variable and what are its levels?
9. What is the dependent variable?
10. Which major category of research design best fits this study (and why)?
11. Calculate the descriptive statistics for each set of scores.
12. Follow the steps in statistical logic to determine whether the students showed significant improvement in their oral skills.

Notes

1 The concept of *variance* is addressed briefly in Chapter Two; it's the squared value of the standard deviation and reflects the *sum of squared errors*. The assumption of equal variances is a way of ensuring that the groups are comparable and drawn from the same population.
2 Calculation and interpretation of the Levene's Test statistic is explained in Chapter Six.
3 See Chapter Five for an introduction to the "exact probability approach" to interpreting statistical significance and Chapter Six for examples in which this approach is followed.
4 Please note that the scales for the x-axes and the y-axes are different. As I pointed out in Chapter Two, how the points on the axes of a histogram are represented should always be considered when reading a histogram.
5 The histogram of the non-experimental group's data was generated in R using this command: hist (non.exp, breaks = 10, col = "salmon", main = "Posttest Motivation Level", xlab = "Non-experimental Group"); the histogram of the experimental group's data was generated in R using this command: hist (exp.group, breaks = 10, col = "pink", main = "Posttest Motivation Level", xlab = "Experimental Group"). You will have to use your imagination to see the colors, though.
6 For this study, the two-tailed, non-directional, alternative hypothesis is: There is a statistically significant difference between the rankings of the posttest motivation scores for the experimental and non-experimental groups.
7 The Shapiro–Wilk test must be supplemented by examination of a histogram when the datasets are very small, because the Shapiro–Wilk is not a very rigorous test of

normality in small samples. Examination of the histograms shows that the distribution of the non-experimental group is flat.

8   The Levene's Test statistic is not a very rigorous measure of equal variances when there's a very small number of participants. In any case, if a researcher really wants to use the parametric Case II Independent Samples t-test statistic, the researcher should plan to have equal group sizes. When it comes to the analysis, if one group is a little larger than the other due to attrition in the other group, randomly deleting one or two participants so the group sizes are equal is a good idea. The researcher should report whether any people were randomly deleted to make the groups the same size.

9   This approach to ranking may seem counterintuitive, but it's used so the highest score has the numerically highest ranking instead of the highest score having the lowest numerical ranking (first), a convention in the calculation and interpretation of the statistic.

10 There is a **rank** command in R, but ranking is programmed into the calculation of the Wilcoxon Rank Sum statistic. If you want to simply rank a set of data for some reason, though, once you've entered the data, you can use the command **rank** followed by the name of the dataset to do the ranking.

11 Note that like many other statistical software programs, the order in which the two levels of the independent variable are entered dictates which of the two values is reported as the observed value; the reported value is the one that's entered first! In contrast, when doing calculations with a calculator, W_E and W_{NE} are both calculated, and the smaller of the two values is identified as the observed value of the statistic. When the data for the two groups are entered separately, as in this example, I recommend doing the **wilcox.test** command two times so *both* values for W are computed—the smaller one should be reported as the observed value of the statistic.

12 An explanation and illustration of the formula that compensates for tied scores can be found on the companion website (www.routledge.com/cw/turner).

13 You'll see when you review the discussion of how to do these calculations using R that the converted z-values for $W_{observed}$ are a bit different. When calculated using a calculator and rounding numbers to a limited number of decimal places, the converted value of $W_{observed}$ is $z = -0.1191$. R calculates with greater precision and reports the converted $W_{observed}$ as $z = -0.0977617$.

14 Notice in these histograms that neither the x-axes nor the y-axes are on exactly the same scales.

15 Notice that R calculated the conversion of $W_{observed}$ to a z-score with greater precision than I did when I used a calculator to convert the score. When calculated using a calculator and rounding numbers of a limited number of decimal places, I determined that the converted $W_{observed}$ is $z = -0.1191$. R reports the converted $W_{observed}$ as $z = -0.0977617$.

16 The pretest histogram was made in R using this command: **hist (pretest, breaks = 10, col = "orange")**; the posttest histogram was made using this command: **hist (posttest, breaks = 15, col = "aquamarine")**. Again you have to use your imagination to see the colors.

17 Corder and Foreman (2009) suggest that the z-approach can be used only when there are 30 or more participants; R uses the z-approach when there are more than 40 participants (Field et al., 2012, p. 664).

18 The Shapiro–Wilk statistics for the two sets of scores show 95% certainty of the scores being normally distributed, though the histograms show that the distributions are

nearly flat. The Shapiro–Wilk statistic is not a very rigorous test of normality when the datasets are very small.

19 Note that *R* uses this approach when there are 40 or more participants (Field et al., 2011, p. 664).

20 With this many values, a researcher may prefer to create an Excel spreadsheet and import the data rather than enter the data directly into *R*. The spreadsheet should have two columns, one for the first set of data (pretest in this example) and the other for the second set of data (posttest). In row 1, each column should be given a simple (memorable and easy to type) label (*R* creates a heading for each column if there isn't one, so be sure to view the dataset after importing it to verify the names of the columns—the names are needed in the commands). The Excel spreadsheet should be saved in the MS-DOS comma separated values (csv) format (for PC users) and in the equivalent csv format for Mac users. The spreadsheet can be imported using the **read.csv = (file. choose(), header = T)** command (see Box 6.1 for additional details).

SECTION III

Analyzing Differences Among More Than Two Sets of Data

8

INTRODUCTION TO THE PARAMETRIC BETWEEN-GROUPS ANALYSIS OF VARIANCE STATISTIC

The statistics that you studied in Chapter Six and Seven can be used in research in language education when a researcher wants to compare the performance of two groups. The Kruskal–Wallis and Friedman's Test statistics that you'll study in Chapter Nine are non-parametric statistics that are used when a researcher's independent variable has more than two levels and the researcher wants to compare the performance of the groups. When the data meet the assumptions for parametric analysis and there are *more* than two groups defined by the independent variable, or when there is one or more moderator variables, analysis using one of the parametric analysis of variance (ANOVA) formulas may be appropriate.

The ANOVA formulas represent a large family of statistics frequently used in research in language education. In this chapter, I introduce you to the family with the goal of helping you read and critique studies in which an ANOVA was done. I give a general explanation of the family using the variance-ratio approach (DeVeaux, Velleman, & Bock, 2008; Field, Miles, & Field, 2012; Hatch & Lazaraton, 1991). I'll also introduce some useful terminology and important concepts for understanding studies that use the ANOVA formulas, including a summary of the different types of ANOVA. I'll address the assumptions for appropriate use of the ANOVA formulas; however, for in-depth explanations of when the various ANOVA formulas can be used and how to calculate and interpret them, I recommend Chapters 28 and 29 in the text by DeVeaux and colleagues, and Chapters 10 through 14 by Field et al. I don't provide an in-depth explanation in this text because my focus is on small-scale research and non-parametric analyses; an in-depth discussion of the many ANOVA formulas, most of which require a rather large number of participants, is truly beyond the scope of this introductory text. Being able to read and critique ANOVA research is a useful skill, though, even for people who generally do small-scale, non-parametric data analyses, because of the number of studies in which an ANOVA formula was used. To help you understand and critique this research for your own purposes, I explain some fundamental concepts in Chapter Eight. To illustrate my discussion, I use a (fabricated) example study.

Example Study

The director for English as a Second Language (ESL) courses at a large private language school decided to investigate the relative effectiveness of three different approaches to teaching advanced ESL. (The advanced level is determined by performance on the Complete English Test, the CLT.) The type of advanced course the school usually offers has a grammar focus (GF), but two new courses were developed. The first is a content-based (CB) course with topics proposed by students and teachers. The second is a project-based (PB) course, in which the students explore topics of their choice and produce multimedia presentations on their topics. From the very large number of advanced-level students, the director randomly chose 36 and randomly assigned 12 to each of the three types of class. There was no attrition. An interval-scale, norm-referenced test, Form A of the CLT, was given as a pretest to establish that there were no significant differences in *knowledge of English*, the dependent variable, among the groups before the period of instruction. Form B of the CLT was given as a posttest after the 10-week period of instruction. The researcher compared the CLT posttest scores for the three classes to determine whether any of the three programs appeared to be more effective than the others in promoting the development of advanced ESL learners' knowledge of English.

Introduction to the 1-Way Between-Groups ANOVA

In this study, the independent variable, *type of instruction*, has three levels and the dependent variable is interval-scale in nature and likely to be normally distributed. The participants seem to have been drawn randomly from a population and each was randomly assigned to one of the three levels of the independent variable. Additionally, the researcher wants to investigate whether there are significant differences among the groups. None of the statistics from Chapter Six, the *t*-test family, or Chapter Seven, the Wilcoxon family, can be used because they're appropriate only when the independent variable has two levels. The parametric 1-way between-groups ANOVA is appropriate when the following general conditions are met:

- The independent variable is nominal and includes more than two levels.
- The participants are drawn randomly from a normally distributed population and are assigned randomly to the levels of the independent variable.
- The dependent variable is interval-scale and normally distributed within the population and the groups formed by the levels of the independent variable.

- The groups defined by the levels of the independent variable include different individuals.
- The researcher is interested in knowing whether there is a difference in dependent variable performance among the groups formed by the levels of the independent variable.

Figure 8.1 shows the three levels of the independent variable, *type of instruction*. The dependent variable is represented by the means and standard deviations for each group.

Type of instruction: grammar focus (GF)	Type of instruction: content-based (CB)	Type of instruction: project-based (PB)
$\bar{X} = 82.41667$	$\bar{X} = 84.16667$	$\bar{X} = 83.75000$
$s = 5.56708$	$s = 6.63097$	$s = 6.95603$

FIGURE 8.1 Three Levels of the Independent Variable in a 1-Way Between-Groups ANOVA Design

We know that the 36 participants' dependent variable scores vary—the scores should be normally distributed, so the participants can't all have the same score! The participants within a single group have different scores and the participants' scores vary across the three groups. The question that the ANOVA formula allows us to explore is whether the amount of variance within the groups is about the same as the amount of variance among the groups. If neither of the experimental conditions had any effect on the participants, we'd see no significant difference in the variance within the groups and the variance among the groups. However, if one or both of the experimental conditions had an effect, there would be a difference between the variance within the groups and the variance among the groups. Using one of the ANOVA formulas and statistical logic allows us to compare the variance within the groups to the variance among the groups and determine whether the groups are probably the same—or probably different.

Variance *within* groups is expected but it's not the focus of a 1-way, between-groups analysis. This part of the variance is typically referred to as *residual variance,* though it is sometimes referred to as *error* (Hatch & Lazaraton, 1991, p. 314). There's error variance within each group and, consequently, among the groups, too. There may also be variance among the groups that reflects the different non-experimental and experimental conditions; this variance is of interest to the researcher and is referred to as the *treatment effect* (p. 314). The ANOVA family contains many formulas but all yield at least one F-ratio, or $F_{observed}$. In the numerator of the *F-ratio* is the error (residual) variance within each group *plus* the variance due to the treatment effect; in the denominator is the error variance itself, as shown in the equation on the next page. When the observed value of an F-ratio is greater than 1, there may be a statistically significant effect, though the steps in statistical logic must be followed to determine whether the F-ratio is large enough to show a statistically significant difference among the groups:

$$F_{observed} = \frac{\text{error variance (residual)} + \text{treatment effect}}{\text{error (residual)variance}}$$

$F_{observed}$ can be interpreted using a chart of critical values or by interpreting the exact probability level of $F_{observed}$; both approaches to interpreting statistical significance allow the researcher to make a probability statement about the apparent differences among the groups that represent the levels of the independent variable.

The 1-way, between-groups ANOVA formula is a parametric statistic, so there's a set of rather rigorous conditions that must be met by researchers who want to use it:

1. The independent variable is nominal and includes more than two levels.
2. The participants are drawn randomly from a normally distributed population and are assigned randomly to the levels of the independent variable.
3. The dependent variable is interval-scale and normally distributed within the population and the groups formed by the levels of the independent variable.
4. The groups defined by the levels of the independent variable include different individuals.
5. The groups defined by the independent variable have exactly the same number of people, or Levene's test shows that the variances are approximately equal.
6. There's a minimum of 5 participants in each level of the independent variable.[1]

Before I discuss how to carry out the steps in statistical logic for the example study, there's a bit more general information about ANOVAs that's helpful to know when reading research that uses one of the ANOVA statistics.

Numbers and Types of Variables in ANOVA Studies

I've been referring to the ANOVA formulas as a family; the first branch of the family is the collection of formulas known as ANOVA. All ANOVA formulas share one characteristic—they have one dependent variable. The ANOVA family of formulas, all of which have one dependent variable, may have moderator variables. In a 2-way ANOVA there's one independent variable and one moderator variable, so there are two variables that the researcher systematically selects or manipulates to determine their impact on the dependent variable. The independent variable represents the researcher's primary concern and question, while the moderator variable represents the researcher's secondary interest. For example, the researcher designing the study on the impact of type of language course on students' knowledge of English could decide to add *learner style,* a moderator variable with three levels—visual, auditory, and kinesthetic—to the study. The levels of the independent variable and the moderator variable are shown in Figure 8.2.

A 2-way ANOVA yields three $F_{observed}$ values, two *main effects,* and *one interaction effect.* The $F_{observed}$ value for the first main effect is interpreted to show whether there's a difference among the participants in the three groups defined by the independent variable: in the example study (Figure 8.2), people who received GF instruction (the first column) versus CB instruction (the second column) versus PB instruction (the third column).

The $F_{observed}$ value for the second main effect is interpreted to show whether there's a difference among the participants in the three groups defined by the moderator variable: as shown in Figure 8.3, everyone who is a visual learner (the first row) versus everyone who is an auditory learner (the second row) versus everyone who is a kinesthetic learner (the third row).

The 2-way ANOVA also yields an $F_{observed}$ value for the interaction. In the example study, the interaction effect value of $F_{observed}$ is interpreted to show whether there is a difference somewhere among all of the nine groups formed by the intersection of the independent and moderator variables (Figure 8.2).

GF Instruction (participants with visual learning style)	CB Instruction (participants with visual learning style)	PB Instruction (participants with visual learning style)
GF Instruction (participants with auditory learning style)	CB Instruction (participants with auditory learning style)	PB Instruction (participants with auditory learning style)
GF Instruction (participants with kinesthetic learning style)	CB Instruction (participants with kinesthetic learning style)	PB Instruction (participants with kinesthetic learning style)

FIGURE 8.2 Representation of a 2-Way ANOVA, First Main Effect, and Interaction Effect

All participants (GF, CB, & PB) from the 3 levels of the independent variable with a visual learning style
All participants (GF, CB, & PB) from the 3 levels of the independent variable with an auditory learning style
All participants (GF, CB, & PB) from the 3 levels of the independent variable with a kinesthetic learning style

FIGURE 8.3 Representation of the Second Main Effect in a 2-Way ANOVA

In a 3-way ANOVA, there's one independent variable (Variable A) and two moderator variables (Variables B and C). A 3-way ANOVA yields three main-effect $F_{observed}$ values and three interaction $F_{observed}$ values, as shown below:

First Main Effect—Analysis of the groups defined by the levels of the independent variable, Variable A

Second Main Effect—Analysis of the groups defined by the levels of the first moderator variable, Variable B

Third Main Effect—Analysis of the groups defined by the levels of the second moderator variable, Variable C

Interaction Effect #1—Analysis of the groups defined by the intersection of Variables A and B

Interaction Effect #2—Analysis of the groups defined by the intersection of Variables A and C

Interaction Effect #3—Analysis of the groups defined by the intersection of Variables B and C

Although more complex ANOVA procedures are possible (4-way, etc.), they require a substantial number of participants and they're very rare in small-scale language education research.

Some researchers describe their ANOVA designs in terms of the number of levels each variable has rather than by the number of independent and moderator variables. These researchers would refer to the 2-way ANOVA presented in Figure 8.2 as a 3×3 ANOVA because the independent variable has three levels and the moderator variable has three levels. A 3-way ANOVA that has an independent variable with five levels, one moderator variable with three levels, and another moderator with two levels would be referred to as a $5 \times 3 \times 2$ ANOVA.

Types of Comparisons in ANOVA Studies

There's another characteristic of ANOVAs that runs across the branches of the family. Some ANOVA statistics are designed for between-groups comparisons, like the Case II Independent Samples t-test formula and the Wilcoxon Rank Sum statistic. There are different people in each of the comparison groups in all between-groups ANOVA studies, regardless of whether the study is 1-way, 2-way, 3-way, or more.

There are also members of the ANOVA family that have *repeated-measure* comparisons; these formulas are appropriate when the comparison groups involve exactly the same people, such as when one wants to compare pretest, midtest, and posttest scores for the same people. The Case II Paired Samples t-test and the Wilcoxon Signed Rank statistic are both repeated-measure statistics too, but they're designed for comparing just two sets of information.

Some members of the ANOVA family involve *mixed design* comparisons, such as shown in Figure 8.4. If I change the design of the example study just a little,

Type of instruction #1 Test at end of 10 weeks	Type of instruction #2 Test at end of 10 weeks	Type of instruction #3 Test at end of 10 weeks
Type of instruction #1 Test 4 weeks later	Type of instruction #2 Test 4 weeks later	Type of instruction #3 Test 4 weeks later

FIGURE 8.4 A 2-Way Mixed Design ANOVA

I can change it from a 1-way between-groups study to a 2-way mixed-design study. Let's say that I have a secondary interest—I want to know whether the students in the three different types of instruction have similar retention of what they learned in their classes—and I administer Form C of the CLT 4 weeks after they completed the initial course. I then would have a 2-way mixed-design ANOVA. The first main-effect comparison is of the different people in the three groups defined by the independent variable. The second main effect involves comparison of the outcomes for the two different test administrations—a comparison of the same people to themselves. The interaction effect involves both comparison of the different people across the types of instruction groups and comparison of the same people to themselves, across the two posttest events.

MANOVA and ANCOVA Designs

In additional to the between-groups, within-group, and mixed-design ANOVA family members, all of which have only one dependent variable, there are formulas for comparison of two dependent variables. These formulas are known as *multiple analysis of variance*, or MANOVA. A 1-way MANOVA has one independent variable and two dependent variables; a 2-way MANOVA has one independent variable, one moderator variable, and two dependent variables.

There are also formulas that compensate mathematically for pre-existing differences among the independent variable groups; these formulas, *analysis of covariance* (ANCOVA), use pretest scores to statistically equate the groups, thereby accounting for any differences among the groups on the pretest. You might also see *multiple analysis of covariance* (MANCOVA). When reading a study that includes these complex analyses, think of them as supercharged ANOVAs, though the basic premises are similar to those for a 1-way, between groups ANOVA.

Additional Considerations

There are two additional considerations in using the ANOVA formulas.

1. If calculations are done by hand rather than by computer, the design must be *balanced*; that is, there should be the same number of participants in each level of the independent variable(s). In small studies, inequalities in the number of participants at each level are particularly problematic. An *orthogonal*

ANOVA has the same number of participants in each level of the independent variable(s)—it has a balanced design.

2. Most ANOVA studies in language education are *fixed effects* studies; that is, the levels of the variables are defined before the data are collected. In *random effects* studies, the levels of the variables are defined after examination of the data confirms what the levels are.

The Essential Post Hoc Analysis

All of the ANOVA formulas are *omnibus* statistics, so the alternative hypothesis for an ANOVA study is two-tailed. When it's accepted, it indicates only that there's a difference somewhere among the levels of the independent variable; it doesn't indicate *which* groups are different from one another. When the alternative hypothesis is accepted, a post hoc analysis must be done to determine which pairs of groups show differences. Though there are many different formulas for locating the differences, including the Bonferroni, Scheffé, Tukey's Honestly Significant Difference, and Newman–Keuls statistics, I'll use the Bonferroni statistic in this chapter.

Calculating Effect Size

As is the case for most of the other statistics you've encountered in this text, there's a formula for calculating effect size—the *omega*^{2} statistic can be used to calculate effect size for the 1-way between-groups ANOVA when the design is balanced.[2]

$$omega^2 = \frac{SSB - [(k-1)MSW]}{SST + MSW}$$

There are some mysterious-looking symbols in the formula for omega:[2] SSB, MSW, and SST. I'll explain what these refer to in the discussion that follows of how to use the variance-ratio approach to calculating $F_{observed}$.

Some researchers believe that effect size should be calculated for the post hoc comparisons rather than for the entire ANOVA study. In this case, and when the ANOVA design is not balanced, the effect size formula for *t*-tests can be used to estimate effect size for each post hoc comparison. This formula is:

$$\sqrt{\frac{t^2}{t^2 + df}}$$

Steps in Calculating a 1-Way Between-Groups ANOVA

Although it isn't difficult to calculate $F_{observed}$ using the 1-way between-groups ANOVA formula for balanced designs, it's time consuming and usually done using statistical software rather than a calculator (though I do illustrate the calculations below). Most statistical software programs present the output of ANOVA in a *source table*, which shows the outcome of several important steps in calculating $F_{observed}$. Researchers often include the source table for their ANOVA in their reports, both by tradition and because reviewing the information in a source table can facilitate understanding of a study. Figure 8.5 is the source table for the research problem introduced earlier in this chapter and is discussed in more detail below. The first column reflects the two elements of the ratio—the variance between the levels of the independent variable and the variance within the levels. The second column reflects the calculation of what's called *sums of squares*, the outcomes of the mathematical process of determining variance between and within the levels of the independent variable. The third column shows the degrees of freedom for the between-groups comparison, the within-group comparison, and the total comparison. The sums of squares values and the degrees of freedom are used to determine the mean square values. The fifth column shows the *F*-ratio, which is calculated using the mean square values. The sixth column shows the exact level of significance for the observed *F*-ratio (added after I used *R* to calculate it). Each of the steps reflected in this table is described in detail in the discussion that follows.

I return to the example study to illustrate where the information in the source table comes from. In Figure 8.6, the posttest data are presented, along with some values that are helpful as I illustrate the steps in calculating the $F_{observed}$ value for a 1-way between-groups ANOVA. Note the sums for the 12 scores in each column. Note, too, the sum of all 36 scores and the square of this value. Finally, note the sum of the squared values of the 36 scores.

When calculating ANOVA using the variance-ratio approach, I determine three critical variances—*sums of squares between groups* (SSB), *sums of squares within groups* (SSW), and *sums of squares total* (SST). (These values are reported in the second column in Figure 8.5, the source table.)

Source of variance	Sum of squares	Degrees of freedom	Mean square values	F-ratio	Significance
Between groups comparison	20.05	2	10.03	.244	.785
Within groups comparison (error)	1356.84	33	41.12		
Total	1376.89	35			

FIGURE 8.5 ANOVA Source Table for the Example Study

First, calculate SST. The formula for SST is:

$$SST = \sum X^2 - \frac{\left(\sum X\right)^2}{N}$$

Student	G-O class n = 12	CB class n = 12	E & I class n = 12	G-O class squared	CB class squared	E & I class squared
1	75	86	88	5625	7396	7744
2	72	85	90	5184	7225	8100
3	81	91	80	6561	8281	6400
4	84	78	72	7056	6084	5184
5	86	76	74	7396	5776	5476
6	92	84	76	8464	7056	5776
7	78	89	82	6084	7921	6724
8	84	88	86	7056	7744	7396
9	82	89	84	6724	7921	7056
10	81	92	92	6561	8464	8464
11	86	70	90	7396	4900	8100
12	88	82	91	7744	6724	8281
	$\bar{X}_1 = 82.42$	$\bar{X}_2 = 84.17$	$\bar{X}_3 = 83.75$			
	$\sum X_1 =$ 989	$\sum X_2 =$ 1010	$\sum X_3 =$ 1005	$\sum X_1^2 =$ 81851	$\sum X_2^2 =$ 85492	$\sum X_3^2 =$ 84701
	N = 36 $\sum X = 3004$			N = 36 $\sum X^2 = 252,044$		
	$(\sum X)^2 = 9,024,016$					

FIGURE 8.6 Values for Calculating $F_{observed}$ for a 1-Way Between-Groups ANOVA

I show the steps in calculating SST below, using relevant values from Figure 8.6.

$$SST = 252,044 - \frac{3004^2}{36} = 252,044 - \frac{9,024,016}{36} =$$
$$252,044 - 250,667.11 = \mathbf{1376.89}.$$

Second, I calculate SSB. The formula for SSB is:

$$SSB = \left[\frac{\left(\sum X_1\right)^2}{n_1} + \frac{\left(\sum X_2\right)^2}{n_2} + \frac{\left(\sum X_3\right)^2}{n_3} \right] - \frac{\left(\sum X\right)^2}{N}$$

Here are the calculations for SSB:

$$SSB = \left[\frac{989^2}{12} + \frac{1010^2}{12} + \frac{1005^2}{12} \right] - \frac{3004^2}{36} =$$
$$\left[\frac{978,121}{12} + \frac{1,020,100}{12} + \frac{1,010,25}{12} \right] - \frac{9,024,016}{36} =$$
$$\left[81510.08 + 85008.33 + 84168.75 \right] - 250667.11 =$$
$$\left[250687.16 \right] - 250667.11 = \mathbf{20.05}.$$

Finally, I calculate SSW:

$$SSW = SST - SSB.$$
$$SSW = 1376.89 - 20.05 = \mathbf{1356.84}.$$

Once I have the values for SST, SSB, and SSW, the next steps in calculating $F_{observed}$ can be done. When you review the next column in Figure 8.5 (the source table), you see two different degrees of freedom—the degrees of freedom for the between-groups comparison and the degrees of freedom for the within-group comparison. To complete the source table and calculate $F_{observed}$, I need the value for each of these different degrees of freedom.

For the between-groups comparison, the formula for degrees of freedom is $k - 1$, where k represents the number of levels of the independent variable. There are 2 degrees of freedom in the between-groups comparison $(3 - 1)$. For the within-group comparison, the formula for degrees of freedom is $N - k$, where N represents the total number of participants and k represents the number of levels of the independent variable. There are 33 degrees of freedom for the within-group comparison $(36 - 3)$. The formula for the total degrees of freedom is $N - 1$, so there are 35 degrees of freedom for the total study $(36 - 1)$.

The next step in calculating the F-ratio is to determine the mean square values: the mean square between and the mean square within.

The formula for mean squares between is: $\dfrac{SSB}{df_{between}}$

$$MSB = \frac{20.05}{2} = \mathbf{10.03}$$

The formula for mean squares within is: $\dfrac{SSW}{df_{within}}$

$$MSW = \frac{SSW}{df_{within}} = \frac{1356.84}{33} = \mathbf{41.12}$$

I transferred this information about the mean square values into the source table in Figure 8.5 and now calculate $F_{observed}$.

The formula for the F-ratio is: $\dfrac{MSB}{MSW}$

$$F = \frac{MSB}{MSW} = \frac{10.03}{41.12} = \mathbf{.24}$$

The value in the last column in Figure 8.5, the exact level of probability for $F_{observed}$, was calculated using R—I'm not going to do that calculation with a calculator!

The $F_{observed}$ value itself has no meaning—it's simply a tool used in statistical logic. Before returning to the steps in statistical logic, I illustrate how to calculate $F_{observed}$ using R. In Box 8.1, I illustrate how to enter the data for each level of the independent variable directly into R and calculate $F_{observed}$; in Box 8.2, I illustrate how to calculate $F_{observed}$ after importing a dataset into R. Although there are several different commands for calculating a 1-way between-groups ANOVA, I use the **aov** command because the output is presented in a source table, a conventional format for presenting ANOVA results.

Box 8.1 *R* Commands for 1-Way, Between-Groups ANOVA With Data for Variable Levels Entered Separately Into *R*

Enter the data for each of the levels of the independent variable. There are three levels in this example.	> **group1 = c(75,72,81,84,86,92,78,84,82, 81,86,88)** > **group2 = c(86,85,91,78,76,84,89,88,89, 92,70,82)** > **group3 = c(88,90,80,72,74,76,82,86,84, 92,90,91)**
Calculate the descriptive statistics for each level of the independent variable. Make a histogram of each group's scores. Add whatever arguments you'd like to the histogram command to add color or labels, or to adjust the number of bars presented in the histograms. If you want to see the histograms for the three groups all at once, create a space for them using the **par (mfrow = c (2,2))** command. Check each set of scores for normality using the Shapiro–Wilk statistic.	> **summary (group1)** > **summary (group2)** > **summary (group3)** > **sd (group1)** > **sd (group2)** > **sd (group3)** > **par (mfrow = c(2,2))** > **hist (group1)** > **hist (group2)** > **hist (group3)** > **shapiro.test (group1)** > **shapiro.test (group2)** > **shapiro.test (group3)**
Write a command that assembles the data for the three groups into a dataset (I named the dataset "d") with two columns of information; one column includes the *values* for each of the individuals in the three groups, and the second indicates whether each individual is in group 1, 2, or 3. You can give the groups names if you'd like, as I did for the "GF" group, the "CB" group, and the "PB" group.	> **d = stack (list("GF" = group1, "CB" = group2, "PB"= group3))**

(Continued)

Box 8.1 (*Continued*)

The **names** command is not required, but it gives the names of the variables in the newly created dataset; *R* assigns the name *values* for the column with the individuals' scores and the name *ind* for the column that indicates the group for each individual, the level of the independent variable to which that individual belongs.	> **names (d)**
Type the name of the dataset, d, after you've created it so you can see the two columns of information, a list of the values, and the corresponding group designation for each value. You can use the **View** command instead.	> **d** OR > **View (d)**

Do Levene's Test before calculating the ANOVA to verify that the assumption of equal variances is met. First you have to install the "car" package and load it into the *R* library.	> **install.packages ("car")**
	> **library (car)**
	> **leveneTest (values~ind,**
	  data = d)
	The output looks like this:
	Levene's Test for Homogeneity of Variance
	  (center = median)
	
	          Df F value Pr(>F)
	Group 2 0.4569 0.6372
	          33

To do the ANOVA analysis, you'll first create the model to which the data are compared; the ANOVA analysis is indicated by the **aov** component of the command. The subsequent **summary** command produces the outcome of the ANOVA in the source table format.[3]	> **study.model = aov (values~ind, data = d)** > **summary (study.model)** Here's the output—the Source Table: Df Sum Sq Mean Sq F value Pr(>F) Ind 2 20.06 10.028 0.2439 0.785 Res 33 1356.83 41.116

Box 8.2 *R* Commands for 1-Way, Between-Groups ANOVA With Data Imported as .csv Formatted Excel Document[4]

To import an Excel csv dataset, use the **read. csv** command. If you import the dataset from the companion website, you'll find that the dependent variable column of information has the header *celt.post* and the independent variable header is *type*. (Details of how to import a document can be found in Box 6.1.)	d = read.csv (file.choose (), header = T)
To view the data, type the name of the dataset, d, or you can use the **View** command instead.	> d OR > View (d)

The **study.model = aov** command tells *R* to do a 1-way, between-groups ANOVA on the data in the dataset called d, using *celt.post* as the dependent variable and treating *type* as the independent variable (that's what the symbol ~ does). The **var.equal = TRUE** component of the command indicates that the formula to be used assumes that the variances for the three groups are equal.
After you enter the command, enter the command **study.model** to see the source table.
	> study.model = aov (celt.post~type,
	    data=d, var.equal=TRUE)
	> **study.model**
	The output is:
	One-way analysis of means
	data:celt.post and type
	F = <u>0.2439</u>, num df = 2, denom df = 33,
	    p-value = <u>0.785</u>

Here's another way to get a source table: The **res** part refers to *residuals* from calculating the sums of squares.	> **res = aov(celt.post~type, data = d)** > **summary (res)** **The Source Table looks like this:** Df Sum Sq Mean Sq F value Pr(>F) Ind 2 20.06 10.028 <u>0.2439</u> <u>0.785</u> Residuals 33 1356.83 41.116

Having illustrated how to calculate an *F*-ratio using either a calculator or *R*, I now explain how ANOVA is used within the framework of statistical logic. I continue using the example study introduced earlier in the chapter.

Using ANOVA Within Statistical Logic

Step 1: State the Formal Research Hypotheses

The null hypothesis for the study is:

> **There is no statistically significant difference in the mean knowledge of English among the participants receiving one of the three types of ESL instruction.**

The alternative hypothesis is:

> **There is a statistically significant difference in the mean knowledge of English among the participants receiving one of the three types of ESL instruction.**

The ANOVA statistic simply indicates whether there's a significant difference somewhere among the three groups. It doesn't indicate where the significant difference or differences are located. Because ANOVAs don't indicate the direction of differences, the two-tailed alternative hypothesis is the only option for an ANOVA study.

Step 2: Set Alpha

I set alpha for this study at .05.

Step 3: Select the Appropriate Statistic for Analysis of the Data

The appropriate statistical formula for analyzing the example study data is a 1-way between-groups ANOVA. A 1-way, between-groups ANOVA is appropriate because in addition to the participants being randomly selected from a normally distributed population and randomly assigned to one of the levels of the independent variable, (1) the independent variable is nominal and has more than two levels, (2) the groups defined by the levels of the independent variable comprise different participants, (3) the dependent variable is interval in nature (and the scores are assumed to be normally distributed in the population and the groups), and (4) the researcher wants to determine whether there is (probably) a difference among the groups defined by the independent variable.

Step 4: Collect the Data

The data are presented in Figure 8.6.

Step 5: Verify That the Assumptions for the Statistic Are Met

The assumptions for ANOVA are:

1. The levels of the independent variable(s) contain exactly the same number of participants OR the variances are approximately equal.
2. The dependent variable is interval or interval-like (continuous) and the scores are normally distributed in the population and the groups.
3. There is a minimum of 5 (or 10) participants in each of the groups defined by the level of the independent variable(s).

I can see from reviewing the data that the independent variable, *type of class*, has three levels, the grammar-oriented program, the content-based program, and the email and Internet-based program, and there is the same number of participants in each group, so the first assumption is satisfied. If the groups were different sizes, I'd have to calculate Levene's Test to verify that the variances are equal. To check the second assumption, I need to review information about the dependent variable and the instrument or procedure used to collect the data to verify that the tool is designed to yield normally distributed data when administered to a population. I'd also calculate the Shapiro–Wilk statistic to check the normality of the distribution of scores for each group. The third assumption can be checked by reviewing the data to verify that there are at least 5 (or 10) participants in each class.

Step 6: Calculate the Observed Value of the Appropriate Statistic

I calculated the observed F-ratio above: $F_{observed} = .24$.

Step 7: Determine the Degrees of Freedom for the Statistic and Use Degrees of Freedom and Alpha to Find the Critical Value of the Statistic OR Calculate the Exact Probability of the $F_{observed}$ Calculated in Step 6

Either of the two approaches described in Step 7 can be used, but the critical value approach is typically used when the calculation of $F_{observed}$ is done using a calculator. The exact probability approach can be used when the calculation of $F_{observed}$ is done using R or some other statistical software programs because the exact probability is reported.

Using the Critical Value Approach

Interpreting the $F_{observed}$ value for ANOVA requires two different degrees-of-freedom values, one from the between-group comparison and one from the within-group comparison. Both degrees of freedom can be found in the source table (Figure 8.5)—in the column labeled degrees of freedom. The degrees of freedom for the between-group comparison is the number of levels of the independent variable minus one, so there are two between-group degrees of freedom. There are 33 within-group degrees of freedom—the total number of participants minus the number of levels of the independent variable.

In Step 2, I set alpha at .05. To find the critical value of F, a chart of critical values for F is needed.[5] Between-groups degrees of freedom are displayed across the top of the chart; within-group degrees of freedom are displayed down the left side of the chart. Go across the top of the chart to the column with the heading *2*. Then, for the degrees of freedom within, read down the chart until you find the row marked *32*. There's no row *33*, so use row *32*, which gives a slightly more rigorous critical value than would be found in row *33*. (By tradition, one uses the stricter critical value when the chart doesn't have the specific degrees of freedom needed.) The critical value of F for alpha at .05 and 2 degrees of freedom between and 32 degrees of freedom within is 3.30. This is the critical value of F used in Step 8.

Using the Exact Probability Approach

When using the exact probability approach to interpreting the outcome, R (or some other statistical program) is used to calculate $F_{observed}$ and the exact level of probability for $F_{observed}$. In Box 8.1 and Box 8.2, $F_{observed}$ has a single underscore ($F = 0.2439$) and the exact probability ($p = .785$) has a double underscore.

Step 8: To Interpret the Outcome of the Analysis, Compare the Observed Value and the Critical Value OR Compare Exact Probability to Alpha

In Step 8 the outcome of the analysis is determined using either the critical value approach (if calculations were done with a calculator) or the exact probability approach (if calculations were done using R).

Using the Critical Value Approach

The rules for comparing $F_{observed}$ and $F_{critical}$ are:

If $F_{observed} \leq F_{critical} \rightarrow$ accept the null hypothesis.

If $F_{observed} > F_{critical} \rightarrow$ reject the null hypothesis.

When $F_{observed}$ and $F_{critical}$ are compared, we see:

$$.2439 < 3.30.$$

$F_{observed}$ is less than $F_{critical}$, so the null hypothesis is accepted.

Using the Exact Probability Approach

The rules for comparing the exact level of probability for $F_{observed}$ to alpha (α) are:

> If exact probability $\geq$ alpha $\rightarrow$ accept the null hypothesis.
>
> If exact probability $<$ alpha $\rightarrow$ reject the null hypothesis.

The output from R indicates that the exact level of probability for $F_{observed}$ is $p = .785$; alpha was set at .05. Because the exact probability is greater than alpha, the null hypothesis is accepted.

Step 9: Interpret the Findings as a Probability Statement

In this step, the formal research hypothesis that was accepted is recast as a probability statement:

> **There's 95% certainty that there's no statistically significant difference in the mean knowledge of English among the participants receiving one of the three types of ESL instruction.**

Step 10: Interpret the Meaningfulness of the Findings

There are two avenues for interpreting meaningfulness, with reference to the research question and through calculating effect size. Regardless of whether the null hypothesis is accepted or rejected, the findings are interpreted with reference to the research question. I embarked on this analysis because I wanted to know whether type of instruction would have a differential impact on students' learning and learned that type of instruction (probably) doesn't have a differential impact.

If I had rejected the null hypothesis and accepted the alternative hypothesis, before calculating effect size I would do a planned post hoc analysis to determine where the significant differences are located—the F-ratio doesn't indicate which groups are different from one another. This is where one of the statistics I mentioned above, Bonferroni, Scheffé, Tukey's Honestly Significant Difference, or Newman–Keuls, would be used. In Box 8.3, I illustrate how to use R to calculate the Bonferroni comparisons for the example study, though a post hoc analysis isn't usually done in studies in which the null hypothesis has been accepted. The Bonferroni command carries out all possible pairwise comparisons and adjusts the p-values to allow for multiple overlapping t-tests.[6]

The output from the post hoc Bonferroni shows that none of the groups is statistically different from the others—but we knew that, because we accepted the null hypothesis. If the value of $F_{observed}$ had been large enough to reject the null hypothesis, after calculating and interpreting the post hoc analysis, some

Box 8.3 Calculating All Possible Pairwise Comparisons in Post Hoc Examination of the Groups

The **paired = FALSE** component of the Bonferroni command is included because there are different people in each of the groups. The values reported are p-values—and because they are greater than alpha (they're all equal to 1), we have confirmation that none of the differences among the three groups is statistically significant.	> **pairwise.t.test (d$values,d$ind, paired = FALSE, p.adjust.method = "bonferroni")** Output: **exper.two** **exper.one** **exper.one** 1 – **non-exper** 1 1

researchers would calculate the effect size for the ANOVA analysis using the omega^2 formula, though it can be used only when the ANOVA study is balanced (Hatch & Lazaraton, 1991).[7] Others, such as Field and colleagues (2012), recommend determining effect size for the post hoc comparisons rather than for the entire ANOVA study. I think determining the effect size for the post hoc comparisons is more useful and informative than the more general effect size determined by the omega^2 formula, but I explain how to calculate the general omega^2 formula before explaining how to determine effect size for the post hoc comparisons.

The omega^2 formula is:

$$omega^2 = \frac{SSB - \left[(k-1)MSW\right]}{SST + MSW}$$

The values needed to calculate omega^2 can be retrieved from the source table in Figure 8.6: SSB is 20.05; MSW is 41.12; SST is 1376.89. Recall that k is the number of levels of the independent variable.

I enter these values in the formula for omega^2, carry out the calculations below, find the square root, and discover that the effect size is (vanishingly) small. The guidelines for interpreting omega^2 are a bit different from those for the other effect size statistics; in a 1996 study cited by Field et al. (2012, p. 45), Kirk recommends that .01 or less be considered a weak or "small" effect, that .06 be considered a "medium" effect, and that .14 or higher be considered a "large" effect.

$$omega^2 = \frac{20.05 - \left[(3-1)41.12\right]}{1376.89 + 41.12} = \frac{20.05 - \left[(2)41.12\right]}{1418.01} = \frac{20.05 - 82.24}{1418.01}$$

$$= \frac{-62.19}{1418.01} = -.044$$

For researchers who believe calculating effect size for the post hoc comparisons is more useful than using the general omega^2 approach, the effect size formula for t-test analyses can be used:

$$\sqrt{\frac{t^2}{t^2 + df}}$$

Each of the t-tests must be performed so that the t-values are available; because we're not using the t-values to interpret probability (we're simply going to use them to calculate effect size), the fact that the three t-tests overlap isn't a problem.[8]

Box 8.4 Using R to Calculate $t_{observed}$ for the Post Hoc Comparisons

To calculate effect size for each of the three comparisons for this ANOVA when the scores for each level of the variable were entered directly as separate sets (see Box 8.1), use **t.test** commands.	> **t.test (group1, group2)** Output: t = -0.7002, df = 21.36, p-value = 0.4914 > **t.test (group1, group3)** Output: t = -0.5184, df = 20.992, p-value = 0.6096 > **t-testIgroup2, group3)** Output t = 0.1502, df = 21.95, p-value = 0.882
For each of the three comparisons, the effect size can be calculated using this formula and the values for $t_{observed}$ and degrees of freedom (df). $$\sqrt{\frac{t^2}{t^2 + df}}$$ A template for the formula written in R is: **sqrt ((t$_{observed}$) ^2 / ((t$_{observed}$) ^2 + df))**	> **sqrt ((-0.7002)^2/ ((-0.7002) ^2 + 21.36))** Output: [1] 0.1497937 > **sqrt ((-0.5184)^2 / ((-0.5184) ^2 + 20.992))** Output: [1] 0.1124283 > **sqrt ((0.1502) ^2 / ((0.1502) ^2 + 21.95))** Output: [1] 0.03204274

The findings can be reported in this way:

> **R** was used to calculate the observed value of F ($F = 0.2439$; $df = 2,33$; $p = .785$). The results indicate with 95% certainty that the type of course an advanced ESL student takes, a grammar-focused course, a content-based course, or a project-based course, does not have an impact on the students' language development. Additionally, the overall effect size for the study was very small (−.044). The effect sizes for the pairwise comparisons were similarly small (group 1 and group 2 = .15; group 1 and group 3 = .11; group 2 and group 3 = .03).

Though many researchers in language education will never have the occasion to use an ANOVA statistic themselves in their own research, almost all will at some time read a study in which an ANOVA has been used. Readers who would like a bit of practice with the concepts can turn to the Practice Problem at the end of the chapter.

R Commands Introduced in Chapter Eight

par (mfrow = c(2,2)) This command creates a space for displaying four histograms in a two-by-two grid.

d = stack (list("name 2" = group1, "name 2" = group2, "name 3"= group3)) This command creates a dataset from data entered separately. The independent variable is given the name *ind*, and the dependent variable is given the name *values*.

study.model = aov (values~ind, data = d) This command creates a model that includes information from the steps in calculating $F_{observed}$ and calculates $F_{observed}$ itself. It yields a source table when **study.model** is entered.

res = aov(celt.post~type, data = d) and > summary (res) The first command creates a model that includes information from the steps in calculating $F_{observed}$ and calculates $F_{observed}$ itself; the second command yields a source table.

pairwise.t.test (d$values,d$ind, paired = FALSE, p.adjust.method = "bonferroni") This command calculates the post hoc comparisons for a 1-way, between-groups ANOVA (based on a dataset named *d* that was created using the **stack (list...** command.

sqrt ((tobserved) ^2 / ((tobserved) ^2 + df)) This command is the formula needed for calculating effect size for *t*-tests.

Practice Problem

The assistant director for ESL courses in a large adult education district in a Western state decided to investigate the effectiveness of the various types of advanced ESL instruction that were offered in the district. There were four types of programs available to advanced students (student level was determined by performance on the CLT). From the population of advanced learners in the district, 48 participants were randomly selected and 12 were randomly assigned to each of the four types of class. There was no attrition. An interval-scale pretest, Form A of the CLT, was given to establish that there were no significant differences among the groups before the period of instruction (the pretest data were analyzed using a 1-way ANOVA and no significant differences were found at the .01 level). Form B of the CLT was given as a posttest after the 10-week period of instruction. The researcher wanted to know whether any of the programs appeared to be more effective for these advanced learners of English. I think it's safe to assume that the data are normally distributed in the populations from which the groups are drawn, but the other assumptions for ANOVA should be checked. You'll find the dataset in the resource section of the companion website. (www.routledge.com/cw/turner).

Notes

1 Some statisticians recommend 10. When the number of people in each group is very small, each individual has a greater effect on the outcome than when there are more people in the group.
2 *Balanced* means there's exactly the same number of participants in each level of the independent variable.
3 The **plot (study.model)** command produces a series of plots that are useful for interpreting the results; please refer to Chapters 28 and 29 by De Veaux, Velleman, and Bock (2008) or Chapters 10 through 14 by Field, Miles, and Field (2012) for detailed discussion of the interpretation of specific types of ANOVAs.
4 The csv file has two columns of information: (1) codes indicating to which level of the independent variable each individual is assigned, and (2) each individual's score on the dependent variable.
5 There is a chart of $F_{critical}$ values in the resources section of the companion website (www.routledge.com/cw/turner).
6. Without the correction factor built into the Bonferroni procedure, the multiple overlapping *t*-tests performed in the analysis lead to a degradation of the level of probability.
7 A reminder that *balanced* means there's exactly the same number of participants in each of the levels of the independent variable.
8 The level of probability is adversely affected in overlapping *t*-tests.

9

THE NON-PARAMETRIC KRUSKAL–WALLIS AND FRIEDMAN'S TEST STATISTICS

Four of the statistics you studied in Chapters Six and Seven, the Case II Independent Samples *t*-test formula, the Case II Paired Samples *t*-test, the Wilcoxon Rank Sum statistic, and the Wilcoxon Signed Rank statistic, are used in research in language education when the researchers' independent variable has two levels and the researchers want to compare the performance of the two different groups. The 1-way between-groups analysis of variance (ANOVA) is a parametric statistic that's used to analyze data for possible differences when the independent variable has more than two levels. The Kruskal–Wallis and Friedman's Test statistics are the "right tools" when researchers have an independent variable with more than two levels and the data are non-parametric—rankable interval or ordinal scale data.

As I noted in Chapter Seven, the goal of small-scale language education research is typically to gain a deep understanding of the local learning environment and learners—the primary goal is not generalization of the findings to a population, as is the case in parametric studies. The participants in these small-scale studies are seldom randomly selected from a normally distributed population; they're often the students in a teacher/researcher's own classes or school. These existing groups are relatively small and may be different sizes; the dependent variable variances[1] may be different because the participants chose their classes on their own rather than being randomly assigned to them. Additionally, the data collection tools used are often designed to measure students' learning and opinions, not to yield a normal distribution of data. In these conditions, non-parametric statistics are appropriate.

In this chapter, I describe the Kruskal–Wallis and Friedman's Test statistics and explain how they are calculated, whether using a calculator or *R*; I also address how and when to calculate effect size and how to handle tied scores when doing Friedman's Test. As in other chapters, I illustrate each statistic with an example study.

A Non-Parametric Statistic for Comparison of More Than Two Samples: The Kruskal–Wallis Statistic

I discuss the Kruskal–Wallis statistic first, using the example study described below.

Example Study

The director of a large adult education program observed that students seemed to become nervous when faced with taking a required multiple-choice test. She decided to try out two new types of preparation for taking multiple-choice tests to determine whether the students' confidence in taking this type of test might be increased. Her independent variable included three levels: a non-experimental group that received no additional instruction on taking tests; an experimental group that completed a number of practice tests; and an experimental group that completed a 2-hour course on test-taking strategies. Data on the dependent variable, *confidence in taking multiple-choice tests*, were collected through a questionnaire that yields confidence scores (between 20 and 60); the questionnaire data are not normally distributed but are rankable (see Table 9.1 for the fabricated data). She used the Kruskal–Wallis statistic to determine whether there was a statistically significant difference in the participants' confidence in taking multiple-choice tests depending on the type of test preparation activities they did.

I follow the 10 steps in statistical logic as I use the Kruskal–Wallis statistic.

1. State the formal research hypotheses, the null hypothesis and the alternative hypothesis/hypotheses.
2. Set alpha, the level of probability for the analysis.
3. Select the appropriate statistic for analysis of the data.
4. Collect the data.
5. Verify that the assumptions for the statistic are met.
6. Calculate the observed value of the appropriate statistic.
7. Determine the degrees of freedom (*df*) for the statistic and use degrees of freedom and alpha to find the critical value of the statistic OR calculate the exact probability for the observed statistic calculated in Step 6.
8. To interpret the outcome of the analysis, compare observed value and the critical value OR compare the exact probability to alpha. Apply one of the appropriate set of rules to the comparison.

   Critical value approach:

      If the observed value ≤ the critical value → accept the null hypothesis.
      If the observed value > the critical value → reject the null hypothesis.

Exact probability approach:

If exact probability ≥ alpha → accept the null hypothesis.
If exact probability < alpha → reject the null hypothesis.

9. Interpret the findings as a probability statement using the hypothesis accepted in Step 8.
10. Interpret the meaningfulness of the findings and calculate the effect size if possible.

Step 1: State the Formal Research Hypotheses

The null hypothesis is:

> **There is no statistically significant difference among the test-taking confidence rankings of the students who received no test training, did a series of practice tests, or studied test-taking strategies.**

The alternative hypothesis is:

> **There is a statistically significant difference among the test-taking confidence rankings of the students who received no test training, did a series of practice tests, or studied test-taking strategies.**

Similar to the ANOVA statistics, the Kruskal–Wallis statistic simply indicates whether there's a significant difference among the rankings of the three groups. The statistic doesn't indicate where the significant differences are located, so there's only one possible alternative hypothesis—the two-tailed, non-directional alternative hypothesis. If the null hypothesis is rejected and the alternative hypothesis is accepted, subsequent comparisons of the pairs of groups must be conducted to identify which of the groups are different from the others. The Wilcoxon Rank Sum statistic can be used to determine which specific pairs of groups differ.

Step 2: Set Alpha

I set alpha for this study at .05.

Step 3: Select the Appropriate Statistic for Analysis of the Data

The appropriate statistical formula for analyzing the data is the Kruskal–Wallis statistic because (1) there's only one independent variable and it has more than two levels, (2) the groups defined by the levels of the independent variable comprise different participants, (3) the dependent variable yields rankable data, and (4) the researcher wants to determine whether there is a difference among the groups defined by the levels of the independent variable.

Step 4: Collect the Data

The fabricated confidence scores for the classes with different types of test-taking strategies are displayed in Table 9.1.

Step 5: Verify That the Assumptions for the Statistic Are Met

The researcher wants to know whether there's a difference strong enough to be due to something other than chance among the three groups of learners defined by the levels of the independent variable. The assumptions for using the Kruskal–Wallis statistic are:

1. The independent variable has three or more levels.
2. The groups defined by the levels of the independent variable comprise different participants.
3. The dependent variable yields rankable data.

I can see from reviewing the data that the independent variable, *type of test preparation*, has three levels and I know that there are different people in each of these three conditions. Review of the data in Table 9.1 shows that the confidence scores are rankable.

TABLE 9.1 Confidence Scores for the Groups With Different Types of Test-Taking Instruction (fabricated data)

Non-experimental Group n = 8		Experimental Group 1 (extended practice) n = 7		Experimental Group 2 (strategy course) n = 5	
1 Nonexperimental	28	1 Experimental 1	25	1 Experimental 2	37
2 Nonexperimental	30	2 Experimental 1	40	2 Experimental 2	27
3 Nonexperimental	26	3 Experimental 1	36	3 Experimental 2	47
4 Nonexperimental	22	4 Experimental 1	19	4 Experimental 2	49
5 Nonexperimental	29	5 Experimental 1	23	5 Experimental 2	51
6 Nonexperimental	35	6 Experimental 1	31		
7 Nonexperimental	18	7 Experimental 1	43		
8 Nonexperimental	20				

Step 6: Calculate the Observed Value of the Appropriate Statistic

Similar to the Wilcoxon Rank Sum and the Wilcoxon Signed Rank statistics, the first step in calculating the Kruskal–Wallis statistic requires combining the groups of participants and ranking them.

After ranking the set of merged outcomes for the participants in the study, the sum of the ranks for each of the three groups is calculated; these values are presented at the bottom of Table 9.2.

The formula for the Kruskal–Wallis statistic yields a value, KW, which is converted to a chi-squared value (χ^2)^2 (see Chapter Twelve). The $KW\chi^2$ value can be interpreted using the chart of critical values for χ^2, though when the Kruskal–Wallis is calculated using R, the outcome can be interpreted using the exact probability for the observed value of the statistic, so there's really no need to use the chart of critical values. I show how to calculate the Kruskal–Wallis statistic using the formula below; however, immediately after, I discuss and illustrate how to calculate the statistic using R.

TABLE 9.2 Rankings for the Three Combined Groups and Sum of Ranks for Each Group

StudentGroup	Questionnaire Outcome	Rank
5 Experimental 2	51	20
4 Experimental 2	49	19
3 Experimental 2	47	18
7 Experimental 1	43	17
2 Experimental 1	40	16
1 Experimental 2	37	15
3 Experimental 1	36	14
6 Nonexperimental	35	13
6 Experimental 1	31	12
2 Nonexperimental	30	11
5 Nonexperimental	29	10
1 Nonexperimental	28	9
2 Experimental 2	27	8
3 Nonexperimental	26	7
1 Experimental 1	25	6
5 Experimental 1	23	5
4 Nonexperimental	22	4
8 Nonexperimental	20	3
4 Experimental 1	19	2
7 Nonexperimental	18	1

ΣR Nonexperimental = 58
ΣR Experimental 1 = 72
ΣR Experimental 2 = 80

Here is the formula for the Kruskal–Wallis statistic, as presented by Corder and Foreman (2009, p. 100):

$$KW\chi^2 = \frac{12}{N(N+1)}\sum_{i=1}^{k}\frac{R_i^2}{n_i} - \left[3(N+1)\right]^{3,4}$$

And here are the calculations:

$$KW\chi^2 = \frac{12}{20(20+1)}\left[\left(\frac{58^2}{8}\right)+\left(\frac{72^2}{7}\right)+\left(\frac{80^2}{5}\right)\right]-\left[3(20+1)\right]$$

$$= \frac{12}{420}\left[\left(\frac{3364}{8}\right)+\left(\frac{5184}{7}\right)+\left(\frac{6400}{5}\right)\right]-\left[3(21)\right]$$

$$= \frac{12}{420}\left[(420.5)+(740.57142)+(1280)\right]-\left[63\right]$$

$$= (.0285714)(2441.0714)-63$$

$$= 69.744827 - 63$$

$$= \mathbf{6.744827}$$

In Boxes 9.1 and 9.2, I describe how to calculate the Kruskal–Wallis statistic using R. In Box 9.1, the data for each group are entered separately; in Box 9.2, I import a spreadsheet that includes a column of information indicating each person's group and another column indicating each individual's dependent variable score.

Box 9.1 *R* Commands for Calculating the Observed Value of the Kruskal–Wallis With Data for Each Group Entered Separately

Enter the data for each level of the independent variable separately, using the **c** notation.	> **nonexp.group = c(28,30,26,22, 29,35,18,20)** > **practice.group = c(25,40,36,19,23,31,43)** > **strategy.group = c(37,27,47,49,51)**
The **d=stack(list …)** command builds a dataset with two columns of information. The **stack** command assigns the label *values* to one column of information, the dependent variable values— the values that I entered using the **c** command. The other column is labeled *ind* and indicates each participant's group, using the names I gave the groups (inside double quotation marks).	> **d = stack (list("Non–experimental Group" = nonexp.group, "Test Practice Group" = practice.group, "Test Strategy Group" = strategy. group))**

(Continued)

Box 9.1 (*Continued*)

When used with a "stacked" dataset, the **plot** command makes a so-called whisker chart for each of the three groups; the **xlab** and **ylab** commands provide labels for the whisker charts.[5]	> plot (values~ind, data=d, xlab = "Group", ylab = "Outcomes", col = "light blue") Here are the whisker charts: 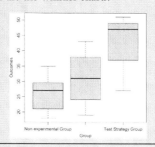
If you prefer histograms, you can make three side-by-side histograms by first creating a space for them using the **par** (mfrow = c(2,2)) command and then making a histogram for each group. (Imagine the different colors when you look at the set of histograms.)	> par (mfrow =c(2,2)) > hist(nonexp.group, breaks =10, main = "Non-experimental Group", xlab = "confi-dence score", col = "light green") > hist (practice.group, breaks = 10, main = "Practice Group", xlab = "confidence score", col = "light blue") > hist(strategy.group, breaks = 10, main = "Strategy Group", xlab = "confidence score", col = "pink") Output: 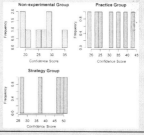
The **kruskal.test** command produces a value labeled *Kruskal-Wallis chi-squared*, which is the observed value of the Kruskal–Wallis statistic. The degrees of freedom are also provided. The exact level of probability for the observed value of the Kruskal–Wallis statistic is reported too.	> kruskal.test (values ~ ind, data = d) Output: data:values by ind Kruskal-Wallis chi-squared = 6.7449, df = 2, p-value = 0.03431

Box 9.2 *R* Commands for Calculating the Observed Value of the Kruskal–Wallis Statistic With Imported Data[6]

Import the csv document that contains the data using the **read.csv (file.choose())** command (see Box 6.1 for more explanation). This command allows you to import a dataset and name it *d*. (You can give the dataset any name you want; simply replace *d* with the name you prefer!)	**d = read.csv (file.choose (), header = T)**
Enter the name that you gave the dataset in the previous command so you can see the values. (You can use the **View** command instead; the **View** command presents the data in a separate, pop-up window.) There should be two columns of information; a list of each of the dependent variable values in one column and the corresponding group designation for each value.	**> d** **OR** **> View (d)**
To view histograms of the data for each of the three groups, first create a space for the three histograms using the **par(mfrow= c(2,2))** command.	**> par (mfrow = c(2,2))**
This command then creates the three histograms.	**> sapply (split (d$confidence, d$practype), hist)** Output:
This command provides the mean for each group. (You'll have to remember which group is 1, which is 2, and which is 3 in the dataset you created and imported. In the Excel document I imported, the non-experimental group is 1, the group that does practice tests is 2, and the group that does the strategy training is 3.)	**> sapply (split (d$confidence, d$practype), mean)** Output: 1 2 3 26.0 31.0 42.2
This command provides the standard deviation for each group.	**> sapply (split (d$confidence, d$practype), sd)** Output: 1 2 3 5.682052 9.073772 10.059821

(Continued)

Box 9.2 (*Continued*)

The **kruskal.test** command provides the observed value of the Kruskal–Wallis statistic, the degrees of freedom, and the exact level of probability for the observed value of Kruskal–Wallis chi-squared.	> **kruskal.test (confidence ~ practype, data = d)** Output: data:confidence by practype Kruskal-Wallis chi-squared = 6.7449, df = 2, p-value = 0.03431

The R output includes the Kruskal–Wallis value, which is 6.7449, reported as the Kruskal–Wallis χ^2 value, the degrees of freedom for the analysis, and the exact level of probability for the observed value of the Kruskal–Wallis statistic.

Step 7: Determine the Degrees of Freedom for the Statistic and Use Degrees of Freedom and Alpha to Find the Critical Value of the Statistic OR Calculate the Exact Probability of the Observed Statistic

Either the critical value or the exact probability approach can be used in Step 7, but the critical value approach is typically used when the calculation of the observed value is done using a calculator. The exact probability approach can be used when the calculation of the statistic is done with R because exact probability is reported.

Using the Critical Value Approach

The formula for the degrees of freedom for the Kruskal–Wallis statistic is $k - 1$: the number of levels of the independent variable minus 1. So for this study, there are 2 degrees of freedom ($3 - 1 = 2$). Using the chart of critical values[7] for χ^2, I find that the critical value for alpha = .05 and $df = 2$ is 5.991.

Using the Exact Probability Approach

With the exact probability approach to interpreting the outcome, I use R (or some other statistical program) to calculate the observed value of the Kruskal–Wallis statistic and the exact probability of that observed value. The Kruskal–Wallis χ^2 value is 6.7449 (with $df = 2$) and the exact probability is $p = .03431$.

Step 8: To Interpret the Outcome of the Analysis, Compare the Observed Value and the Critical Value, OR Compare the Exact Probability to Alpha

In Step 8, the outcome of the analysis is determined using either the critical value approach (if calculations were done with a calculator) or the exact probability approach (if calculations were done using R).

Using the Critical Value Approach

To interpret the statistical significance for the Kruskal–Wallis statistic using the observed value of Kruskal–Wallis χ^2, these rules are followed:

If $KW\,\chi^2_{observed} \leq \chi^2_{critical} \rightarrow$ accept the null hypothesis.

If $KW\,\chi^2_{observed} > \chi^2_{critical} \rightarrow$ reject the null hypothesis.

If the observed value of the statistic (the one that was calculated) is less than the critical value (the one from the chart), the null hypothesis is accepted. If the observed value of the statistic (the one that was calculated) is greater than the critical value, the null hypothesis is rejected and the alternative hypothesis is accepted.

The observed value of $KW\,\chi^2$ is 6.744827 (according to my calculations done with a handheld calculator), which is greater than 5.991, the critical value for χ^2, so I reject the null hypothesis and accept the alternative hypothesis.

Using the Exact Probability Approach

When statistical significance is interpreted using the exact level of probability rather than a chart of critical values for χ^2, these rules should be followed:

If exact probability $\geq$ alpha $\rightarrow$ accept the null hypothesis.

If exact probability $<$ alpha $\rightarrow$ reject the null hypothesis.

The exact level of probability, .03431, is less than alpha, .05, so the null hypothesis is rejected and the alternative hypothesis is accepted.

Because the alternative hypothesis was accepted, pairwise comparisons of the groups must be calculated using the Wilcoxon Rank Sum statistic to determine which of the pairs show statistically significant differences. The independent variable has three levels—the non-experimental group, the practice group, and the strategy group—so there are three possible comparisons: (1) non-experimental to practice, (2) non-experimental to strategy, and (3) practice to strategy. The effect size for each of the pairwise comparisons would be calculated too, if there were enough participants to justify converting the Wilcoxon Rank Sum values to z-scores. Due to the small number of participants in this study, effect size will not be calculated (see Chapter Seven).

In Box 9.3 and Box 9.4, I show how to use R to make the three possible pairwise comparisons, first for when the data are entered directly into R in three separate groups and then when a dataset is imported into R.

Box 9.3 Using *R* for Pairwise Comparison Using the Wilcoxon Rank Sum Statistic (Data Entered Directly Into *R*)

The data for each level of the independent variable were entered directly into R.	> **nonexp.group = c(28,30,26,22, 29,35,18,20)** > **practice.group = c(25,40,36,19, 23,31,43)** > **strategy.group = c(37,27,47,49,51)**
Enter the command for the first pairwise comparison. (If there are ties among the values add **exact = FALSE** to the command. See Chapter Seven for details.)	> **wilcox.test (nonexp.group, pratice.group)** Output: W = 18, p-value = <u>0.281</u>
Enter the command for the second pairwise comparison. (Add **exact = FALSE** if needed.)	> **wilcox.test (nonexp.group, strategy.group)** Output: W = 4, p-value = <u>0.01865</u>
Enter the command for the third pairwise comparison. (Add **exact = FALSE** if needed.)	> **wilxox.test (practice.group, strategy.group)** Output: W = 6, p-value = <u>0.07323</u>

Box 9.4 Using *R* for Pairwise Comparison Using the Wilcoxon Rank Sum Statistic (Dataset Imported)

The dataset was imported using this command, so the complete dataset is named *d*. The independent variable is labeled *practype*.	> **d = read.csv (file.choose (), header = T)**
Create (and View) three separate datasets, one for each group.	> **nonexp.group.dataset = subset (d,d$practype == "1")** > View (**nonexp.group.dataset**) > **practice.group.dataset = subset (d, d$practype == "2")** > View (**practice.group.dataset**) > **strategy.group.dataset = subset (d, d$practype == "3")** > View (**strategy.group.dataset**)
Calculate the observed value of the Wilcoxon Rank Sum statistic for the first comparison. (If there are ties among the values, add **exact = FALSE** to the command. See Chapter Seven for details.)	> **wilcox.test (nonexp.group. dataset$confidence, practice. group.dataset$confidence)** Output: W = 18, p-value = <u>0.281</u>

(Continued)

Box 9.4 (*Continued*)

Calculate the observed value of the Wilcoxon Rank Sum statistic for the second comparison. (Add **exact = FALSE** if needed.)	> **wilcox.test (nonexp.group. dataset$confidence, strategy.group. dataset$confidence)** Output: W = 4, *p*-value = <u>0.01865</u>
Calculate the observed value of the Wilcoxon Rank Sum statistic for the third comparison. (Add **exact = FALSE** if needed.)	> **wilxox.test (practice.group. dataset$confidence, strategy.group. dataset$confidence)** Output: W = 6, p-value = <u>0.07323</u>

In the output from the three pairwise comparisons in Boxes 9.3 and 9.4, the exact *p*-values have a single underscore or a double underscore. The exact probability rules for interpreting statistical significance are:

If exact probability ≥ alpha → accept the null hypothesis.

If exact probability < alpha → reject the null hypothesis.

The exact *p*-value that has a double underscore in Boxes 9.3 and 9.4 is statistically significant; the exact *p* for the comparison of the non-experimental group with the group that had strategy training, $p = .01865$, is less than alpha, .05. The exact *p*-values that have a single underscore in Boxes 9.3 and 9.4 are not statistically significant. The exact *p*-value of the comparison between the non-experimental group and the group that did practice tests ($p = .281$) and the exact *p*-value for the comparison of the practice group and the strategy training group ($p = .07323$) are greater than alpha, .05, showing that there's no statistically significant difference between the groups. As I noted above, effect size for the pairwise comparisons can't be calculated because there are too few participants to justify converting the observed values of the Wilcoxon Rank Sum statistic to *z*-scores.[8]

Step 9: Interpret the Findings as a Probability Statement

In this step, I make the probability statement based on the hypothesis that was accepted, the alternative hypothesis in this example:

There's 95% certainty that there's a statistically significant difference among the test-taking confidence rankings of the students

who received no test training, did a series of practice tests, or studied test-taking strategies.

10: Interpret the Meaningfulness of the Findings

Meaningfulness is interpreted with reference to the research question, "Is there a statistically significant difference in participants' test-taking confidence depending on the type of test preparation activities they did?"

When possible, effect size is also reported but effect size can't be calculated for this study because there aren't enough participants to meet the conditions necessary for its calculation.[9] The researcher's interpretation of the outcomes might look something like this:

> For these students, the researcher concludes with 95% certainty that training in test-taking strategies may be more effective in promoting test-taking confidence than no instruction (Kruskal–Wallis χ^2 = 6.7449, df = 2, p = .03431). This impact was apparent in the significant difference in the level of confidence for the group that received strategy training and the practice test group (Wilcoxon Rank Sum = 4, p = .01865). There was no significant difference in level of confidence for the practice group and the no-instruction group (Wilcoxon Rank Sum = 18, p = .281) or the practice group and the strategy group (Wilcoxon Rank Sum = 6, p = .07323). Though the participants may have differed in their level of confidence at the outset of the study, the findings indicate a need for further research on the possible impact of strategy training on learners' confidence when taking tests. Effect size cannot be calculated for any of the pairwise comparisons due to the small number of participants.

A Non-Parametric Statistic for Comparison of More Than Two Paired Samples: Friedman's Test Statistic

The Friedman's Test statistic can be considered the partner to the Kruskal–Wallis statistic. Both are used to analyze non-parametric data when the independent variable has more than two levels. The Kruskal–Wallis statistic is used when there are different individuals in the comparison groups. The Friedman's Test statistic is used when individuals are compared to themselves. The Kruskal–Wallis statistic parallels the Wilcoxon Rank Sum statistic and Friedman's Test parallels the Wilcoxon Signed Rank statistic. I'll use a fabricated expansion of Professor Oliva's research to illustrate how the Friedman's Test statistic works.

Example Study

Professor Oliva, in his study on factors affecting the motivation of learners of Spanish, collected data on his participants' level of motivation at three times during the term: at the beginning of the term, at midterm, and at the end of the term after a period of instruction during which they received feedback designed to promote learners' motivation to study Spanish. I want to determine whether their level of motivation was affected incrementally, so I plan to compare the outcomes from these three data collection events. The research question that guides this investigation is: "Is there a statistically significant difference in the pre-feedback, midterm-feedback, and post-feedback levels of motivation for students who received feedback designed to promote autonomy and motivation?" To do this analysis, I'll use the Friedman's Test statistic. The fabricated motivation scores for Professor Oliva's participants are displayed in Table 9.3.

I now follow the 10 steps in statistical logic to the analyze the data.

Step 1: State the Formal Research Hypotheses

The null hypothesis and alternative hypothesis are both stated.

> **Null hypothesis: There is no significant difference in the rankings of the pre-feedback, midterm-feedback, and post-feedback motivation scores for participants who received feedback designed to promote autonomy and motivation.**

> **Alternative hypothesis: There is a significant difference in the rankings of the pre-feedback, midterm-feedback, and post-feedback**

TABLE 9.3 Motivation Scores at Three Points in Time for Participants Who Receive Experimental Feedback (fabricated data)

Pretest Total	Midtest Total	Posttest Total
38	40	44
42	51	52
32	42	46
40	42	50
35	48	45
46	53	52
38	45	47
38	42	43
47	48	49
41	51	50

motivation for participants who received feedback designed to promote autonomy and motivation.

Similar to the ANOVA statistics and the Kruskal–Wallis statistic, the alternative hypothesis for the Friedman's Test statistic indicates simply whether there's a significant difference among the rankings of three sets of scores; the statistic doesn't indicate where the significant differences are located. If the null hypothesis is rejected and the alternative hypothesis is accepted, subsequent comparisons are conducted to identify which of the sets of scores are different from one another. The Wilcoxon Signed Rank statistic can be used to determine which specific sets of scores differ.

Step 2: Set Alpha

This research is exploratory in nature, but the researcher may make decisions about his pedagogical practice based on the outcomes, so alpha is set at .01.

Step 3: Select the Appropriate Statistic for Analysis of the Data

The researcher wants to know whether there's a statistically significant difference in the pre-feedback, midterm-feedback, and post-feedback motivation scores for participants who received feedback designed to promote autonomy and motivation. The independent variable, represented by the participants' level of motivation at the outset of the term, at midterm, and at the end of the term, forms three categories, or levels. The dependent variable, *participants' degree of motivation*, yields rankable data, though the actual values aren't normally distributed. Friedman's Test statistic is appropriate because the researcher wants to determine whether there's a difference among the pretest, midterm, and posttest outcomes. Additionally, (1) the three sets of data come from exactly the same participants, and (2) the dependent variable yields rankable outcomes. A non-parametric statistic is appropriate because the participants aren't drawn from a population and the tool used to collect the dependent variable scores isn't designed to yield normally distributed data.

Step 4: Collect the Data

The data are presented in Table 9.3.

Step 5: Verify That the Assumptions for the Statistic Are Met

There are three conditions that must be met when using Friedman's test.

1. The independent variable is *nominal* and has more than two levels.
2. Comparison is of outcomes for exactly the same set of participants.
3. The dependent variable yields rankable data.

Before using R to calculate the observed value of the Friedman's Test statistic, the data must be checked to verify that there are no tied scores for any of the individual participants, as I demonstrate later in the chapter. When there are ties for individuals the observed value of the statistic should not be calculated using the **friedman.test** command in *R*.

The first assumption is met by the fact that the independent variable is represented by the participants' pre-feedback, midterm-feedback, and post-feedback states; these three states represent three categories. The second is met by verifying that there's exactly the same people in the pre-, midterm, and post-comparison groups; review of Table 9.3 confirms that there are three scores from each person. The third is met by verifying that the questionnaire used to collect the information on the dependent variable yields rankable data, and taking a look at the scores in Table 9.3, the scores are rankable. Finally, I'll check the data as I rank them to verify that there are no ties within any individual's scores.

Step 6: Calculate the Observed Value of the Appropriate Statistic

Friedman's Test is another non-parametric statistic; the model for determining statistical significance is based on rankings rather than the normal distribution model. The first step in calculating Friedman's Test is to rank the three outcome scores for each individual. The lowest outcome for each individual is ranked 1, and because the independent variable has three levels, the highest outcome for each individual is ranked 3. The middle outcome is given the rank of 2. The sum of the ranks for each level is calculated and these sums are then squared. The data, their rankings, and the sums of the ranks and the squared ranks are displayed in Table 9.4. (As I noted above, when the calculations are done using *R*, the data must first be

TABLE 9.4 Individuals' Rankings for Pretest, Midterm, and Posttest (fabricated data)

	Pretest Total	Pretest Rank	Midtest Total	Midtest Rank	Posttest Total	Posttest Rank
1	38	1	40	2	44	3
2	42	1	51	2	52	3
3	32	1	42	2	46	3
4	40	1	42	2	50	3
5	35	1	48	3	45	2
6	46	1	53	3	52	2
7	38	1	45	2	47	3
8	38	1	42	2	43	3
9	47	1	48	2	49	3
10	41	1	51	3	50	2
		$\sum R_{Pre} = 10$		$\sum R_{Mid} = 23$		$\sum R_{Post} = 27$
		$\sum R_{Pre}^2 = 100$		$\sum R_{Mid}^2 = 529$		$\sum R_{Post}^2 = 729$

checked to verify that there are no tied scores for any of the individuals—if there are tied scores, Friedman's Test statistic should be calculated with a calculator. I discuss this problem and how to carry out the calculations with a hand calculator in the final section in this chapter using data displayed in Table 9.5.)

With the values from Table 9.4 I can calculate the observed value of the Friedman's Test statistic using this formula (12 and 3 are constant values; n = number of participants; k = the number of levels of the independent variable):

$$\frac{12}{nk(k+1)}(\sum R^2) - [(3n)(k+1)]$$

$$\frac{12}{(10)(3)(3+1)}(100 + 529 + 729) - [(3)(10)(3+1)]$$

$$= \frac{12}{(30)(4)}(1358) - [(30)(4)]$$

$$= (.1)(1358) - [120]$$

$$= 135.8 - 120 = \mathbf{15.8}$$

I am going to use R to carry out the calculations too, but I have to massage the dataset I create so R can read it—the data must be presented as a matrix. In Box 9.5, I explain how to convert the dataset to the necessary format and how to calculate the observed value of the Friedman's Test statistic.

Box 9.5 Preparing Data for and Calculating the Observed Value of the Friedman's Test Statistic

You'll need to create and import a dataset. Make an Excel spreadsheet with three columns of information—the pretest score, midterm score, and posttest score for each individual. Give each column of information a simple title, such as *pre.data, mid.data.,* and *post.data.* All of the data in each column must be numerical, and there can be no missing values. Save the spreadsheet in the csv (MS-DOS) format and then import it into R using the **read.csv** command.	> **friedman.data = read.csv (file. choose(), header = T)**
Calculate the mean and the standard deviation for the pretest data—the researcher would probably want to report these descriptive statistics for each of the three tests.	> **mean (friedman.data$pre.data)** Output: [1] 39.7 > **sd (friedman.data$pre.data)** Output: [1] 4.595892

(Continued)

Box 9.5 (*Continued*)

Calculate the mean and the standard deviation for the midtest data.	> **mean (friedman.data$mid. data)** Output: [1] 46.2 > **sd (friedman.data$mid.data)** Output: [1] 4.613988
Calculate the mean and the standard deviation for the posttest data.	> **mean (friedman.data$post.data)** Output: [1] 47.8 > **sd (friedman.data$post.data)** Output: [1] 3.259175
Convert the dataset into a data matrix (which is what the Friedman's Test command requires). Give the matrix you're creating a name (I use the name *Friedman.matrix*), then type the equal sign and give the name of the dataset you want to convert to a matrix.	> **Friedman.matrix = as.matrix (friedman.data)**
View the matrix.	> **View (Friedman.matrix)**
Calculate the observed value of the Friedman's Test statistic and its exact level of probability.	> **friedman.test (as. matrix(Friedman.matrix))** Output: data:as.matrix(Friedman.matrix) Friedman chi-squared = 15.8, df = 2, p-value = 0.0003707

Step 7: Determine the Degrees of Freedom for the Statistic and Use Degrees of Freedom and Alpha to Find the Critical Value of the Statistic, OR Calculate the Exact Probability of the Observed Statistic

Either the critical value approach or the exact probability approach can be used in Step 7, but the critical value approach requires a chart of critical values for χ^2.[10] The exact probability approach can be used when the calculation of the observed statistic is done using R because the exact probability is reported.

Using the Critical Value Approach

The formula for the degrees of freedom for the Friedman's Test statistic is $k - 1$; the number of levels of the independent variable minus 1. So for this study, there are 2 degrees of freedom $(3 - 1 = 2)$. Using the chart of critical values for χ^2, I find that the critical value for alpha $= .01$ and $df = 2$ is 9.210.

Using the Exact Probability Approach

Using the exact probability approach, the observed value of the Friedman's Test statistic and the exact probability of that observed value are retrieved from the output. The observed value of Friedman's Test χ^2 is 15.8 $(df = 2)$ and the exact probability is the p-value (.0003707).

Step 8: To Interpret the Outcome of the Analysis, Compare the Observed Value and the Critical Value OR Compare the Exact Probability to Alpha

In Step 8, the outcome of the analysis is determined using either the critical value approach or the exact probability approach.

Using the Critical Value Approach

When interpreting the Friedman's Test statistic using this approach, the observed value of Friedman's Test (15.8) is compared to the critical value of $\chi^2_{critical}$ for 2 degrees of freedom and alpha $= .01$; $\chi^2_{critical} = 9.210$.

If Friedman's Test $\chi^2_{observed} \leq \chi^2_{critical} \rightarrow$ accept the null hypothesis.

If Friedman's Test $\chi^2_{observed} > \chi^2_{critical} \rightarrow$ reject the null hypothesis.

In this case, $\chi^2_{observed}$ (15.8) is greater than $\chi^2_{critical}$ (9.210), so the null hypothesis is rejected and the alternative hypothesis is accepted.

Using the Exact Probability Approach

Here are the rules for interpreting exact probability:

If exact probability $\geq$ alpha $\rightarrow$ accept the null hypothesis.
If exact probability $<$ alpha $\rightarrow$ reject the null hypothesis.

Alpha was set at .01 and the exact probability, $p = .0003707$, is less than alpha, so the null hypothesis is rejected and the alternative hypothesis is accepted.

> **Alternative hypothesis: There is a significant difference in the rankings of the pre-feedback, midterm-feedback, and post-feedback motivation for participants who received feedback designed to promote autonomy and motivation.**

Notice that the alternative hypothesis allows us to say that there's a difference, but it doesn't indicate where the difference or differences are. A *post hoc* analysis must be carried out to identify which pairs of scores show a significant difference. In Box 9.6, I illustrate how to do multiple Wilcoxon Signed Rank analyses to compare each of the possible pairs of data: (1) pretest to posttest, (2) midtest to posttest, and (3) pretest to midtest. The phrase **exact = FALSE** is added to each analysis to account for any tied scores within and among the <u>two</u> sets of scores being compared.

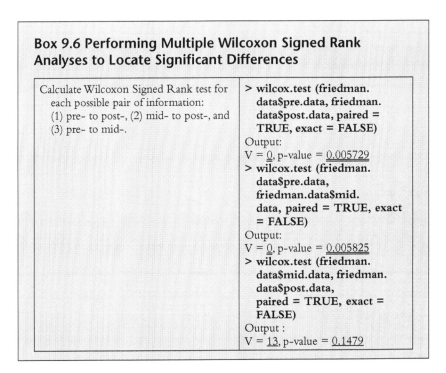

Box 9.6 Performing Multiple Wilcoxon Signed Rank Analyses to Locate Significant Differences

Calculate Wilcoxon Signed Rank test for each possible pair of information: (1) pre- to post-, (2) mid- to post-, and (3) pre- to mid-.	> wilcox.test (friedman. data$pre.data, friedman. data$post.data, paired = TRUE, exact = FALSE) Output: V = <u>0</u>, p-value = <u>0.005729</u> > wilcox.test (friedman. data$pre.data, friedman.data$mid. data, paired = TRUE, exact = FALSE) Output: V = <u>0</u>, p-value = <u>0.005825</u> > wilcox.test (friedman. data$mid.data, friedman. data$post.data, paired = TRUE, exact = FALSE) Output : V = <u>13</u>, p-value = <u>0.1479</u>

Alpha was set in Step 2 at .01, so this is the level of significance used to interpret the outcomes of the Wilcoxon Signed Rank values (the relevant information in the R output is underscored in Box 9.6). Two of the observed values of the Wilcoxon Signed Rank statistic show a statistically significant difference between the pairs of data, the values that have double underscoring. The comparison of the pretest and posttest scores shows a statistically significant difference ($V = 0, p = .005729$) as does the comparison of the pretest and midtest scores ($V = 0, p = .005825$); however, the comparison of the midtest and posttest scores (single underscoring) doesn't show a significant difference ($V = 13, p = .1479$).

Step 9: Interpret the Findings as a Probability Statement

The probability statement for Friedman's Test statistic should look something like this:

> **There's 99% certainty of a significant difference in the rankings of the pre-, mid-, and post-level motivation scores for these participants who received feedback designed to promote autonomy and motivation.**

Step 10: Interpret the Meaningfulness of the Findings

Meaningfulness is interpreted with reference to the research question: "Is there a statistically significant difference in the pre-, mid-, and post-level of motivation for students who received feedback designed to promote autonomy and motivation?" The outcomes of the pairwise comparisons are also reported. When possible, effect size for the pairwise comparisons is reported, though effect size can't be calculated for this study because the number of participants is too small to justify converting the observed values of the Wilcoxon Signed Rank statistic to z-scores, a necessary condition for calculating effect size.[11]

The findings might be reported something like this:

> **For these students there's 99% certainty that receiving a type of feedback designed to promote autonomy and motivation had a significant impact on their level of motivation (Friedman's $\chi^2 = 15.8$, $df = 2$, $p = .0003707$). This impact was apparent in the significant differences between the pretest and posttest scores (pretest mean = 39.7, pretest $s = 4.60$; posttest mean = 47.8, posttest $s = 3.26$, Wilcoxon Signed Rank = 0, $p = .005729$) and the pretest and midtest scores (midtest mean = 46.2, midtest $s = 4.62$, Wilcoxon Signed Rank = 0, $p = .005825$), though comparison of the midtest with the posttest did not show a significant difference (Wilcoxon Signed Rank = 13, $p = .1479$).**

A Postscript: Calculating the Friedman's Test Statistic With Tied Scores

When calculating the Friedman's Test statistic, a critical step is ranking the scores for each individual. When there are tied rankings within the scores for an

TABLE 9.5 Individual's Rankings for Pretest, Midtest, and Posttest With Some Tied Scores (fabricated data)

	Pretest total	Pretest rank	Midtest total	Midterm rank	Posttesttotal	Posttest rank
1	38	1	40	2	44	3
2	42	1	51	2	52	3
3	32	1	46	2.5	46	2.5
4	40	1	42	2	50	3
5	35	1	48	2.5	48	2.5
6	46	1	53	3	52	2
7	38	1	45	2	47	3
8	38	1	42	2	43	3
9	47	1.5	47	1.5	49	3
10	41	1	51	2.5	51	2.5
		$\sum R_{Pre} = 10.5$		$\sum R_{Mid} = 22$		$\sum R_{Post} = 27.5$
		$\sum R_{Pre}^2 = 110.25$		$\sum R_{Mid}^2 = 484$		$\sum R_{Post}^2 = 756.25$

individual, the non-parametric convention is to assign a mean rank to tied scores. If the scores presented in Table 9.5 had been collected instead of those presented in Table 9.4, the researcher would have to deal with some tied scores for individuals. For example, for the third person in Table 9.5, the pretest value is assigned the rank of 1 because it's the lowest of the three scores for that individual. The midterm score and the posttest scores are each assigned a ranking of 2.5 because the individual received the same score on these two tests, which represent the second and third ranks. (The rank places are added, 2 + 3, and divided by the number of tied scores, 2. The result is assigned to each of the tied scores.) Similarly, the ninth person had tied scores on the pretest and midtest, a tie for first and second place, so a ranking of 1.5 was assigned to each (1 + 2/2 = 1.5).

When a researcher uses the Friedman's Test statistic, a table similar to Table 9.4 and Table 9.5 should be created and the researcher should verify whether there are any tied values for individuals before using R to perform the calculation. If there are ties for individuals, the calculation of the statistic should be done with a calculator, using the formula I presented above, rather than with R. Although R *will* calculate a value for the Friedman's Test statistic when there are ties for indivduals, the outcome is not accurate according to the mathematical rules expressed in the formula for the Friedman's Test statistic.[12]

With the rankings from Table 9.5, I calculate the observed value of the Friedman's Test using the same formula as above:

$$\frac{12}{(10)(3)(3+1)}(110.25+484+756.25)-[(3)(10)(3+1)]$$

$$=\frac{12}{(30)(4)}(1350.50)-[(30)(4)]$$

$$=\frac{12}{120}(1350.50)-[120]$$

$$=(.1)(1350.50)-[120]$$

$$=135.05-120=\mathbf{15.05}$$

To interpret the outcome of the analysis, I use the critical value approach. There are 2 degrees of freedom, so when alpha is set at .01, $\chi^2_{critical}$ is 9.210. When the observed value of the statistic (Friedman's χ^2 = 15.05) is greater than the critical value ($\chi^2_{critical}$ = 9.210), the null hypothesis is rejected and the alternative hypothesis is accepted:

> **There's 99% certainty of a statistically significant difference in the rankings of the pre-, mid-, and post-level motivation scores for these participants who received feedback designed to promote autonomy and motivation.**

Because the alternative hypothesis was accepted, post hoc analyses like those carried out in Box 9.6 must be done to identify which pairs of scores show a significant difference. Box 9.7 shows how to perform these analyses.

Box 9.7 Performing Multiple Wilcoxon Signed Rank Analyses to Locate Significant Differences

Enter the data for the pretest, the midtest, and the posttest.	> **pre = c(38, 42, 32, 40, 35, 46, 38, 38, 47, 41)** > **mid = c(40, 51, 46, 42, 48, 53, 45, 42, 47, 51)** > **post = c(44, 52, 46, 50, 48, 52, 47, 43, 49, 51)**

(Continued)

Box 9.7 (*Continued*)

Calculate Wilcoxon Signed Rank test for each possible pair of information: (1) pre- to post-, (2) mid- to post-, and (3) pre- to mid-. (The phrase **exact = FALSE** is added to each analysis to account for tied scores within and among the <u>two</u> sets of scores being compared.)	> **wilcox.test (pre, post, paired = TRUE, exact = FALSE)** Output: V = <u>0</u>, p-value = <u>0.005761</u> > **wilcox.test (pre, mid, paired = TRUE, exact = FALSE)** Output: V = <u>0</u>, p-value = <u>0.00903</u> > **wilcox.test (mid, post, paired = TRUE, exact = FALSE)** Output: V = <u>2</u>, p-value = <u>0.04983</u>

The findings could be reported something like this:

> **For these students there is 99% certainty that receiving a type of feedback designed to promote autonomy and motivation had a significant impact on their level of motivation (Friedman's χ^2 = 15.05, $\chi^2_{critical(df = 2, \alpha = .01)}$ = 9.210). This impact was apparent in the significant differences between the pretest and posttest scores (pretest mean = 39.7, pretest s = 4.60; posttest mean = 48.2, posttest s = 3.19, Wilcoxon Signed Rank = 0, p = .005761) and the pretest and midtest scores (midtest mean = 46.5, midtest s = 4.35, Wilcoxon Signed Rank = 0, p = .00903), though comparison of the midtest with the posttest did not show a significant difference (Wilcoxon Signed Rank = 2, p = .04983).**

R Commands Introduced in Chapter Nine

plot (values ~ ind, data = d, xlab = "Group", ylab = "Outcomes", col = "light blue") This command creates whisker plots using a dataset called *d* created using the **stack (list. . . .** command. This command includes labels for the *x*-axis and the *y*-axis. The whisker plots themselves are light blue.

kruskal.test (values ~ ind, data = d) This command for the Kruskal–Wallis statistic is used when the dataset, named *d*, was created using the **stack (list. . . .** command.

kruskal.test (dependent.variable.name ~ independent.variable.name, data = d) This command for the Kruskal–Wallis statistic is used when a dataset named *d* was imported.

sapply (split (d$dependent.variable.name, d$independent.variable.name), hist) When this command is preceded by the **par (mfrow = c(2,2)** command, up to four histograms are displayed in a two-by-two grid. The format of the command is appropriate when a dataset is imported with two columns of information (one column with values of the dependent variable and one indicating each individual's level of the independent variable).

sapply (split (d$dependent.variable.name, d$independent.variable.name), mean) This command gives the mean for each level of the independent variable when a dataset is imported with two columns of information (one column with values of the dependent variable and one indicating each individual's level of the independent variable).

sapply (split (d$dependent.variable.name, d$independent.variable.name), sd) This command gives the standard deviation for each level of the independent variable when a dataset is imported with two columns of information (one column with values of the dependent variable and one indicating each individual's level of the independent variable).

group1.dataset = subset (d,d$independent.variable.name == "1") This command separates out the data for one level of the independent variable from a dataset that was imported and has all levels of the independent variable. This creates a new dataset named *group1.dataset*. The command can be used as a template to create a separate dataset for each level of the independent variable.

dataset.matrix = as.matrix (dataset.name) This command must be used to convert a dataset to a matrix in preparation for calculating the observed value of the Friedman's Test statistic. It is the first in a set of two commands.

friedman.test (as.matrix(dataset.matrix)) This is the command for calculating the Friedman's Test statistic. This is the second in a set of two commands.

Practice Problem

The Practice Problem is based on data collected by Rebecca Noreen. The data are presented in Table 9.6; you'll also find the data in the resource section of the companion website (www.routledge.com/cw/turner).

Rebecca was interested in exploring whether native speakers of English (NSEs) who have relatively few interactions with non-NSEs perceive those whose English is strongly affected by their first language differently than people who have more interaction with non-NSEs. She thought the findings of a study in this area would help raise the awareness of her non-NSE students of the role of standard English expression in NSEs' perceptions of non-NSEs, but more importantly, she hoped to raise the awareness of NSEs that it is important to have an open mind toward all members of society. The independent variable (*interact*) in her study is represented by NSEs with three different levels of interaction with non-NSEs: few interactions with non-NSEs (1), moderate amount of interaction with non-NSEs (2), and extensive amount of interaction with non-NSEs (3). All were asked to listen to a recording of a learner of English whose language contains many grammatical errors. They then completed a series of Likert-scale items that yielded scores for five different dependent variables: the speaker's degree of attractiveness, the speaker's level of education (*educate*), the speaker's level of friendliness (*friendly*), the speaker's level of intelligence (*intell*), and the speaker's perceived degree of politeness (*polite*).

For practice, choose one of the dependent variables and follow the steps in statistical logic to determine whether there's a statistically significant difference in the perception of the participants depending on the amount of interaction they've had with non-NSEs. Remember that the independent variable is *interact*, the sixth column of information.

TABLE 9.6 Rebecca Noreen's Dataset

educate	intell	attract	friendly	polite	interact
1	1	2	1	1	1
2	2	3	3	2	1
3	3	3	1	1	1
1	1	2	1	1	1
3	4	2	1	2	1
2	3	1	2	1	1
1	1	2	3	2	1
2	2	3	2	2	1
2	3	3	3	3	1
2	1	4	2	1	1
1	3	3	3	1	1
2	2	3	3	4	1
2	2	2	1	1	1
3	3	2	1	1	1
2	2	3	2	1	1
1	2	2	2	1	1
1	1	3	4	1	1
1	1	2	1	1	1
3	1	1	2	1	1
2	5	3	3	2	1
1	5	3	2	2	1

(Continued)

TABLE 9.6 (*Continued*)

educate	intell	attract	friendly	polite	interact
1	1	1	2	2	1
1	2	2	2	5	1
1	1	2	2	5	1
3	2	4	3	1	1
1	1	1	1	1	1
1	1	3	1	1	1
2	2	3	2	1	1
1	4	2	1	1	1
1	1	2	2	2	1
1	1	2	3	4	1
1	1	2	1	1	2
2	2	3	2	2	2
2	3	3	3	1	2
2	3	1	4	4	2
3	3	3	3	1	2
4	2	4	4	4	2
1	2	4	1	2	2
3	2	5	3	2	2
3	2	3	1	1	2
3	3	3	2	2	2
2	1	2	3	2	2
2	3	2	2	1	2
2	2	4	2	2	2
1	1	3	2	2	2
3	3	3	2	1	2
2	3	3	4	3	2
3	3	4	2	1	2
1	1	2	2	1	2
2	2	3	2	1	2
1	1	3	3	2	2
3	4	3	1	1	2
1	1	3	2	2	2

(*Continued*)

TABLE 9.6 (*Continued*)

educate	intell	attract	friendly	polite	interact
1	1	1	1	1	2
2	2	4	4	4	2
1	1	3	1	1	2
2	1	1	2	3	2
1	2	2	4	3	2
2	3	2	1	1	2
2	2	3	1	1	2
1	1	3	1	1	2
3	1	3	1	1	2
1	1	2	1	1	3
3	2	3	2	2	3
3	3	3	2	1	3
4	4	1	3	2	3
2	2	3	2	2	3
3	3	2	2	2	3
3	3	3	3	3	3
5	4	3	3	3	3
4	4	3	1	1	3
4	3	5	2	2	3
4	4	3	1	1	3
5	4	4	3	2	3
3	1	3	2	3	3
3	3	3	2	3	3
2	2	4	2	3	3
2	2	1	1	2	3
4	2	3	2	3	3
3	2	2	2	2	3
3	2	3	3	3	3
3	3	3	2	1	3
2	1	3	3	2	3
1	2	2	1	2	3

(*Continued*)

TABLE 9.6 (*Continued*)

educate	intell	attract	friendly	polite	interact
2	2	4	1	1	3
2	2	2	1	1	3
4	5	1	1	1	3
2	2	2	2	1	3
4	5	2	1	1	3
3	3	4	3	2	3
1	1	3	1	1	3
4	3	3	2	2	3
5	3	3	1	1	3

Notes

1 The concept of *variance* is addressed briefly in Chapter Two; it's the squared value of the standard deviation and reflects the *sum of squared errors*. The assumption of equal variances is a way of ensuring that the groups are comparable and drawn from the same population.

2 Chi-squared statistics are discussed in Chapter Twelve.

3 The notations above and below the symbols Σ, R, and n in this formula indicate that the summing operation should be done for each separate group.

4 Note that 12 and 3 are constant values—they remain the same regardless of the number of participants or the number of levels of the independent variable.

5 Whisker charts (also referred to as box-whisker plots) can be made instead of histograms, and in some cases may give a better sense of whether there are any extreme scores. The center line in a whisker plot represents the median. The box includes the middle 50% of the scores; 25% of the scores fall between the bottom of the box and the horizontal line at the bottom (or the lowest dots representing score, if there are any that are extremely lower than the others). The remaining 25% of the scores are between the top of the box and the horizontal line at the top. When there are dots representing scores beyond the whiskers, those scores might be examined to make certain that they're entered correctly—or they might represent participants who are *outliers*, people who are very different from the other participants, perhaps so different that they should be removed from the analysis (see Chapter Two).

6 A dataset can be created in Excel, with one column for the independent variable (an individual's group designated by 1, 2, or 3) and the dependent variable score for each participant included in another column. Save the document in the comma separated values format as an MS-DOS document (PC) or in a comparable Mac format.

7 A chart of critical values for χ^2 can be found on the companion website (www.routledge.com/cw/turner).

8 See Chapter Seven for details on when the Wilcoxon Rank Sum statistic can be converted to a z-score.

9 Yep, see Chapter Seven for details.
10 A chart of critical values for χ^2 can be found on the companion website (www. routledge.com/cw/turner).
11 See Chapter Seven for details on calculating effect size for the Wilcoxon Signed Rank statistic.
12 For the data displayed in Table 9.5, with ties, the R output is Friedman's $\chi^2 = 16.7222$, $df = 2$, $p = 0.0002338$, which is not accurate according to the formula for calculating Friedman's Test. R doesn't print a warning, so the researcher must check the data for ties before using R to calculate this statistic.

Analyzing Patterns Within a Variable and Between Two Variables

10

THE PARAMETRIC PEARSON'S PRODUCT MOMENT CORRELATION COEFFICIENT STATISTIC

In Chapter Ten, we take a look at one of the statistics designed for investigating the correlational relationship between variables, Pearson's product moment correlation coefficient, also known as Pearson's r. Pearson's r is a parametric statistic used to calculate the strength of the correlational relationship between two normally distributed variables, an independent variable and a dependent variable. When it's used in the context of statistical logic, Pearson's r allows a researcher to make a probability statement about the degree of correspondence between two sets of data. Unlike the statistics addressed in Chapters Six through Nine, which allow a researcher to explore differences among groups, correlation formulas are used to determine the extent to which two sets of data vary together. A correlation is a numerical expression of the strength of the relationship between the two variables.

Researchers in language education often want to know whether there's a significant relationship between variables; they can gain a deeper understanding of the learners in their classes and their learning environment by knowing how the variables are related to one another. There's a practical application too, of knowing the strength of the relationship between two variables—when two variables are strongly related, we can estimate or predict a person's behavior on the second variable, given his or her performance on the first. It's important, though, to remember that even a strong relationship between two variables can't be interpreted as evidence of causality. To illustrate, I'd like to tell you about a little study I did quite a while ago, just out of curiosity. I was teaching oral skills courses for international undergraduate students at a university and it seemed to me that the type of shoe a student usually wore was related to the level of his or her oral skills. I collected some data and found there was a statistically significant relationship between the two variables, a strong one—the participants who wore a particular kind of sport shoe definitely tended to have a higher degree of oral language proficiency than did people who wore other types of shoes. So, yes, on the basis of that small study, I can say that there was a statistically significant relationship between the type of shoe an international undergraduate student wears and the level of his or her oral skills, but there's no causality there—buying a different type of shoe isn't going to help anyone become more fluent in English!

There's a large family of statistical formulas for calculating correlation values. In addition to Pearson's *r*, other frequently used correlation statistics include Spearman's rho, Kendall's tau, and in the area of testing, point biserial, Cronbach's alpha, KR-20, and KR-21. The specific statistic used to calculate a correlation is determined by the type of data. In this chapter, I address the characteristics of correlations in general through discussion of Pearson's *r* before illustrating how Pearson's *r* is used within the 10 steps in statistical logic.

Features of Correlation Coefficients

Correlation values have a possible range from −1 to +1. A correlation of +1 indicates a perfect pattern of correspondence between the two variables—a perfect correlation. A correlation of −1 indicates a perfect correlation too, though the pattern of correspondence is reversed. A correlation of zero indicates that there's no pattern of correspondence between the two variables. When two variables are plotted together on a two-dimensional graph called a *scatterplot*, or *scattergram*, with one variable represented on the *x*-axis and the other on the *y*-axis, the scatterplot reflects the strength of the correlation between the variables. When the correlation is perfect, the points of intersection for the two variables can be connected to form a straight line.

Here's a set of scores from five people illustrating a perfect correlation:

Participant	Variable A (*x*)	Variable B (*y*)
1	5	5
2	4	4
3	3	3
4	2	2
5	1	1

As shown in Figure 10.1, these scores show a perfect positive correlation ($r = +1.00$): a straight line that climbs uphill.[1]

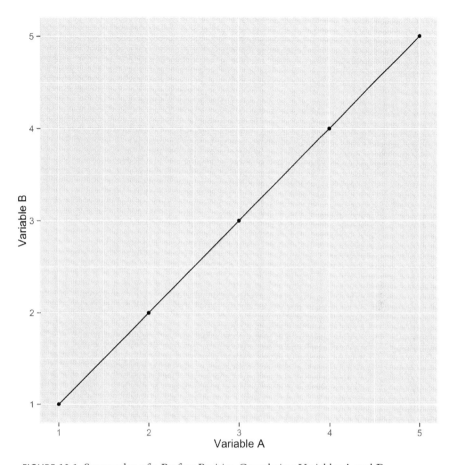

FIGURE 10.1 Scatterplot of a Perfect Positive Correlation, Variables A and B

The scores for the two variables don't have to be exactly the same to form a straight line—the scores for Variables C and D form a straight line too—because there's a perfect correspondence between the two sets of data ($r = +1.00$).

Participant	Variable C (x)	Variable D (y)
1	18	15
2	16	13
3	14	11
4	12	9
5	10	7

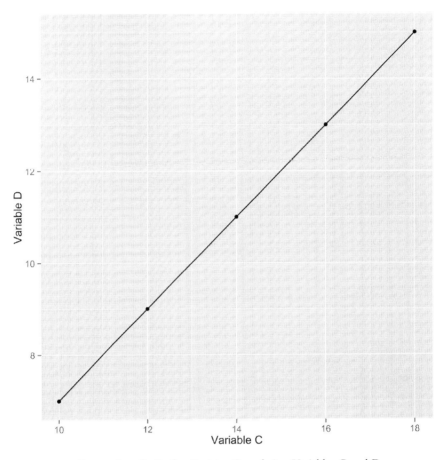

FIGURE 10.2 Scatterplot of a Perfect Positive Correlation, Variables C and D

The third set of data shows a perfect negative correlation ($r = -1.00$).

Participant	Variable E (x)	Variable F (y)
1	1	5
2	2	4
3	3	3
4	4	2
5	5	1

When these values for x and y are plotted on a scatterplot, the line is straight but goes downhill, as shown in Figure 10.3.

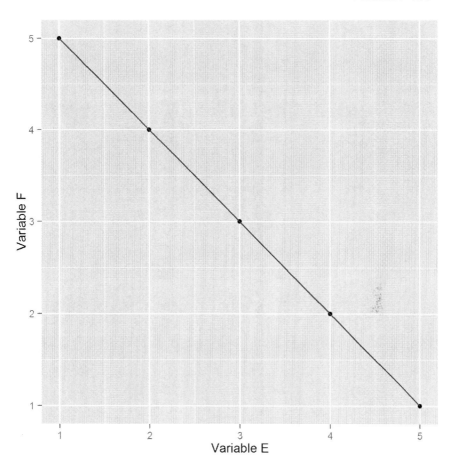

FIGURE 10.3 Scatterplot of a Perfect Negative Correlation, Variables E and F

As shown in Figure 10.4, a scatterplot of two variables that aren't related to one another looks like a collection of rather isolated dots or a blob; a straight line that's superimposed on the scatterplot doesn't connect very many, if any, of the data points ($r \approx +.28$).

Participant	Variable G (x)	Variable H (y)
1	2	1
2	4	2
3	2	3
4	3	3
5	4	3

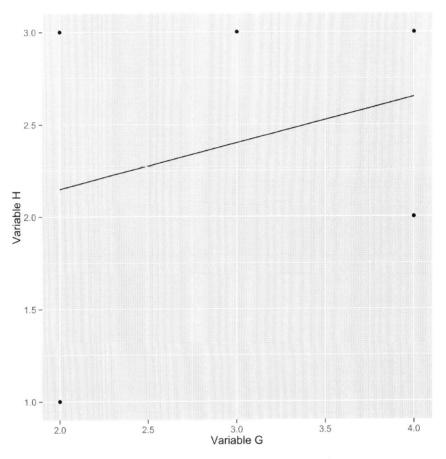

FIGURE 10.4 Scatterplot of a Lack of Correlation, Variables G and H

The moderately strong positive correlation ($r = +0.85$) based on the data below is shown in Figure 10.5. The superimposed straight line doesn't connect all of the data points, but all of the points are somewhat near the line.

Participant	Value for I (x)	Value for J (y)
1	5	5
2	4	4
3	3	5
4	2	3
5	1	2

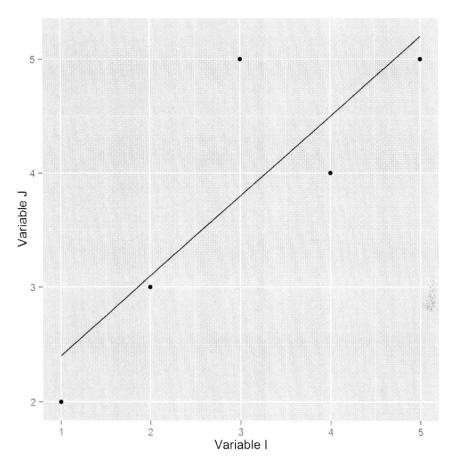

FIGURE 10.5 Scatterplot of a Moderately Strong Positive Correlation, Variables I and J

Assumptions for Pearson's *r*

The Pearson's *r* statistic can be used simply to determine the strength of the relationship between two interval-scale variables; however, it can also be used as an inferential statistic in the framework of statistical logic to investigate whether the correlation between two interval-scale variables is strong enough to be considered statistically significant. Pearson's *r* is a parametric statistic, so the conditions for the use of parametric statistics that you encountered previously must be met. In addition to the assumption that the data are collected from participants randomly drawn from a normally distributed population, the specific assumptions for Pearson's *r* are:

1. The independent and dependent variables are measured on an interval scale.
2. Each of the two variables is normally distributed in the population and the sample of participants.

3. Each observation is independent from all the others.
4. The relationship between the two variables is linear.

The first assumption for Pearson's *r* requires that the data for both the independent and the dependent variable be measured on an interval scale, while the second requires that the data for both the independent and the dependent variable be checked to verify that they're normally distributed.

The third assumption, that each observation is independent from all the others, means that there can be no overlap in the collection of the independent and dependent variables. There are two aspects to this condition. First, there can be no items or tasks that appear on both of the data collection instruments. For example, let's say that we want to find the relationship between test takers' performance on the listening subsection and the reading subsection of a test. The score report for each person provides a listening subscore and a reading subscore; there's also a total score. The listening and reading sections are entirely distinct from one another—there are no questions or tasks that provide information for both listening and reading. Because the listening subtest and reading subtest have no shared items or tasks, they are independent; the second assumption for Pearson's *r* is met. However, Pearson's *r* shouldn't be used to find the correlation between the listening subscore and the total score because the listening section is part of the total test—the listening items contribute to the total score, so the two sets of scores aren't entirely independent.

The second aspect related to the independence of the observation is that each participant in the study must perform independently from the others on the data collection tools; there can be no collaboration among the participants (or cheating!) during administration of the tests.

The fourth assumption reflects the point made earlier in the chapter about plotting the independent and dependent variables against one another in a scatterplot. Pearson's *r* requires that the relationship between the two variables be linear, not curvilinear or wavelike, but some approximation of a straight line. Once a researcher has collected the data and before calculating the strength of the correlation between the variables, a scatterplot should be made to verify that the relationship between the variables approximates a straight line.

The Formal Research Hypotheses for Pearson's *r*

The phrasing of the formal research hypotheses, the null and alternative hypotheses, is different for correlations than for the statistics addressed in Chapters Six through Nine.

The null hypothesis looks like this:

There is no statistically significant correlation between the independent and dependent variables. (The null hypothesis is represented by these symbols: $H_0 : r = 0$.)

The two-tailed alternative hypothesis looks like this:

There is a statistically significant correlation between the independent and dependent variables. (In symbols, the two-tailed alternative hypothesis is $H_1 : r \neq 0$.)

The one-tailed alternative hypotheses look like this:

Positive one-tailed alternative hypothesis: There is a statistically significant positive correlation between the two variables. ($H_1 : r > 0$)

Negative one-tailed alternative hypothesis: There is a statistically significant negative correlation between the two variables. ($H_2 : r < 0$)

Researchers typically propose the null hypothesis and only one one-tailed, directional, alternative hypothesis. Generally, there's a sufficient amount of previous research to indicate the direction of the relationship between two variables, so there's no need to propose both of the one-tailed, directional, alternative hypotheses. For example, it's generally accepted as a fact that the correlation between foreign language aptitude and foreign language learning is positive rather than negative; that is, individuals with high language aptitude scores tend to have stronger language learning outcomes than do individuals with low language aptitude scores. Given that the direction of the relationship is known, a researcher conducting a study on the relationship between performance on an aptitude test and language learning success would probably pose the null hypothesis and the one-tailed, positive, alternative hypothesis. A person doing research on the correlation between proficiency in the sport of golf and actual performance on a golf course would be likely to propose the null hypothesis and just one one-tailed hypothesis too, but this researcher would propose the one-tailed negative version of the alternative hypothesis—it's generally known that individuals with high golf proficiency tend to have lower golf scores than players with a low level of golf proficiency.

Using Pearson's *r* in the 10 Steps in Statistical Logic

A researcher who wants to make a probability statement about the relationship between two variables should follow the steps in statistical logic.

1. State the formal research hypotheses, the null hypothesis and the alternative hypothesis/hypotheses.
2. Set alpha, the level of probability for the analysis.
3. Select the appropriate statistic for analysis of the data.

4. Collect the data.
5. Verify that the assumptions for the statistic are met.
6. Calculate the observed value of the appropriate statistic.
7. Determine the degrees of freedom for the statistic and use degrees of freedom and alpha to find the critical value of the statistic OR calculate the exact probability for the observed statistic calculated in Step 6.
8. To interpret the outcome of the analysis, compare the observed value and the critical value OR compare the exact probability to alpha. Apply one of the appropriate sets of rules to the comparison.

   Critical value approach:

   If $r_{observed} \leq r_{critical} \rightarrow$ accept the null hypothesis.
   If $r_{observed} > r_{critical} \rightarrow$ reject the null hypothesis.

   Exact probability approach:

   If exact probability $\geq$ alpha $\rightarrow$ accept the null hypothesis.
   If exact probability $<$ alpha $\rightarrow$ reject the null hypothesis.

9. Interpret the findings as a probability statement using the hypothesis accepted in Step 8.
10. Interpret the meaningfulness of the findings and calculate the effect size if possible.

Example Study

The director of an organization that supports foreign language summer camps for native English-speaking children wanted to conduct a study on the potential usefulness of a foreign language aptitude test for identifying children who would be most likely to be successful in the intensive summer camp program. To do so, he needed to know how strong the relationship is between performance on the aptitude test and success in foreign language learning in the summer camp environment. From all of the children with no exposure to Spanish who registered at one camp to study beginning Spanish he randomly selected 15. During the first day of orientation for the summer camp, the 15 children took the aptitude test. At the end of the camp, all of the students took the final test, a test of their Spanish ability. He collected the final test scores of these 15 children so he could determine whether the relationship between the children's performance on the aptitude test and their level of communicative language ability was strong enough to be considered statistically significant.

Step 1: State the Formal Research Hypotheses

The first step in statistical logic is stating the hypotheses. I state the null hypothesis first and then, because I have sufficient evidence to indicate that there's a positive relationship between language aptitude and subsequent language learning, I propose a single, positive, one-tailed alternative hypothesis. These hypotheses ultimately allow me to make a probability statement about the absence (if I accept the null hypothesis) or the presence (if I reject the null hypothesis and accept the alternative hypothesis) of a statistically significant relationship between the two variables.

> **Null hypothesis: There's no statistically significant correlation between language aptitude and language learning, as measured by the final test.**

> **Alternative hypothesis: There is a statistically significant, positive correlation between language aptitude and language learning, as measured by the final test.**

Step 2: Set Alpha

I set alpha at .05 because this is exploratory research.

Step 3: Select the Appropriate Statistic for Analysis of the Data

The researcher is interested in making a general conclusion about the strength of the relationship between performance on the aptitude test and foreign language learning, so a correlation statistic should be used. He randomly selected the participants in this study from a small population of learners, and the tests he chose to use are designed to yield normally distributed data. The aptitude test and the final test are entirely distinct, and the administrations of the tests were carefully monitored to ensure that all the participants worked independently. Finally, the data will be checked once they're collected to confirm that both sets of scores are normally distributed. A scatterplot will also be made to check that the relationship between the two variables is linear. It appears that the use of the parametric Pearson's r may be justified.

Step 4: Collect the Data

The fabricated values for the independent variable, *language aptitude*, and the dependent variable, *language learning success*, are displayed in Table 10.1.

TABLE 10.1 Independent and Dependent Variable Values for the Example Study (fabricated data)

Student	Language aptitude	Language learning outcome
1	29	39
2	33	39
3	25	36
4	30	38
5	33	46
6	26	38
7	28	43
8	40	54
9	29	51
10	35	51
11	32	43
12	32	51
13	35	46
14	32	41
15	30	43

Step 5: Verify That the Assumptions for the Statistic Are Met

In Step 5, the four assumptions for appropriate use of Pearson's r are checked.

1. The independent and dependent variables are measured on an interval scale.
2. The data for each of the two variables are normally distributed in the population from which the participants were randomly drawn and in the two groups.
3. Each pair of observations is independent.
4. The relationship between the two variables is linear.

The aptitude test and the final test are norm-referenced, designed to yield a normal distribution when administered to a population, but the participants' scores must be checked to verify that they approximate a normal distribution too. Histograms should be created to take a look at the distributions, and as I noted in Chapter Two, the Shapiro–Wilk statistic[2] should be calculated and interpreted. (In Boxes 10.1 and 10.2, I show how to enter data into R in the two different ways you've encountered, directly or by importing a spreadsheet, and how to write the commands for the histograms, the Shapiro–Wilk statistic, and descriptive statistics.)

The histogram of the independent variable values, the 15 children's scores on the aptitude test, is displayed in Figure 10.6.[3] The distribution looks slightly skewed by the two scores on the far left of the distribution, but the Shapiro–Wilk statistic indicates that the data approximate a normal distribution ($W = .9662$, $p = .7976$). The histogram of the dependent variable scores, the test scores from the administration of the final test, also shows a small cluster of scores at the lower end of the scale, but the Shapiro–Wilk statistic indicates that these data approximate a normal distribution too ($W = .9235, p = .2175$).[4]

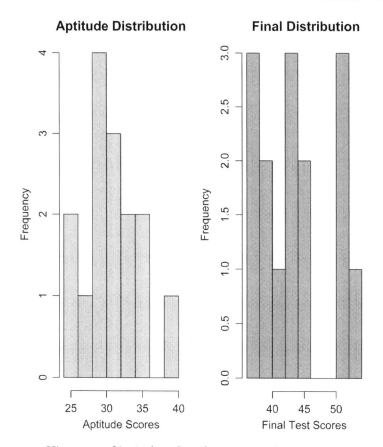

FIGURE 10.6 Histograms of Aptitude and Final Test Data (Fabricated Data)

Box 10.1 Using *R* to Create Histograms and Calculate the Shapiro–Wilk Test of Normality and Descriptive Statistics—Data Entered Directly

Enter the data for first one variable and then the other.	> **apt = c (29, 33, 25, 30, 33, 26, 28, 40, 29, 35, 32, 32, 35, 32, 30)** > **final.test = c (39, 39, 36, 38, 46, 38, 43, 54, 51, 51, 43, 51, 46, 41, 43)**
Make a space for side-by-side histograms using the **par (mfrow = c(1,2))** command.	> **par (mfrow = c(1,2))**
Make a histogram of the aptitude data (Figure 10.1).	> **hist (apt, col = "light blue", breaks = 10, xlab = "Aptitude Scores", main = "Aptitude Distribution")**

(Continued)

Box 10.1 (*Continued*)

Make a histogram of the final test data (Figure 10.1).	> **hist (final.test, col = "lime green", breaks = 10, xlab = "Final Test Scores", main = "Final Distribution")**
Calculate the Shapiro–Wilk statistic for the independent variable (*aptitude*) and the dependent variable (*final.test*).	> **shapiro.test (apt)** Output: W = 0.9662, p-value = 0.7976 > **shapiro.test (final.test)** Output: W = 0.9235, p-value = 0.2175
Calculate the descriptive statistics you wish to report (I calculated the mean and the standard deviation).	> **mean (apt)** Output: [1] 31.26667 > **sd (apt)** Output: [1] 3.807261
Calculate the descriptive statistics you wish to report.	> **mean (final.test)** Output: [1] 43.93333 > **sd (final.test)** Output: [1] 5.687915

Box 10.2 Using *R* to Create Histograms and Calculate the Shapiro–Wilk Test of Normality and Descriptive Statistics—Data Imported

Import the data in a csv spreadsheet with the values for the independent variable in one column and the values for the dependent variable in another column. Each column should be given a simple name as a header; I used *apt* for the aptitude test scores and *final. test* for the final test scores. Note that I've given the dataset that I import a name too—*data*.	**data = read.csv (file.choose(), header = T)**

(Continued)

Box 10.2 (*Continued*)

View the dataset after you import it. Check the column names and take a look at the data to check that everything was entered correctly and all of the participants were included.	> **View (data)**
To create a space for making side-by-side histograms, use the **par (mfrow = c (1,2))** command.	> **par (mfrow = c(1,2))**
Make a histogram of the aptitude data (Figure 10.1). (When you import a dataset, to access a variable within that dataset, the name of the dataset is given first, then a dollar sign, then the name of the variable.)	> **hist (data$apt, col = "light blue", breaks = 10, xlab = "Aptitude Scores", main = "Distribution of Aptitude Scores")**
Make a histogram of the final test data (Figure 10.1).	> **hist (data$final.test, col = "lime green", breaks = 10, xlab = "Final Test Scores", main = "Distribution of Final Exam Scores")**
Check the normality of the distribution of the data for the independent variable (*aptitude*) and the dependent variable (*outcome*).	> **shapiro.test(data$apt)** Output: W = 0.9662, p-value = 0.7976 > **shapiro.test(data$final.test)** Output: W = 0.9235, p-value = 0.2175
Calculate the descriptive statistics for the aptitude scores that you'd like to report. (I calculated mean and standard deviation.)	> **mean (data$apt)** Output: [1] 31.26667 > **sd (data$apt)** Output: [1] 3.807261
Calculate the descriptive statistics for the final test scores that you'd like to report. (I calculated mean and standard deviation.)	> **mean (data$final.test)** Output: [1] 43.93333 > **sd (data$final.test)** Output: [1] 5.687915

The third assumption, that the two sets of data are independent of one another, is satisfied; none of the items from the aptitude test appear on the teacher-made final test, or vice versa, and observation of the test administrations confirmed that all of the participants worked independently on the tests.

The fourth assumption, that the two sets of data are in a linear relationship, as opposed to a curvilinear or wavelike relationship, is checked by making a scatterplot of the two variables. In Box 10.3, I explain how to create a scatterplot in *R* using data that are entered directly or a dataset that is imported into *R*.

Box 10.3 Using *R* to Make a Scatterplot When Data Are Entered Directly or Imported as a Dataset

Data entry option 1 (data are entered directly into *R*): Create a scatterplot (give the scatterplot a title, and label both the *x*-axis and the *y*-axis).	> plot(apt, final.test, main = "Scatterplot of Independent & Dependent Variables", xlab = "independent variable (aptitude performance)", ylab = "dependent variable (final exam outcomes)", col = "red")
Data entry option 2 (data are imported as an Excel dataset): Create a scatterplot (give the scatterplot a title, and label both the *x*-axis and the *y*-axis).	> plot(data$apt, data$final.test, main = "Scatterplot of Independent & Dependent Variables", xlab = "independent variable (aptitude performance)", ylab = "dependent variable (final exam outcomes)", col = "red")

The scatterplot is displayed in Figure 10.7. The one or two individuals who diverge from the group have rather low aptitude scores and rather high final test scores, but the data appear to be in a linear relationship, not a curvilinear or wavelike pattern.

Having verified that the assumptions were met, I go to the next step in statistical logic, calculating the observed value of Pearson's *r*.

Scatterplot of Independent and Dependent Variables

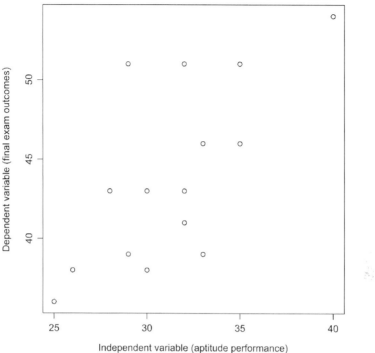

FIGURE 10.7 Scatterplot of Independent and Dependent Variable Values

Step 6: Calculate the Observed Value of the Appropriate Statistic

Calculating Pearson's r with a calculator doesn't involve any really weird math, but it does require attention to detail. It's really helpful at the start to set up a chart like Figure 10.8 and determine the mean and the standard deviation of each set of data. (The descriptive statistics can be retrieved from the R output.)
Here's the formula for Pearson's r.

$$r_{xy} = \frac{N(\Sigma XY) - (\Sigma X)(\Sigma Y)}{\sqrt{[N\Sigma X^2 - (\Sigma X)^2][N\Sigma Y^2 - (\Sigma Y)^2]}} =$$

First, I fill in the values from the chart and add the information for N (there are 15 participants):

$$\Sigma X = 469 \quad \Sigma Y = 659 \quad \Sigma X^2 = 14867 \quad \Sigma Y^2 = 29405 \quad \Sigma XY = 20821$$

$$r_{xy} = \frac{15(20821) - (469)(659)}{\sqrt{[(15)(14867) - 469^2][(15)(29405) - 659^2]}} =$$

Student	X	Y	X²	Y²	XY
1	29	39	841	1521	1131
2	33	39	1089	1521	1287
3	25	36	625	1296	900
4	30	38	900	1444	1140
5	33	46	1089	2116	1518
6	26	38	676	1444	988
7	28	43	784	1849	1204
8	40	54	1600	2916	2160
9	29	51	841	2601	1479
10	35	51	1225	2601	1785
11	32	43	1024	1849	1376
12	32	51	1024	2601	1632
13	35	46	1225	2116	1610
14	32	41	1024	1681	1321
15	30	43	900	1849	1290
	$\Sigma X = 469$	$\Sigma Y = 659$	$\Sigma X^2 = 14867$	$\Sigma Y^2 = 29405$	$\Sigma XY = 20821$

$$\bar{X} = 31.26 \quad \bar{Y} = 43.93$$
$$S_x = 3.81 \quad s_y = 5.69$$

FIGURE 10.8 Chart to Guide Calculation of Pearson's r

Now I carry out the calculations:

$$\frac{312315 - 309071}{\sqrt{[223005 - 219961][441075 - 434281]}}$$

$$= \frac{3244}{\sqrt{[3044][6794]}}$$

$$= \frac{3244}{\sqrt{20680936}}$$

$$= \frac{3244}{4547.63} = .71$$

Pearson's r for the correlation between aptitude (x) and students' performance on the final test (y) is .71. This is a moderately strong relationship, but is it strong enough to be statistically significant? Before addressing this question by following the remaining steps in statistical logic, I demonstrate in Box 10.4 how to use R to calculate Pearson's r using data that are entered directly into R or a dataset that's imported.

Box 10.4 Using *R* to Calculate Pearson's *r* When Data Are Entered Directly or Imported (relevant output underscored)

Calculate Pearson's *r* when data were entered as two separate sets, *apt* and *final.test*.	**cor.test (apt, final.test)** Output: data:apt and outcome t = 3.3775, df = 13, p-value = 0.004952 alternative hypothesis: true correlation is not equal to 0 95 percent confidence interval: 0.2637621 0.8857257 sample estimates: cor 0.6836528
Calculate Pearson's *r* when data are imported as a dataset with the independent variable values in one column and the dependent variable values in another.	**cor.test (data$apt, data$final. test)** Output: data:data$apt and datt$outcome t = 3.3775, df = 13, p-value = 0.004952 alternative hypothesis: true correlation is not equal to 0 95 percent confidence interval: 0.2637621 0.8857257 sample estimates: cor 0.6836528

Step 7: Use Degrees of Freedom and Alpha to Find the Critical Value of the Statistic OR Determine the Exact Probability of the Observed Value of the Statistic

Either approach is fine, but when the calculations are done with a calculator, the critical value approach must be used and a chart of critical values of *r* is needed;[5] the exact probability approach can be used when calculations are done using *R* because the exact probability is reported.

Using the Critical Value Approach

The degrees of freedom formula for Pearson's *r* is *number of pairs* − 2. The degrees of freedom for this study are 13 (15 − 2 = 13). I set alpha at .05; using alpha and the degrees of freedom, I look up the $r_{critical}$ value in a chart of critical values of *r* and find that $r_{critical}$ is .5139.

Using the Exact Probability Approach

The **cor.test** output shows that R uses a t-test formula to calculate the exact probability of the observed Pearson's r (Field, Miles, & Field, 2012, p. 211).[6] The observed value of Pearson's r is .6836528; the exact probability is .004952.

Step 8: To Interpret the Outcome of the Analysis, Compare the Observed Value and the Critical Value OR Compare the Exact Probability to Alpha

In Step 8, the outcome of the analysis is determined using either the critical value approach (if calculations were done with a calculator) or the exact probability approach (if calculations were done using R).

Using the Critical Value Approach

Here are the rules for interpreting $r_{critical}$:

$$\text{If } r_{observed} \leq r_{critical} \rightarrow \text{accept the null hypothesis.}$$

$$\text{If } r_{observed} > r_{critical} \rightarrow \text{reject the null hypothesis.}$$

When $r_{observed}$ (the value of r that I calculated with a calculator) and $r_{critical}$ (the value I looked up in a chart of critical values) are compared, I see:

$$.71 > .5139.$$

When $r_{observed}$ is greater than $r_{critical}$, as is the case here, the null hypothesis is rejected and the alternative hypothesis is accepted.

Using the Exact Probability Approach

Here are the rules again for interpreting the exact level of probability. The observed value of Pearson's r is 0.6836528; the exact probability is 0.004952. In Step 2, alpha was set at .05.

$$\text{If exact probability} \geq \text{alpha} \rightarrow \text{accept the null hypothesis.}$$

$$\text{If exact probability} < \text{alpha} \rightarrow \text{reject the null hypothesis.}$$

The exact level of probability, .004952, is less than .05, so the null hypothesis is rejected and the alternative hypothesis is accepted:

H_1: **There is a statistically significant, positive correlation between language aptitude and language learning, as measured by the final test in students' first foreign language class.**

Step 9: Interpret the Findings as a Probability Statement

I now make the appropriate probability statement:

> **There's 95% certainty of a statistically significant, positive correlation between language aptitude and language learning, as measured by the final test in students' first foreign language class.**

Step 10: Interpret the Meaningfulness of the Findings

Meaningfulness is interpreted with reference to the research question and purpose regardless of whether the null hypothesis is accepted or rejected. Effect size is also calculated.

The researcher wanted to know whether there's a significant correlational relationship between language aptitude and learners' performance on their final exam, which he considers a measure of the learners' success in their first language class. The researcher learned through this study that there's 95% certainty of a statistically significant correlational relationship between the two variables.

The formula for the effect size of Pearson's r is a simple one: r^2. For $r = .68$,[7] the effect size, r^2, is .47. Almost half of the variation in performance on the final test, 47%, overlaps with or can be predicted by performance on the aptitude test. The remaining 53% of what might be related to performance on the final test is unsystematic and a mystery. Guidelines for interpreting effect size indicate that an effect size greater than .3 can be considered "strong" (Field et al., 2012), so the findings would be reported as something like this:

> **We found that there's 95% certainty of a statistically significant correlation between performance on the aptitude test and the summer camp's final test ($r = .6836528$, $df = 13$, $p = .004952$). The effect size ($r^2 = .47$) can be considered strong.**

The researcher thought that if he found a statistically significant relationship between children's performance on the aptitude test and their performance in the summer camp language program, he might be able to use the aptitude test for making selection decisions for a new accelerated curriculum that he plans to implement. In the next section of this chapter I explain how $r_{observed}$ can be used to estimate, or predict, dependent variable performance from independent variable performance.

Calculating an Estimated *y* from *x*

A statistically significant correlational relationship is useful for predictive purposes. When we have only an individual's score on the independent variable, that individual's performance on the second variable can be estimated. Being able to estimate, or predict, an individual's performance on the dependent variable from performance on the independent variable means we can make informed estimates of a person's performance on the dependent variable without the person's actually taking the test. This predicting (or estimating), called *linear regression*, is based on the underlying assumption that the correlation is expressed as a straight line in a scatterplot of the variables' values. The distance of the data points from this line is a visual representation of the strength of the correlation.

We know (based on the fabricated data!) that the statistically significant relationship between language aptitude and language learning is $r = 0.6836528$ (let's round this to 0.68). How might a person who received a score of 27 on the aptitude test (the independent variable, x) perform in the language program and on the final test (the dependent variable, y)? With the means and standard deviations of the two tests and the correlation, the score for that person can be estimated, or predicted.

These are the formulas and the information needed to estimate performance on y from performance on x:

$$\hat{Y} = \bar{Y} + b(X - \bar{X})$$ $[\hat{Y}$ is the estimated or predicted value of Y]

$$b = \left(r_{xy}\right)\frac{S_y}{S_x}$$ $[b$ is called *slope*]

$$SEE = S_y\sqrt{1 - r_{xy}^2}$$ [SEE is the standard error of the estimate]

$\bar{X} = 31.3$ $\bar{Y} = 43.9$ [the means and standard deviations]

$s_x = 3.81$ $s_y = 5.69$ [the correlation between x and y]

$r_{xy} = .68$

The first step is to calculate the slope of the line, b:

$$b = (.68)\frac{5.69}{3.81} = .69(1.49) = \mathbf{1.0132}$$

The second step is to calculate the estimated score on the final test ($\hat{Y}$) for a person who has a score of 27 on the aptitude test:

$\hat{Y} = 43.93 + 1.0132\,(27-31.27) = 43.93 + 1.0132\,(-4.27) = 43.93 - 4.327218 = \mathbf{39.602782}$. (I'm rounding this off to 39.60.)

The third step is to calculate the value of the SEE so that a confidence band for the $\hat{Y}$ value can be established:

$$SEE = S_y\sqrt{1 - r_{xy}^2} =$$
$5.69\sqrt{1 - .68^2} = 5.69\sqrt{1 - .4624} = 5.69\sqrt{.5376} = 5.69(.7332121) = 4.17$

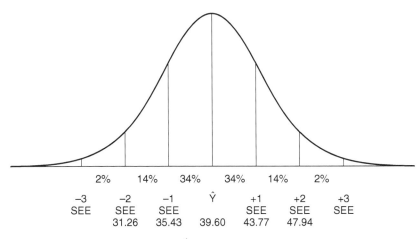

FIGURE 10.9 Model Distribution of $\hat{Y}$ Values

SEE can be considered a cousin of the standard deviation. We can assume there is a normal distribution of possible $\hat{Y}$s, with the one we calculated in the middle (Figure 10. 9).

To establish a 68% confidence band, we add one SEE value (4.17 points) to the $\hat{Y}$ value to establish the upper boundary of this student's likely performance on y, and we subtract one SEE value (4.17 points) to establish the lower boundary. So we can be 68% certain that a student who received a score of 27 on the aptitude test would earn a score between 35.43 and 43.77 on the summer camp final exam.

To establish a 96% confidence band, we add two SEE values to the $\hat{Y}$ value to establish the upper boundary of this student's likely performance on y and we subtract two SEE values to establish the lower boundary. We can be 96% certain that a student who received a score of 27 on the aptitude test would earn a score between 31.26 and 47.94 on the final exam for the language class. (An explanation of how to perform linear regression using R will be found on the companion website.)

If you'd like to practice applying statistical logic to the use of Pearson's r or practice estimating an individual's performance on the dependent variable from performance on the independent variable, take a look at the Practice Problem.[8]

R Commands Introduced in Chapter Ten

plot (independent.variable, dependent.variable, main = "Name of Scatterplot", xlab = "Name of x-axis", ylab = "Name of y-axis", col = "name.of.color") This command creates a scatterplot of two variables when the data are entered directly into R as two separate sets.

plot (dataset.name$independent.variable, dataset.name$dependent. variable, main = "Name of Scatterplot", xlab = "Name of x-axis",

ylab = "Name of y-axis", col = "name.of.color") This command creates a scatterplot of two variables when the data are imported into a dataset with two columns of information, one column for the independent variable values and one column for the dependent variable values.

cor.test (independent.variable, dependent.variable) This command yields the observed value of Pearson's r and the exact probability of that value when data for the independent and dependent variables were entered directly into R in two separate sets.

cor.test (dataset.name$independent.variable, dataset.name$independent. variable) This command yields the observed value of Pearson's r and the exact probability of that value when the data are imported into a dataset with two columns of information, one column for the independent variable values and one column for the dependent variable values.

Practice Problem

An answer key is available on the companion website (www.routledge.com/cw/turner).

A group of researchers is interested in determining whether teachers' perception of the importance of a particular learning strategy is related to the frequency of their use of the strategy. The researchers used a questionnaire to collect data regarding teachers' perception of the importance of the strategy; they had a team of research assistants who did observations of the same teachers to determine how often they used the strategy. The perceived importance scale yields scores between 1 and 5; the frequency of use scale yields scores between 0 and 45. The (fabricated) data for 16 of the teachers who were randomly selected from the population are presented below:

Participant	Perceived Importance	Reported Frequency of Use
1	3.75	37
2	4.57	44
3	3.67	36
4	3.32	33
5	3.94	38
6	4.22	41
7	3.02	25
8	4.03	37
9	4.02	38
10	4.00	35
11	4.28	40

Participant	Perceived Importance	Reported Frequency of Use
12	4.25	40
13	3.77	36
14	3.63	33
15	4.14	41
16	2.80	25

1. Follow the steps in statistical logic to determine whether there is a statistically significant relationship between teachers' perceived importance of this strategy and their use of the strategy.
2. Based on the relationship between these two variables, what do you think the frequency of use would be for a teacher who perceived the importance of the strategy to be 3.20?

Notes

1 The scatterplot was created in R using these commands: **scatter.AB = ggplot(dataset, aes(varA, varB))** and **scatter.AB + geom_point()+ geom_smooth(method = "lm", col = "green", se = F) + labs(x = "Variable A", y = "Variable B")**. These commands are found in the ggplot2 package—the package must be added to R. [To add a package to R, use the **install.packages ("ggplot2")** command and the **library (ggplot2)** command.]

2 When there are more than 200 cases in a dataset, the researcher should check the kurtosis and skewedness separately (see Chapter Two for details).

3 Please recall that the data for this problem are fabricated.

4 See Chapter Two for a detailed explanation of the interpretation of the Shapiro–Wilk statistic.

5 A chart of critical values for r can be found in the resource section of the companion website (www.routledge.com/cw/turner).

6 The t-test formula that's used is $t_r = \frac{r\sqrt{N-2}}{\sqrt{1-r^2}}$ (Field, Miles, & Field, 2012, p. 211).

7 The value of r from R is used here because it's more precise than my calculations with a calculator (I rounded off the numbers in my calculations to the hundredth place).

8 Additional Practice Problems can be found on the companion website (www.routledge.com/cw/turner).

11

THE NON-PARAMETRIC SPEARMAN'S RHO AND KENDALL'S TAU STATISTICS

Spearman's rho and Kendall's tau are the non-parametric counterparts to Pearson's r. Like Pearson's r, the Spearman rank order correlation coefficient—Spearman's rho—and Kendall's tau can be used to determine the degree of correspondence between two variables. However, Spearman's rho and Kendall's tau are appropriate when the values for the independent and dependent variables are rankable ordinal-scale or interval-scale data. They are both non-parametric statistics and unlike Pearson's r, can be used when the relationship between the independent and dependent variable isn't linear (DeVeaux, Velleman, & Bock, 2008; Verzani, 2005).

Spearman's rho has been more commonly used than Kendall's tau; however, rho is adversely affected when there are a lot of tied values in the data. As Field et al. noted (2012), "when you have a small data set with a large number of tied ranks" Kendall's tau gives a "better estimate of the correlation" (p. 225). There are three formulas for tau; R uses the tau-b formula, which accommodates tied scores. (Kendall's tau is calculated based on the number of concordant and discordant pairs rather than by finding the difference between paired scores as is done when calculating Spearman's rho; therefore, tied scores do not present the same problem that they do in calculating rho.)

The possible range for values of Spearman's rho and Kendall's tau is −1.00 to +1.00. Both −1.00 and +1.00 represent a perfect correlational relationship between two variables; when rho or tau equals zero, there's no correlational relationship, no correspondence, between the values of the two variables.

Teachers who want to gain a deeper understanding of their learners and their learning environment are often very interested in knowing the strength of the relationship between variables. To gain a deeper understanding of his learners, Derek Yiu (2011), for example, wanted to know whether there was a statistically significant relationship between their perceptions of their extroversion (or intro-version) and how much they interacted with their classmates and teacher. I won-der, in my own classes, whether there's a relationship between how much my students write in the journal entries that they submit to me and how much I write in response. I *think* I write more when a student writes a lot, but I'm not sure how strong that relationship is. I also wonder about the relationship between the length of my response and how long it takes me to write it—it seems like a longer response would take more time, but I've got a feeling there are other fac-tors involved, and the relationship might not be as strong as I think. Spearman's rho and Kendall's tau are useful for investigating the impressions that teachers have about their learners and what goes on in the learning environment. I've got some data we can take look at to see if the impressions I have about responding to journal entries are accurate.

Though neither Spearman's rho nor Kendall's tau requires normally distrib-uted data and the relationship between the two variables need not be linear, there are two assumptions for their use:

1. The data are measured on interval or ordinal scales and are rankable.
2. Each pair of values is independent.

When there is a small number of participants and there are tied values, Kendall's tau should be used instead of Spearman's rho.

Let's investigate this question: "Is there a relationship between how much my students write in the journal entries and how much I write in response?" I *do* believe I write more when a student writes a lot, but let's find out how strong the relationship is and whether it's strong enough to be due to something other than chance.

Using Spearman's rho (or Kendall's tau) in the 10 Steps of Statistical Logic

In the discussion that follows, I explain how Spearman's rho is used in the context of statistical logic and how it's calculated using a calculator and R. I also illustrate how to calculate Kendall's tau using R. I illustrate the discussion using data from 19 of my students' journal entries (and I thank them again for their permission to use the data!).

Step 1: State the Formal Research Hypotheses

The first step in statistical logic is to state the hypotheses. I state the null hypoth-esis and two one-tailed directional alternative hypotheses. I chose to pose two alternative hypotheses because I have no evidence of the possible direction of the relationship between the variables.

Null hypothesis: There is no statistically significant correlation between the amount that students write in journal entries and how much their teacher writes in her responses to the entries.

Alternative hypothesis 1: There is a statistically significant positive correlation between the amount that students write in journal entries and how much their teacher writes in her responses to the entries.

Alternative hypothesis 2: There is a statistically significant negative correlation between the amount that students write in journal entries and how much their teacher writes in her responses to the entries.

Step 2: Set Alpha

I'll set alpha at .01 because although this is exploratory research, after so many years of simply having an impression of the relationship between the length of students' journal entries and the length of my responses, it will feel good to know if my impression is probably accurate—or not. It's time for more rigor!

Step 3: Select the Appropriate Statistic for Analysis of the Data

My study is small-scale and the participants are my students, not a sample randomly selected from a population. Additionally, I'm reasonably certain the data won't be normally distributed, so a non-parametric statistic is needed. For these reasons, I propose to use Spearman's rho to determine the relationship between the two variables. I'll check the data once I've collected them to determine whether there are a lot of tied values—if there are, I'll use Kendall's tau instead of Spearman's rho.

Step 4: Collect the Data

I present the values for the independent and dependent variables in Table 11.1. [I threw in a third variable, *how much time I spend writing each entry*, because that might be interesting to investigate too (interesting to me anyway).]

Step 5: Verify That the Assumptions Are Met

In Step 5, the three assumptions for the appropriate use of Spearman's rho are verified.

1. The data for the independent and dependent variables are measured on interval or ordinal scales and are rankable.
2. Each observation is independent from the others.
3. There are very few tied values within the data.

TABLE 11.1 Length of Student Journal Entries and Length of Teacher's Responses to Entries ($n = 19$)

author.wds	my.wrds	my.time
582	553	14
658	386	23
667	334	19
637	933	45
1060	665	27
899	897	39
1143	980	54
633	227	17
525	446	32
645	349	22
361	495	27
385	206	18
730	362	27
506	394	20
462	516	33
793	501	21
847	320	24
723	673	32
388	522	29

A review of the values in Table 11.1 shows that the two variables are rankable. The distributions approximate a normal distribution (Figure 11.1), but regardless of the distribution shape, the fundamental conditions of the parametric paradigm aren't met—the participants are not drawn randomly from a population and the primary goal of the research is not generalization to a population. I simply want to gain a better understanding of one aspect of my teaching practice.

The two sets of values are independent from one another—the students wrote their file entries individually and without any intervention from me. I wrote my responses to their file entries without any direct consultation with the individual authors and each response was independent from the others. Finally, I take a look at the values in Table 11.1 for both variables and verify that there are no tied values. Having verified that these assumptions are met, I continue to Step 6.

Step 6: Calculate the Observed Value of the Appropriate Statistic

In Step 6, the observed value of the statistic is calculated. In the discussion below, I first explain how Spearman's rho is calculated using a calculator, then I explain how to do the calculations using R. (I don't illustrate how to calculate Kendall's tau using a calculator; I recommend using R.)

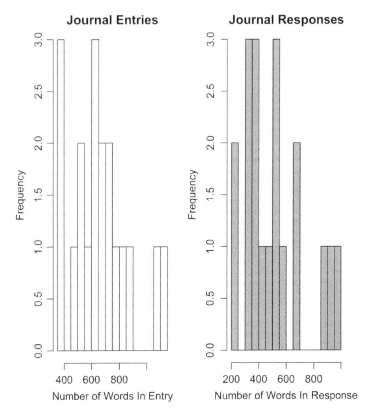

FIGURE 11.1 Histograms of Length of Journal Entries and Length of Teacher's Responses to Entries

Here's the formula for Spearman's rho. The 6 in the numerator is a constant.

$$rho = 1 - \frac{6\left(\sum D^2\right)}{N\left(N^2 - 1\right)}$$

To calculate Spearman's rho, I first rank the data for each of the two variables. Then I determine the difference between the ranks for each paired set of values and I square the differences. These steps are shown in Table 11.2. Then I find the sum of the squared differences (D^2)[1] (Table 11.2).

The sum of the squared differences, 802, can then be put in the formula, as can the number of participants ($n = 19$). I then calculate the observed value of Spearman's rho:

$$\mathbf{rho} = 1 - \frac{6(802)}{19(19^2 - 1)} = 1 - \frac{4812}{19(361 - 1)} = 1 - \frac{4812}{19(360)} = 1 - \frac{4812}{6840}$$

$$= 1 - .70351 = \mathbf{0.29649}$$

TABLE 11.2 Steps in Calculating Spearman's rho

Student	Entry Length	Rank of Entry Length	Response Length	Rank of Response Length	D (difference in ranks)	D^2
1	361	1	495	10	−9	81
2	385	2	206	1	−1	1
3	388	3	522	13	−10	100
4	462	4	516	12	−8	64
5	506	5	394	8	−3	9
6	525	6	446	9	−3	9
7	582	7	553	14	−7	49
8	633	8	227	2	+6	36
9	637	9	933	18	−9	81
10	645	10	349	5	+5	25
11	658	11	386	7	+4	16
12	667	12	334	4	+8	64
13	723	13	673	16	−3	9
14	730	14	362	6	+8	64
15	793	15	501	11	+4	16
16	847	16	320	3	+13	169
17	899	17	897	17	0	0
18	1060	18	665	15	+3	9
19	1143	19	980	19	0	0
					$\Sigma D^2 = 802$	

In Box 11.1, I explain how to use R to make histograms of the data for the two variables, how to calculate descriptive statistics, and how to calculate Spearman's rho. In Box 11.1 there's also a shortcut for calculating Spearman's rho and Kendall's tau.[2]

Box 11.1 Using *R* to Calculate Spearman's rho and Kendall's tau

In this example, I imported an Excel document[3] that contains the values for the three variables presented in Table 11.1. (I could have entered the values for the two variables of interest directly into *R*—see Box 10.1 for details on how to enter the data directly if that's your preference.)	> **data = read.csv (file.choose(), header = T)** > **View (data)**

(*Continued*)

Box 11.1 (*Continued*)

View the dataset to check that the correct document was imported and that all of the values were entered accurately.	> View (data)
Create a space for side-by-side histograms.	> par (mfrow = c(1,2))
Make a histogram of the independent variable, *length of journal entry* (and imagine it being yellow, ok?).	> hist (data$author.wds, breaks = 15, col = "yellow", xlab = "Number of Words In Entry", main = "Journal Entries")
Make a histogram of the dependent variable, *length of my responses to entries* (imagine this histogram is lime green—why not?).	> hist (data$my.wrds, breaks = 15, col = "lime green", xlab = "Number of Words In Response", main = "Journal Responses")
Calculate the mean for each of the two variables.	> mean (data$author.wds) Output: [1] 665.4737 > mean (data$my.wrds) Output: [1] 513.6316
Calculate the standard deviation for each of the two variables.[4]	> sd (data$author.wds) Output: [1] 215.9144 > sd (data$my.wrds) Output: [1] 226.3982
Rank the data for each of the variables using the **rank** command (to check the rankings I did that are presented in Table 11.2).	> rank (data$author.wds) Output: [1]7 11 12 9 18 17 19 8 6 10 1 2 14 5 4 15 16 13 3 > rank (data$my.wrds) Output: [1]14 7 4 18 15 17 19 2 9 5 10 1 6 8 12 11 3 16 13
The command **cor** can be used with an embedded **rank** command.	> cor (rank(data$author.wds), rank (data$my.wrds)) Output: [1] 0.2964912
Alternatively, the "**method**" argument can be used with **cor** to calculate Spearman's rho. (Note that the "s" in "spearman" must be lowercase.)	> cor (data$author.wds, data$my.wrds, method = "spearman") Output: [1] 0.2964912

(*Continued*)

Box 11.1 (*Continued*)

Even better, use the shortcut **cor. test** command; it reports exact probability.[5]	> **cor.test (data$author.wds, data$my.wrds, method = "spearman")** Output: S = 802, p-value = 0.2171 sample estimates: rho 0.2964912
Kendall's tau is considered more appropriate when there are many tied scores within the data. There aren't any ties within this dataset, but just for fun, let's see what the value of Kendall's tau is. It's slightly lower than Spearman's rho, but if there were a lot of tied values in the data, I'd calculate and report Kendall's tau instead of Spearman's rho. (There is a special *R* package for calculating Kendall's tau, but **cor.test,method = "kendall"** is fine for computing tau and its exact probability (McLeod, 2013). The **exact = FALSE** component is needed when there are tied values because exact probability is then calculated using an approach appropriate for tied data rather than the default approach.)	> **cor.test (data$author.wds, data$my.wrds, method = "kendall", exact = FALSE)** Output: T = 102, p-value = 0.2669 sample estimates: tau 0.1929825

Step 7: Determine the Degrees of Freedom for rho$_{observed}$ and Use Degrees of Freedom and Alpha to Find the Critical Value of the Statistic OR Calculate the Exact Probability of rho$_{observed}$

Either of the two approaches in Step 7 can be used, but the critical value approach is typically used when the calculation of rho$_{observed}$ is done with a calculator. The exact probability approach can be used when the calculation of rho$_{observed}$ is done with *R* because the exact probability is reported (if you use the **cor.test** command).

Using the Critical Value Approach

The formula for the degrees of freedom (*df*) for Spearman's rho is the *number of pairs of data*, 19 in this study. If I use the critical value approach to determining statistical significance, I use degrees of freedom and alpha to find the critical value for rho in a chart of critical values for rho.[6] I set alpha at .01; with alpha and the degrees of freedom, I find that the critical value of rho is 0.625.[7]

Using the Exact Probability Approach

When choosing the exact probability approach to interpreting the outcome, I use R to calculate the observed value of rho and from the output I retrieve the value of rho$_{observed}$ (single underscored in the output), rho =.2964912 *and* the exact level of probability for rho$_{observed}$ (double underscored in the output), *p*-value =.2171.

Step 8: To Interpret the Outcome of the Analysis, Compare the Observed Value and the Critical Value OR Compare the Exact Probability to Alpha

Remember that you don't need to use both approaches—choose one. I prefer the exact probability approach and recommend using the **cor.test** command in R that provides the exact probability.

Using the Critical Value Approach

The rules for interpreting the outcome using the critical value approach are:

If rho$_{observed}$ ≤ rho$_{critical}$ → accept the null hypothesis.

If rho$_{observed}$ > rho$_{critical}$ → reject the null hypothesis.

My calculation of rho$_{observed}$ using a calculator (as opposed to R) is .29649, less than rho$_{critical}$, 0.625. Rho$_{observed}$ < rho$_{critical}$, so I accept the null hypothesis.

Using the Exact Probability Approach

If I use the exact probability approach to determine statistical significance, these are the rules:

If exact probability ≥ alpha → accept the null hypothesis.

If exact probability < alpha → reject the null hypothesis.

The exact *p*-value is .2171 and I set alpha at .01. The exact *p*-value is greater than alpha, so I accept the null hypothesis.

Step 9: Interpret the Findings as a Probability Statement

In Step 9, the probability statement is made using alpha and the hypothesis accepted in the previous step.

There's 99% certainty of no statistically significant correlation between the amount that students write in journal entries and how much their teacher writes in her response to the entries.

Step 10: Interpret the Meaningfulness of the Findings

Now, I interpret the meaningfulness of the outcome. Meaningfulness is usually interpreted with reference to the research question and by reporting effect size. Unlike Pearson's *r*, it's not generally recommended that rho be squared to interpret the overlap between the two variables, though there's current ongoing discussion about the appropriateness of doing so for some purposes. As Jeremy Anglim (2012) wrote on Cross Validated, an online question and answer site for statisticians, "People often square a correlation coefficient because it has a nice verbal interpretation as the proportion of shared variance. . . . It does not seem to be customary to square Spearman's rho. That said, you could square it if you wanted to. It would then represent the proportion of shared variance in the two ranked variables." I decided that there is some usefulness in reporting the shared variance, though the shared variance is very small, .087907.

My report of the outcomes of this analysis might look something like this:

On the basis of this small study, there's 99% certainty that there's no significant correlation between how much a student writes in a journal entry and how much I write in my response to it (rho = .297; *df* = 19, *p* =.2171). The shared variance (Anglim, 2012) is very small, .088. I am surprised by the outcome of this investigation and am reminded of how important it is that I continue to systematically collect and analyze data to explore the accuracy of my impressions regarding my professional practice.

R Commands Introduced in Chapter Eleven

rank (dataset.name$variable.name) This command ranks the values of the variable that's named inside the parentheses when the variable is located in a dataset.

rank (variable.name) This command ranks the values of the variable that's named inside the parentheses when the values for the variable were entered directly into *R*.

cor (dataset.name$independent.variable, dataset.name$dependent.variable, method = "spearman") This command for Spearman's rho gives only the observed value of rho. The variables are located in an imported dataset.

cor (independent.variable, dependent.variable, method = "spearman") This command for Spearman's rho gives only the observed value of rho; the values for the variables were entered directly into *R*.

cor.test (dataset.name$independent.variable, dataset.name$independent. variable, method = "spearman") This command for Spearman's rho gives the observed value of rho and the exact probability of that observed value. The data are located in an imported dataset.

cor.test (data$author.wds, data$my.wrds, method = "kendall", exact = FALSE) This command for Kendall's tau gives the observed value of tau and the exact probability of that observed value. The data are located in an imported dataset. The **exact = FALSE** component of the command indicates that instead of the default formula for calculating exact probability the formula that's appropriate when there are ties among the data is used.

Practice Problems

An answer key is available on the companion website (www.routledge.com/cw/turner).

1. In the dataset in Table 11.3 there are three variables: students' performance on a debate, students' performance on a brief, and students' performance on a final report. Choose two and use statistical logic to determine whether there is a statistically significant relationship between the two variables you have chosen.

TABLE 11.3 Data From Three Variables for Practice Problem 1

debate	brief	report
99	94	98
78	80	86
88	92	93
97	96	95
93	94	94
94	92	98
91	90	90
95	94	94
98	96	95
79	83	84
85	83	89
94	92	95
95	92	95
94	96	95
90	94	92
92	94	87
94	92	93
94	90	92
89	76	77
97	90	89
94	90	89
88	90	89

2. Derek Yiu (2011) gave permission for us to examine his dataset. His data include his participants' self-assessment of their introversion/extroversion and their self-perception of how much they participate in class interactions (Table 11.4). Follow the steps in statistical logic to determine whether there is a statistically significant relationship between the two variables.

TABLE 11.4 Derek Yiu's Introversion/
Extroversion and Class Participation Data

intro.extro	part
89	30
69	32
62	27
57	38
101	41
84	35
59	28
95	34
105	35
75	20
70	36
48	48
116	31
121	35
45	14
97	29
62	37
90	33
93	42
85	48
56	16
120	51
84	30
116	52
74	34
94	42
101	26
69	54
71	34
101	38
103	35
70	30
107	44

(*Continued*)

TABLE 11.4 (*Continued*)

intro.extro	part
52	39
67	16
87	38
76	39
74	37
58	33
96	26
56	18
62	39

Notes

1 The order of the participants in the table doesn't coincide with their order in the dataset; I reordered the participants after ranking the entry length to make the table easier to read.

2 I don't show how to calculate Kendall's tau using a calculator, though I have included information on the *R* command for Kendall's tau in Box 11.1.

3 The dataset can be found in the resources section of the companion website (www.routledge.com/cw/turner).

4 I was really surprised by the size of the standard deviations. I had never calculated the standard deviation for either the length of the journal entries or my responses until now—I didn't have any idea that they had such wide dispersion. I learned something new about my students and me—I love it when that happens—really. I decided I needed to know the mean time I spend writing the responses and how much dispersion there is in that variable too—the mean for *my.time* is 27.52632 minutes and the standard deviation is 10.08502. I'm surprised again—I had the impression that there wasn't that much difference in the number of minutes I spend responding to different individuals' journal entries. I'll have to do some thinking about these new insights into my teaching practice.

5 I'm generally in favor of sensible shortcuts, and this one gives the exact probability of the observed value of Spearman's rho. I can interpret the probability instead of locating a chart of critical values for rho.

6 A chart of critical values for rho is included in the resource section of the companion website (www.routledge.com/cw/turner).

7 I used the critical value for $df = 18$ because the critical value for $df = 19$ is not provided in the chart. (The critical value for $df = 19$ is a tiny bit more rigorous than the critical value for $df = 20$; by tradition, I use the slightly more rigorous critical value when the exact critical value isn't provided in the chart.)

12

THE NON-PARAMETRIC CHI-SQUARED STATISTICS

The two statistics examined in Chapter Twelve, the 1-way chi-squared (χ^2)[1] and 2-way chi-squared statistics, allow the statistical analysis of frequency data, that is, data that are simple tallies or counts. The 1-way chi-squared formula allows a researcher to make a probability statement about the likelihood of there being a pattern in frequency count data for a single nominal variable. For example, 1-way chi-squared can be used to determine whether there's a significant pattern in diners' use of politeness markers in their responses to a server's initial greeting. The 2-way chi-squared formula allows a researcher to make a probability statement about the likelihood of a relationship between two nominal variables; such as diners' use of politeness markers and the sex of their server.

The chi-squared statistics are non-parametric; they aren't based on an assumption of normally distributed data. In small-scale language education research, the chi-squared formulas are often used to analyze survey and observation data. Imagine, for example, that on October 26, we survey 210 students at the Monterey Institute because we want to know whether they plan to attend the school's Halloween Party—having a sense of how many party animals to expect would help the party organizers work out details of the event, like how many pumpkins they need for the pumpkin carving contest. The questionnaire respondents could choose one of three answers: "I think so," "No way," or "Maybe, but I don't like parties." We then count how many people responded "I think so," how many responded "no way," and how many responded "Maybe, but I don't like parties." The variable is *participants' intention regarding Halloween party attendance*. The 1-way chi-squared statistic can be used to determine whether there's a statistically significant pattern within the frequency data—a strong enough tendency to be probably due to something other than chance. We might decide to sort the responses on an additional variable too—for example, whether the participants are domestic or international students. The 2-way chi-squared formula allows us to analyze the data to determine whether there is a relationship between the two nominal variables; are the domestic or international students more likely to choose one of the possible responses than another?

The actual tally, or frequency count, is known as the *observed frequency.* Another important concept in calculating a chi-squared value is *expected frequency.* Determining expected frequency is simple for a 1-way chi-squared analysis; expected frequency is simply the total number of participants divided by the number of levels of the variable. In the Halloween party data we expect the 210 participants to be distributed evenly across the three levels of the independent variable, 70 in each category, as shown in Figure 12.1 if there is no pattern to their responses.

The concept of expected frequency for a 2-way chi-squared analysis is also straightforward, but the calculation of expected frequency requires several steps. I illustrate these steps below after adding the dependent variable, *international versus domestic status*, to the example study. The observed frequencies, the tallies themselves, are presented in Figure 12.2 as well as the *marginals,* the sums of the tallies for each row and column of data. The expected frequency for each of the six cells in the analysis is found by multiplying the marginal for the cell's row by the marginal for the cell's column and dividing that number by the total number of participants, as I illustrate later in this chapter.

The chi-squared statistics allow comparison of the observed frequencies and the expected frequencies to determine whether there's a statistically significant pattern within a variable (1-way chi-squared) or a statistically significant relationship between two variables (2-way chi-squared).

Maiya Saunders (2011) shared some of her data from a language variation study to illustrate how a 1-way chi-squared analysis works.

Example Study

Maiya's curiosity about how customers in a sandwich shop respond to a polite inquiry and greeting from the sandwich maker was piqued one day while she waited in line for her own turn to order a sandwich. She noticed that the employees solicited customers' attention with a polite inquiry, such as "May I

"I think so"	"No way"	"Maybe, but I don't like parties"
70	70	70

FIGURE 12.1 Expected Frequency for a 1-Way Analysis of Halloween Party Survey Data ($N = 210$)

	"I think so"	**"No way"**	**"Maybe, but I don't like parties"**	*Marginals for the rows*
International students	Observed frequency = 47	Observed frequency = 26	Observed frequency = 11	*Sum of the frequencies in this row: Marginal = 84*
	Expected frequency = (61)(84) / 210 = 24.4	*Expected frequency = (65) (84) / 210 = 26*	*Expected frequency = (149)(84) / 210 = 59.6*	
Domestic students	Observed frequency = 14	Observed frequency = 39	Observed frequency = 73	*Sum of the frequencies in this row: Marginal = 126*
	Expected frequency = (61)(126) / 210 = 36.6	*Expected frequency = (65) (126) / 210 = 39*	*Expected frequency = (149)(126) / 210 = 89.4*	
Marginals for the columns	*Sum of the frequencies in this column: Marginal = 61*	*Sum of the frequencies in this column: Marginal = 65*	*Sum of the frequencies in this column: Marginal = 149*	*total number of respondents = 210*

FIGURE 12.2 The Observed Frequencies, Marginals, and Expected Frequencies for a 2-Way Chi-Squared Analysis

help you?" or a greeting and polite inquiry, such as "Hi, can I help you?" Customers, on the other hand, seemed to respond in various ways—some greeted the employee and placed their order using a similarly polite form, such as, "Hi, can I please have . . ." Some didn't exchange a greeting but simply placed their order using a polite form, such as in these responses: "Could I have . . ." and "Can I get a . . ." Finally, some may have greeted the sandwich maker, but used an imperative verb to place their order, as in this example: "Hi. Let me have . . ." Maiya decided to conduct a study to determine whether there was a statistically significant pattern in the manner in which the customers responded to the sandwich maker and placed their orders. The research question that guided this part of her study was: "Is there a pattern of politeness in how customers respond to a sandwich maker's greeting and offer of assistance?"

Before following the steps in statistical logic to determine whether there's a statistically significant pattern of politeness in the customers' responses to the sandwich maker, several features of the chi-squared analysis should be examined, including the assumptions for using the chi-squared formulas and some other important considerations when using them.

The Assumptions for Using the Chi-Squared Statistics

There are five assumptions for using the chi-squared formulas:

1. For a 1-way chi-squared, there's one nominal variable. For a 2-way chi-squared, there are two variables: an independent variable and a dependent variable, and both are nominal.
2. The data are frequency counts.
3. Each piece of information is independent from every other (no influenced votes!).
4. Each piece of information is counted in only one level of a variable (in only one cell).
5. When the degree of freedom for a chi-squared analysis is 1, all expected frequencies must be equal to or greater than 10; when the degrees of freedom are greater than 1, all expected frequencies must equal to or greater than 5.

The data for the 1-way and 2-way chi-squared statistics must be nominal scale and the data must be frequency counts. In studies in which one of the chi-squared statistics has been used, researchers often report percentages in figures similar to those in Figure 12.3. (I present information on students' intentions regarding Halloween party attendance.) The percentages are more informative for reporting purposes than are tallies because a percentage shows proportion, but the chi-squared calculations must be done on the frequency counts rather than the percentages.

The third and fourth assumptions, that each piece of information is independent from every other and each can be counted in only one cell, require particularly careful planning of the data collection procedures. A problematic approach to collecting data might be something like this: Researchers interested in characterizing the classroom behavior of international and domestic students in language classes at a liberal arts college plan to observe classes to determine whether international students are as likely to express their opinions when engaged in group work as domestic students. The researchers create a data collection instrument with two columns—one for tallying each time an international student expresses an opinion while working in a student group (during class) and one

	"I think so"	"No way"	"Maybe—but I don't like parties"
International students	22%	12%	5%
Domestic Students	6%	19%	34%

FIGURE 12.3 Percentages for Each Category of Response for Halloween Party Survey Data

for tallying each time a domestic student expresses an opinion in a student group (during class). Prior to each observation event, the researchers ensure that they can identify the international and domestic students in the class so they can enter their tallies in the appropriate column. At the conclusion of the observation, the researchers count the number of tally marks in each column. The data collected in this manner violate two assumptions. Any person who expresses more than one opinion while working in the group contributes to the tally more than one time, and consequently represents a violation of the assumption of the independence of each piece of information. Data can be collected, though, in such a way that this violation doesn't occur (Hatch & Lazaraton, 1991).

Instead of using a data collection instrument with only two columns, a data collection instrument can be created to indicate when each student, domestic or international, expresses an opinion while engaged in group work, such as in Figure 12.4.

After a sufficient period of data collection with a sufficient number of students and observations, the researchers can create a chart that categorizes each participant according to the number of times that person expressed an opinion as well as his or her status as an international or domestic student. A segment of the final chart might look something like Figure 12.5.

Student	Tally of questions	Student status
1	I I I I I I I	D(omestic)
2	I I I	I(nternational)
3	I	I
4	I I I	D
5	I I I I I I I I I	I
6	I	D

FIGURE 12.4 Example Segment of a Poorly Designed Observation Tool

	International students	Domestic students
total # of students who expressed < 3 opinions	23	57
total # of students who expressed 4 – 9 opinions	18	36
total # of students who expressed 10 – 15 opinions	22	20

FIGURE 12.5 Example Segment of a Well-designed Observation Tool

This chart presents a solution to collecting observational data without violating any of the assumptions, but it requires more observations than the problematic technique I described above.

Finally, there are assumptions about the size of the expected frequencies. These assumptions are related to the degrees of freedom for a study. The formula for the degrees of freedom in a 1-way chi-squared is $(k - 1)$, the number of levels of the variable minus 1. The degrees of freedom formula for a 2-way chi-squared is the number of levels of the independent variable minus 1 multiplied by the number of levels of the dependent variable minus 1.

When there's one degree of freedom, all *expected* frequencies must be equal to or greater than 10. When there are two or more degrees of freedom, all *expected* frequencies must be equal to or greater than 5. The expected frequencies are calculated after the data are collected to verify that the expected frequency assumption has been met. If the expected frequency assumption is not met, the researcher might be able to combine some of the levels of the variable if doing so doesn't have an adverse impact on the variable construct and the research question. If it's impossible to combine any levels of the variable to form fewer groups, the researcher must collect more data following the same systematic data collection procedures that were used to collect the original set of data.

Important Considerations in Using the Chi-Squared Statistics

In addition to the five assumptions, there are several other important considerations when using the chi-squared statistics. The first is that the levels of the variables should form natural, logical categories. Participants shouldn't be forced to choose from among categories of response that don't accurately represent their opinions or position. A well-designed data collection instrument allows the participants to accurately indicate their opinion or position. In the Halloween party study described above, the three options, "I think so," "No way," and "Maybe, but I don't like parties," could be replaced by options that are more natural (and neutral), and possibly more informative: "yes," "no," and "I haven't decided."

The second consideration when using a chi-squared formula is related to the degrees of freedom. When there's only one degree of freedom, a procedure called the Yates correction factor should be used to calculate the chi-squared value. For a 1-way design, the Yates correction factor requires two operations (Shavelson, 1996, p. 561):

1. If the observed frequency is greater than the expected frequency, 0.5 must be subtracted from the observed frequency when carrying out the calculation of χ^2.
2. If the observed frequency is less than the expected frequency, 0.5 must be added to the observed frequency when carrying out the calculation of χ^2.

For a 2-way design with one degree of freedom (where both the independent and the dependent variables have two levels), the Yates correction factor is a bit more complex, as described in Hatch and Lazaraton (1991). First, one makes a chart like this one to identify *a, b, c,* and *d* in the formula with the correction factor:

	Independent variable	
Dependent variable	*a*	*b*
	c	*d*

This formula provided by Hatch and Lazaraton (p. 404) can then be used to calculate a 2-way chi-squared with the correction factor:

$$\chi^2 = \frac{N[(ad - bc) - N/2]^2}{(a+b)(c+d)(a+c)(b+d)}$$

R uses the Yates correction factor when it's appropriate.

Type of Chi-Squared Analysis

The chi-squared statistics can be interpreted using one of two different models. The type of model used in the discussion in this chapter involves a "test for independence": The model is created based on the expected frequencies. The alternative model involves testing "goodness of fit": For this type of analysis a model is known and the data are compared against that model.[2] In small-scale language education research, the goal is often to gain a deeper understanding of the local environment, and there's rarely a model to which the local students are compared. I chose not to discuss the goodness of fit type of chi-squared analysis here because it is very rarely used in small-scale education research. I recommend readers who are interested in learning about the goodness of fit model for interpreting chi-squared statistics to the discussion by Corder and Foreman (2009, pp. 155–63).

The Formal Research Hypotheses for the Chi-Squared Statistics

The phrasing of the null and alternative hypotheses is different for chi-squared statistics than for the statistics addressed in previous chapters. The null hypothesis looks like this:

> **The observed and expected frequencies are independent; that is, there's no systematic pattern within the variable (1-way chi-squared) or relationship between the variables (2-way chi-squared).**

Lowercase *f* is used to represent *frequency* in the symbolic representation of the null hypothesis, so the symbolic representation of the null hypothesis is:

$$\mathbf{H}_0 : f_o = f_e$$

The chi-squared statistics don't indicate which part of the pattern is significant, so the alternative hypothesis is two-tailed:

> **The observed and expected frequencies are related; that is, there is a systematic pattern within the variable (1-way chi-squared) or relationship between the variables (2-way chi-squared).**

The symbolic representation of the alternative hypothesis is:

$$H_1 : f_o \neq f_e$$

Using the 1-Way Chi-Squared Statistic in Statistical Logic

I illustrate this discussion of using the 1-way chi-squared statistic in the framework of statistical logic with Maiya's sandwich shop study, which was guided by the research question: "Is there a pattern of politeness in how customers respond to a sandwich maker's greeting and offer of assistance?" The calculations for a 1-way chi-squared are very simple, so I demonstrate how to carry out the calculations with only a calculator. R could be used to calculate the observed value of the 1-way chi-squared statistic, but a short string of commands to carry out the steps for a particular study would have to be made. (There's a one-word command for the 2-way chi-squared statistic, but there isn't one for the 1-way analysis.)

Step 1: State the Null and Alternative Hypotheses

Both the null and the alternative hypotheses are set in this step.

> **Null hypothesis: The observed and expected frequencies are independent; that is, there's no systematic pattern within customers' responses to the sandwich maker's greeting and inquiry. ($H_0 : f_o = f_e$)**

> **Alternative hypothesis: The observed and expected frequencies are related; that is, there is a systematic pattern within the customers' responses to the sandwich maker's greeting and inquiry. ($H_1 : f_o \neq f_e$)**

Step 2: Set Alpha

I am not certain what level of probability Maiya set in her own analysis, but for this example I'll set it at .05. The study is exploratory in nature and I believe 95% certainty is sufficiently rigorous.

Step 3: Select the Appropriate Statistic for Analysis of the Data

Maiya, the researcher, is interested in knowing whether there's a statistically significant pattern of politeness within customers' responses to the sandwich maker's greeting and order inquiry. The data are frequency counts, as shown in Figure 12.6.[3] Because the data are frequency counts and the researcher is investigating the possibility of there being a pattern within the data, one of the two chi-squared formulas is an appropriate choice for the analysis. Because there's just one variable, the 1-way chi-squared is used.

Step 4: Collect the Data

The dataset is presented on the companion website (www.routledge.com/cw/turner).

Step 5: Check the Assumptions

There are five assumptions for the analysis:

1. The variable is nominal.
2. The data are frequency counts.
3. Each piece of information is independent from every other.
4. Each piece of information can be counted in only one level of the variable.
5. When the degree of freedom is 1, expected frequencies must be 10 or more. When the degrees of freedom are greater than 1, all expected frequencies must be 5 or more.

The first assumption requires that the variable is nominal, which is true; each participant's response to a sandwich maker's greeting and inquiry is counted in one of the three independent variable categories. The data are indeed frequency counts, as shown in Figure 12.6, so the second assumption is met too.

Maiya's description of how the data were collected (Saunders, 2011) shows that both the third and fourth assumptions are met. Each of the interactions was independent of the others; though some individuals ordered more than one sandwich during their turn, no individual was greeted and invited to place an order more than one time and no individual sought assistance from another customer when ordering.

Finally, because the independent variable has three levels and the formula for degrees of freedom for a 1-way chi-squared is $k - 1$, there are 2 degrees of freedom for this study; therefore, the expected frequencies must all be 5 or more. There are 59 participants, and the independent variable has three levels, so the expected frequency for each group is 19.66 (59/3). Each of the expected frequencies is greater than 5, so this assumption is met as well.

Step 6: Calculate the Observed Value of the Statistic

In the discussion below, I illustrate how to perform the calculations for the observed value of the 1-way chi-squared statistic using a calculator. First, I created

Figure 12.6, which displays the observed frequency for each level of the variable. The levels, called cells when calculating a chi-squared value, are labeled with letters.

Response with greeting & request marked by politeness modal	Request without greeting, marked by politeness modal	Request made using imperative verb
Cell A: 23	Cell B: 16	Cell C: 20

FIGURE 12.6 Levels of the Independent Variable With Observed Frequencies and Lettered Cell Labels

The formula for the 1-way chi-squared statistic is:

$$\chi^2 = \sum \frac{(f_o - f_e)^2}{f_e}$$

I generally make a chart similar to Table 12.1 to guide my steps in calculating the observed value of the statistic. The first column presents the cell labels; the second presents the observed frequency for each cell; the third presents the expected frequency for each cell (the total number of participants divided by the number of levels of the independent variable, 59/3 = 19.66).

In the fourth column, I report the difference between the observed frequency and the expected frequency. The fifth column presents the next step in the calculations—I square each of the differences between the observed and the expected frequency. In the final column, for each cell I divide the squared difference between the observed and the expected frequency by the expected frequency. Chi-squared is the sum of the values in the last column, so to complete the calculation of the observed value of the 1-way chi-squared statistic, I add the values in the last column:

TABLE 12.1 1-Way Chi-Squared Calculations

Cell	f_o	f_e	$f_o - f_e$	$(f_o - f_e)^2$	$\dfrac{(f_o - f_e)^2}{f_e}$
A	23	19.66	23 − 19.66 = + 3.34	+3.34² = 11.1556	11.1556 / 19.66 = 0.5674
B	16	19.66	16 − 19.66 = − 3.66	−.36² = 13.3956	13.3956 / 19.66 = 0.6814
C	20	19.66	20 − 19.66 = + 0.34	+0.34² = 0.1156	0.1156 / 19.66 = 0.0059

$$\sum \frac{(f_o - f_e)^2}{f_e} = 1.2547$$

$$\sum\frac{(f_o - f_e)^2}{f_e} = 1.2547$$

The observed value of the 1-way chi-squared analysis is 1.2547.

Step 7: Determine the Degrees of Freedom for $\chi^2_{observed}$ and Use the Degrees of Freedom and Alpha to Find the Critical Value of χ^2

I use only the critical value approach to interpreting statistical significance for the 1-way chi-squared statistic.[4] There is a chart of critical values for chi-squared.[5] The degrees of freedom (df) for this study are 2 (I used the formula $k - 1$, where k is the number of levels of the variable). I then find the appropriate column in the chart for $df = 2$ and alpha = .05; $\chi^2_{critical}$ with 2 degrees of freedom and alpha set at .05 is 5.991.

Step 8: To Interpret the Outcome of the Analysis, Compare $\chi^2_{observed}$ to $\chi^2_{critical}$

To determine whether to accept or reject the null hypothesis I compare the observed value of the statistic to the critical value. Here are the rules for Step 8:

If $\chi^2_{observed} \leq \chi^2_{critical} \rightarrow$ accept the null hypothesis.

If $\chi^2_{observed} > \chi^2_{critical} \rightarrow$ reject the null hypothesis.

$\chi^2_{observed} = 1.2547$ and $\chi^2_{critical} = 5.991$; the observed value is less than the critical value, so the null hypothesis is accepted.

> **Null hypothesis: The observed and expected frequencies are independent; that is, there's no systematic pattern within customers' responses to the sandwich maker's greeting and inquiry.**

Step 9: Interpret the Findings as a Probability Statement

The probability statement for this study is:

> **There's 95% certainty of no statistically significant pattern within customers' responses to the sandwich maker's greeting and inquiry.**

Step 10: Interpret the Meaningfulness of the Findings

As with the statistics presented in previous chapters, meaningfulness is interpreted with reference to the research question and purpose regardless of whether the null hypothesis is accepted or rejected. Effect size is also calculated and reported when possible. Effect size can be calculated for the observed value of the 2-way chi-squared statistic using the formula for Cramer's V (Corder & Foreman, 2009, p. 173; Hatch & Lazaraton, 1991, pp. 415–16); however, effect size is not calculated for the one-variable, 1-way chi-squared statistic.

Maiya's research question was: "Is there a pattern of politeness in how customers respond to a sandwich maker's greeting and offer of assistance?" She found that she could be reasonably certain there wasn't a pattern of politeness in customers' response to the sandwich maker's greeting and offer of assistance. She should include the $\chi^2_{observed}$ value and the $\chi^2_{critical}$ value showing the degrees of freedom and alpha in her summary of the findings, so she might report something like this:

> **On the basis of this small study, I can be 95% certain that for these customers there's no statistically significant pattern of politeness in how sandwich shop customers respond to a sandwich maker's greeting and offer of assistance ($\chi^2_{observed} = 1.2547$, $\chi^2_{critical(df = 2, \alpha = .05)} = 5.991$).**

Using the 2-Way Chi-Squared Statistic in Statistical Logic

Calculating a two-way chi-squared is facilitated by making a frequency chart and a calculation table, as shown in Figure 12.7 and Table 12.2. After I demonstrate how to calculate a 2-way chi-squared using a calculator, I present the commands needed to do the calculations using *R*.

Here's the research situation: A survey was conducted at a large private English language school in San Diego to determine the preferences of students of different ages with regard to type of instruction. The researcher wants to know whether there's a relationship between age and the type of learning environment the participants prefer.

The (fabricated) data are presented in Figure 12.7 along with the marginals—the subtotals for each row and column.

The steps in statistical reasoning are followed when conducting a 2-way chi-squared analysis.

Step 1: State the Hypotheses

Both the null and the alternative hypotheses are stated.

> **Null hypothesis: The observed and expected frequencies are independent; that is, there's no systematic relationship between age and preference. (H$_0$: f$_o$ = f$_e$)**

> **Alternative hypothesis: The observed and expected frequencies are related; that is, there is a systematic relationship between age and preference. (H$_1$: f$_o$ ≠ f$_e$)**

	Prefers teacher-fronted	Prefers student-centered	Prefers combination	Doesn't like either or the combination	*marginals for the rows*
ages 17–21	Cell A: 13	Cell B: 22	Cell C: 47	Cell D: 5	*marginal for observed values in this row = 87*
ages 22–29	Cell E: 7	Cell F: 25	Cell G: 36	Cell H: 18	*marginal for observed values in this row = 86*
ages 30 up	Cell I: 25	Cell J: 11	Cell K: 29	Cell L: 16	*marginal for observed values in this row = 81*
marginals for the columns	*marginal for observed values in this column = 45*	*marginal for observed values in this column = 58*	*marginal for observed values in this column = 112*	*marginal for observed values in this column = 39*	*total number of respondents = 254*

FIGURE 12.7 2-Way Chi-Squared Chart of Observed Frequencies and Marginals

Step 2: Set Alpha

This is exploratory research, so I set alpha at .05.

Step 3: Select the Appropriate Statistic for Analysis of the Data

I plan to use the formula for 2-way chi-squared because I want to know whether there is a statistically significant relationship between two nominal variables, and the data are frequency counts.

Step 4: Collect the Data

The data are summarized in Figure 12.7.

Step 5: Verify That the Assumptions Are Met

Here are the five assumptions for using chi-square; each must be confirmed.

- The two variables are nominal.
- The data are frequency counts.
- Each piece of information is independent from every other.

- Each piece of information can be counted in only one level of a variable (in only one cell).
- When the degree of freedom is 1, all expected frequencies must be greater than or equal to 10. When the degrees of freedom are more than 1, all expected frequencies must be greater than or equal to 5.

Each of the two variables is nominal scale, and review of the information in Figure 12.7 confirms that the data are frequency counts. The third assumption was checked by verifying that the questionnaires used to collect the data were completed privately by the individual participants and that although their teachers were present, they didn't advise the students how to respond. None of the participants submitted more than one questionnaire, so the fourth assumption is met too. As for the fifth assumption, the degrees of freedom formula for a 2-way chi-squared analysis is (the number of levels for the independent variable − 1) multiplied by (the number of levels of the dependent variable − 1). The *preference* variable has four levels and the *age* variable has three, so there are 6 degrees of freedom [(4 − 1) (3 − 1) = 6]. Because there are 6 degrees of freedom, each of the expected frequencies must be five or more. When I do the calculations with a calculator, one of the steps involves calculating the expected frequencies—when I've completed that step I review the expected frequency values to make sure that each is at least 5. When I use R to calculate the observed value of the 2-way chi-squared statistic, a warning message is given if the expected frequencies aren't high enough. In either case, if the assumption regarding the size of the expected frequencies isn't met, the researcher should examine the levels of the variables to determine whether any can be combined[6] or more data must be collected.[7] In Table 12.2, the expected frequencies are bolded so they can be checked easily—each is greater than 5.

Step 6: Calculate the Observed Value of 2-Way Chi-Squared

Table 12.2 shows the steps in calculating the 2-way chi-squared. The first calculation, shown in the third column, is determining the expected frequency for each of the cells. I refer to the marginals for each cell to calculate its expected frequency (see Figure 12.7). In the fourth column, I find the difference between the observed frequency and the expected frequency for each cell, $f_o - f_e$. In the fifth column, I square that difference, $(f_o - f_e)^2$. In the sixth column, I divide each of the values for $(f_o - f_e)^2$ by the *expected* frequency for that cell, $(f_o - f_e)^2/f_e$. The sum of these values of $(f_o - f_e)^2/f_e$ is the observed value of the 2-way chi-squared statistic.

The formula for the 2-way chi-squared statistic is the sum of the values in the final column of Table 12.2:

$$\chi^2 = \sum \frac{(f_o - f_e)^2}{f_e} = \textbf{28.78}$$

TABLE 12.2 Calculation of the 2-Way Chi-Squared Statistic

Cell	f_o	f_e^1	$f_o - f_e$	$(f_o - f_e)^2$	$\dfrac{(f_o - f_e)^2}{f_e}$
A	13	$(45)(87)/254 = \mathbf{15.41}$	$13 - 15.41 = -2.41$	5.81	$5.81 / 15.41 = .38$
B	22	$(58)(87)/254 = \mathbf{19.87}$	$22 - 19.87 = 2.13$	4.54	$4.54 / 19.87 = .23$
C	47	$(112)(87)/254 = \mathbf{38.36}$	$47 - 38.36 = 8.64$	74.65	$74.65 / 38.36 = 1.95$
D	5	$(39)(87)/254 = \mathbf{13.36}$	$5 - 13.36 = -8.36$	69.89	$69.89 / 13.36 = 5.23$
E	7	$(45)(86)/254 = \mathbf{15.24}$	$7 - 15.24 = -8.24$	67.90	$67.90 / 15.24 = 4.46$
F	25	$(58)(86)/254 = \mathbf{19.64}$	$25 - 19.64 = 5.36$	28.73	$28.73 / 19.64 = 1.46$
G	36	$(112)(86)/254 = \mathbf{37.92}$	$36 - 37.92 = -1.92$	3.69	$3.69 / 37.92 = 0.10$
H	18	$(39)(86)/254 = \mathbf{13.20}$	$18 - 13.20 = 4.80$	23.04	$23.04 / 13.20 = 1.75$
I	25	$(45)(81)/254 = \mathbf{14.35}$	$25 - 14.35 = 10.65$	113.42	$113.4\,2 / 14.35 = 7.90$
J	11	$(58)(81)/254 = \mathbf{18.50}$	$11 - 18.50 = -7.5$	56.25	$56.25 / 18.50 = 3.04$
K	29	$(112)(81)/254 = \mathbf{35.72}$	$29 - 35.72 = -6.72$	45.16	$45.16 / 35.72 = 1.26$
L	16	$(39)(81)/254 = \mathbf{12.44}$	$16 - 12.44 = 3.56$	12.67	$12.67 / 12.44 = 1.02$

$$\sum \frac{(f_o - f_e)^2}{f_e} = 28.78$$

[1] The expected frequencies are bolded as a reminder to check the assumption that each is equal to or greater than five.

In Box 12.1 I illustrate the calculations using R.

Box 12.1 Using R to Calculate the Observed Value of the 2-Way Chi-Squared Statistic

Import the dataset for the 2-way chi-squared problem from the companion website by entering the site and saving the dataset on your computer. Then use the **read.csv(file. choose( ), header = T)** command to import it. Don't forget to give the imported dataset a name—I named it unimaginatively d.	> **d = read.csv(file.choose( ), header = T)**
View the dataset d and note the label for each variable in the header; the independent variable is *age* and the dependent variable is *prefer*.	> **View (d)**
Calculate the observed value of the 2-way chi-squared statistic. The name of the independent variable is $d\$age$ (the variable labeled *age* in the dataset named d). The name of the dependent variable is $d\$prefer$ (the variable labeled *prefer* in the dataset named d). (Note: If you enter the data directly into R, naming the first variable x and the second variable y, the command for calculating chi-squared would be **chisq.test (x,y)**.)	> **chisq.test (d\$age, d\$prefer)** Output: Pearson's Chi-squared test data:d\$age and d\$prefer X-squared = 28.7619, df = 6, p-value = 6.748e-05[8]

Step 7: Determine the Degrees of Freedom for $\chi^2_{observed}$ and Use Degrees of Freedom and Alpha to Find the Critical Value of the Statistic OR Calculate the Exact Probability of $\chi^2_{observed}$

Either of the two approaches described in Step 7 can be used, but the critical value approach is typically used when the calculation of $\chi^2_{observed}$ is done using a calculator. The exact probability approach can be used when the calculation of $\chi^2_{observed}$ is done using R because the exact probability of $\chi^2_{observed}$ is reported.

Using the Critical Value Approach

As noted above, the formula for calculating the degrees of freedom for the 2-way chi-squared statistic is (the number of independent levels − 1) multiplied by (the number of dependent variable levels − 1). For this study there are 6 degrees of freedom [(4 − 1)(3 − 1) = 6]. Using a chart of critical values for chi-squared,[9] I find that the critical value when there are 6 degrees of freedom and alpha is set at .05 is 12.592.

Using the Exact Probability Approach

When using the exact probability approach to interpreting the outcome, I use R (or some other statistical program) to calculate $\chi^2_{observed}$ (single underscore in the output, $\chi^2_{observed} = 28.7619$), and the exact level of probability for $\chi^2_{observed}$ (double underscore in the output, $p = .00006748$).

Step 8: To Interpret the Outcome of the Analysis, Compare the Observed Value and the Critical Value OR Compare the Exact Probability to Alpha

In Step 8, the outcome of the analysis is determined using either the critical value approach (if calculations were done with a calculator) or the exact probability approach (if calculations were done using R).

Using the Critical Value Approach

The rules for comparing $\chi^2_{observed}$ and $\chi^2_{critical}$ are:

$$\text{If } \chi^2_{observed} \leq \chi^2_{critical} \rightarrow \text{accept the null hypothesis.}$$

$$\text{If } \chi^2_{observed} > \chi^2_{critical} \rightarrow \text{reject the null hypothesis.}$$

Table 12.2 shows the outcome when doing the work with a calculator; $\chi^2_{observed} = 28.78$. From Step 7, I know that $\chi^2_{critical} = 12.592$. When I compare $\chi^2_{observed}$ to $\chi^2_{critical}$, I see:

$$28.78 > 12.592$$

According to the steps in statistical logic, when the observed value of the statistic is greater than the critical value, the null hypothesis is rejected and the alternative hypothesis is accepted.

Using the Exact Probability Approach

The rules for comparing the exact level of probability for $\chi^2_{observed}$ with alpha (α) are:

> If exact probability of $\chi^2_{observed} \geq$ alpha $\rightarrow$ accept the null hypothesis.
>
> If exact probability of $\chi^2_{observed} <$ alpha $\rightarrow$ reject the null hypothesis.

For these data, the exact probability is $p = .00006748$; alpha is .05. Because the exact level of p is less than alpha, the null hypothesis is rejected and the alternative hypothesis accepted.

> **Alternative hypothesis: The observed and expected frequencies are related; that is, there's a systematic relationship between age and preference.**

Step 9: Interpret the Findings as a Probability Statement

In Step 9, the probability statement is made using the hypothesis accepted in Step 8.

> **There's 95% certainty of a systematic relationship between the age of these students and their preference for how their classes are conducted.**

Step 10: Interpret the Meaningfulness of the Findings

As noted in Chapter Five, there are two avenues for interpreting the meaningfulness of an inferential statistic; first, with reference to the research question and second, by calculating effect size. In this study, the researcher wanted to know whether there was a significant relationship between learners' age and their preference for how their classes were designed. The school's director was considering separating the younger and older learners and designing courses that reflected their different interests and concerns, but she wanted to know if there was a significant pattern to their preferences before she separated the students by age.

She also calculated the effect size to determine the strength of the relationship. Because there are 6 degrees of freedom, she first calculated *phi*, then used phi to calculate Cramer's V.

Here's the formula for phi:

$$phi = \sqrt{\frac{\chi^2}{n}}$$

Below, I fill in the observed value for chi-squared ($\chi^2_{observed}$ = 28.78) and the number of participants (n = 254). I then carry out the calculations:

$$phi = \sqrt{\frac{28.78}{254}} = \sqrt{.11331} = \mathbf{.33662}$$

Now I use the value of phi in the formula for Cramer's V. Here's the formula for Cramer's V:

$$\text{Cramer's } V = \sqrt{\frac{phi^2}{(r-1)\,or\,(c-1)\,\star}}$$

$\star$Use either *number of independent variable levels* ($r - 1$) or *number of dependent variable levels* ($c - 1$), whichever is smaller.

$$\sqrt{\frac{phi^2}{(r-1)\,or\,(c-1)\,\star}} = \sqrt{\frac{.33662^2}{3-1}} = \sqrt{\frac{.11331}{2}} = \sqrt{.05666} = \mathbf{.23803}$$

Cramer's V tells us how much overlap there is between the two variables—about 24% in this case. Though statistically significant, the relationship between the two variables is only modestly strong (Corder & Foreman, 2009, p. 169).

After consulting with the director of the school, the researcher reported:

> **On the basis of the analysis, the director has decided to design different courses for the younger and older learners because there is a modestly strong, statistically significant relationship between the age of students at the school and their preference for how their courses are conducted (χ^2 = 28.78, *df* = 6, *p* = .00006748, Cramer's V = .23803). However, both teacher-fronted and student-centered activities will be incorporated into the classes for younger and older students. The new classes will be trialed for one term and participants in the classes and their teachers will be questioned to determine their degree of satisfaction with the new design before establishing a policy separating the younger and older learners.**

R Commands Introduced in Chapter Twelve

chisq.test (d$independent.variable, d$dependent.variable) This command calculates the observed value of the 2-way chi-squared statistic (based on an imported dataset named *d* that includes an independent and a dependent variable).

chisq.test (independent.variable, dependent.variable) This command calculates the observed value of the 2-way chi-squared statistic when the values for the two variables are entered directly into *R* as separate datasets.

Practice Problems

An answer key is available on the companion website (www.routledge.com/cw/turner).

Study A. You might take another look at Maiya's data (Table 12.3), which include a variable labeled *sex*. Use the 2-way chi-squared formula and statistical logic to determine whether there's a statistically significant relationship between customers' type of response and their sex.

TABLE 12.3 Some of Maiya Saunders's Data

Type of Response[1]	Sex[2]
2	1
1	1
3	2
2	1
1	1
3	1
3	2
2	1
3	2
1	2
2	2
2	1
2	2
3	2
2	2
1	2
1	1
1	1
1	2
2	1
2	2
1	2

(Continued)

TABLE 12.3 (*Continued*)

Type of Response[1]	Sex[2]
1	1
3	1
1	1
1	1
1	1
2	1
3	1
2	1
3	2
3	1
2	2
2	1
1	2
3	2
1	2
1	2
1	2
1	1
2	2
1	1
2	2
3	2
3	2
3	1
1	1
1	2
2	2
1	2
3	2
1	1
3	2
3	2
1	2
3	2
3	1
3	2
3	2

[1] 1 = greeting + politeness modal;
2 = politeness modal; 3 = possible greeting
+ imperative verb.
[2] Female = 1; male = 2.

Study B. A researcher is interested in investigating whether there is a statistically significant pattern of attitude toward the pedagogical use of computers among 40 incoming students. *Attitude* is a nominal variable with three levels: negative (1), ambivalent (2), and positive (3). On the basis of their responses on a questionnaire, the 40 participants were placed into one of the three categories (the data are presented in Table 12.4). Determine whether there's a statistically significant pattern to their responses about their attitude toward pedagogical uses of computer technologies. The researcher also wanted to explore whether there was a statistically significant relationship between attitude and sex. Follow the steps in statistical reasoning to calculate and interpret these data.

TABLE 12.4 Data for Study B

Attitude	Age	Sex
3.00	1.00	1.00
3.00	1.00	1.00
2.00	1.00	1.00
1.00	1.00	1.00
3.00	1.00	1.00
3.00	1.00	1.00
3.00	1.00	1.00
2.00	1.00	2.00
2.00	1.00	2.00
2.00	1.00	2.00
1.00	1.00	2.00
3.00	1.00	2.00
3.00	2.00	2.00
3.00	2.00	2.00
3.00	2.00	1.00
2.00	2.00	1.00
3.00	2.00	1.00
3.00	2.00	1.00
1.00	2.00	2.00
1.00	2.00	2.00
2.00	2.00	2.00
3.00	2.00	2.00
3.00	2.00	1.00
3.00	2.00	1.00
3.00	2.00	1.00
1.00	2.00	1.00
3.00	2.00	2.00
3.00	3.00	2.00
2.00	3.00	2.00
2.00	3.00	2.00

(Continued)

TABLE 12.4 (*Continued*)

Attitude	Age	Sex
2.00	3.00	1.00
3.00	3.00	1.00
3.00	3.00	1.00
3.00	3.00	2.00
3.00	3.00	2.00
3.00	3.00	2.00
3.00	3.00	1.00
3.00	3.00	1.00
3.00	3.00	2.00
3.00	3.00	2.00

Notes

1 Until writing this text, I used the term *chi-square* instead of *chi-squared* but *R* uses *chi-squared* in some output reports. For consistency, I use the term *chi-squared* throughout my discussion here—at least I hope I did.

2 I remember doing a "goodness of fit" problem in one of the classes I took while studying *R*. I had to buy a small pack of M&M's and count how many red, green, yellow, orange, blue, and brown M&M's there were. I then compared my count with a model count (established by the M&M manufacturer—did you know there are company specifications for that kind of thing?) to determine the goodness of fit between the number of each color in my pack and the numbers in the model. My M&M's fit the model and I ate them.

3 Though Maiya collected 60 cases, the response for one participant was not indicated, so the analysis includes 59 participants.

4 There is no handy one-word command in *R* for calculating the observed value of the 1-way chi-squared statistic and the exact probability of $\chi^2_{observed}$. It's possible to write a program for calculating the observed value of 1-way chi-squared and its exact probability, but when an aid like Table 12.1 is made, the calculations are quite simple, so I suggest using the critical value approach for interpreting 1-way $\chi^2_{observed}$.

5 Check the companion website for a chart of critical values for χ^2 (www.routledge.com/cw/turner).

6 In this study, for example, I think it would be all right to combine the two older groups to form one group, age 21.

7 The additional data have to be collected following the same systematic procedures used to collect the original set of data.

8 The exact probability is reported as 6.748^{e-05}. The e-05 notation means "move the decimal place five places to the left," so exact probability is .00006748.

9 A chart of critical values of χ^2 is included in the resources section of the companion website (www.routledge.com/cw/turner).

REFERENCES

American Council on the Teaching of Foreign Languages. (1999). *ACTFL proficiency guidelines—speaking.* Alexandria, VA: American Council on the Teaching of Foreign Languages.

Anglim, J. (2012, June 14). Re: Reporting coefficient of determination using Spearman's rho [Online forum comment]. Retrieved from http://stats.stackexchange.com/questions/44268/reporting-coefficient-of-determination-using-spearmans-rho

APA. (2001). *Publication manual of the American Psychological Association* (5th ed.). Washington, DC: American Psychological Association.

———. (2010). *Publication manual of the American Psychological Association* (6th ed.). Washington, DC: American Psychological Association.

Association of Classroom Teacher Testers. (1993). *Combined English language skills assessment in a reading context.* Montecito, CA: Author.

Bailey, K.B. (1998). *Learning about language assessment: Dilemmas, decisions, and directions.* Boston, MA: Heinle/Cengage Learning.

———. (2005). Looking back down the road: A recent history of language classroom research. *Review of Applied Linguistics in China: Issues in Language Learning and Teaching, 1,* 6–46.

Borkovska, N. (2007). *The effect of specialized vocabulary presentation technique on non-native speakers' vocabulary retention.* (Unpublished article presented in author's Program Portfolio for MA in TESOL, Monterey Institute of International Studies, Monterey, CA.)

Brown, J. D. (1988). *Understanding research in second language learning.* New York: Cambridge University Press.

Burns, A. (2010). *Doing action research in English language teaching.* New York: Routledge.

Carroll, J.B., & Sapon, S.M. (2002). *Modern Language Aptitude Test—Elementary.* North Bethesda, MD: Second Language Testing.

Corder, W.G., & Foreman, D. L. (2009). *Non-parametric statistics for non-statisticians.* Hoboken, NJ: John Wiley & Sons.

De Veaux, R.D., Velleman, P.F., & Bock, D.E. (2008). *Stats: Data and models* (2nd ed.). Boston, MA: Pearson Education.

Douglas, D. (2010). *Understanding language testing.* London: Hodder Education.

easycalculation. com. (2013). Retrieved 6/17/2013 from http://easycalculation.com/statistics/critical-t-test.php

Educational Testing Service. (2010). *2010–2011 interpreting your GRE scores.* Retrieved from www.ets.org/s/gre/pdf/gre_interpreting_scores.pdf

ESPN. (2012). 2012 Summer Olympics results—swimming. Women's 100m butterfly, final. Retrieved from http://espn.go.com/olympics/summer/2012/results/_/sport/39

Field, A., Miles, J., & Field, Z. (2012). *Discovering statistics using R.* Los Angeles: Sage.

Fulcher, G. (2010). *Practical language testing.* London: Hodder Education.

Grode, J. (2011). *Authentic or instructional? An examination of learners' perceptions.* (Unpublished research project included in MA TESOL Program Portfolio, Monterey Institute of International Studies, Monterey, CA).

Hatch, E., & Lazaraton, A. (1991). *The research manual: Design and statistics for applied linguistics.* New York: Newbury House Publishers.

Johnson, D.M. (1992). *Approaches to research in second language learning.* White Plains, NY: Longman Publishing Group.

Kuncel, N.R., Hezlett, S.A., & Ones, D. S. (2001). A comprehensive meta-analysis of the predictive validity of the graduate record examinations: Implications for graduate student selection and performance. *Psychological Bulletin, 127*(1), 162–81.

Language Testing International. (2004). *Oral proficiency interviews (OPI).* Retrieved from www.languagetesting.com/corp_opi.htm

Larimer, R. E., & Schleicher, L. (Eds.) (1999). *New ways in using authentic materials in the classroom.* Alexandria, VA: TESOL.

McLeod, A. I. (2011). Package 'Kendall' (Version 2.2). Retrieved 11/20/2013 from http://cran.r-project.org/web/packages/Kendall/index.html

McMillan, J.H. (2000). *Educational research: Fundamentals for the consumer* (3rd ed.). New York: Longman.

Nunan, D., & Bailey, K. (2009). *Exploring second language classroom research.* Boston, MA: Heinle/Cengage Learning.

Oliva, P. (2011). *Motivation and autonomy in an advanced Spanish class that follows the individualization approach in content-based instruction.* Madrid, Spain: Defense for the Diploma of Advanced Studies, Universidad de Nebrija.

Pearson Education. (2011). *Inside Versant.* Retrieved from www.versanttest.com/products/spanish.jsp

R Foundation for Statistical Computing. (2010). R version 2.11.1 (2010–05–31) ISBN 3–900051–07–0.

Saunders, M. (2011). *Polite requests in service encounters.* (Unpublished paper, Graduate School of Translation, Interpretation, and Educational Linguistics, Monterey Institute of International Studies, Monterey, CA).

Second Language Testing. (2010). MLAT—Elementary (MLAT-E). Retrieved from www.2lti.com/htm/Test_mlate.htm, retrieved 11/6/2011

Shavelson, R.J. (1996). *Statistical reasoning for the behavioral sciences* (3rd ed.). Boston, MA: Allyn & Bacon.

Siegel, S. (1956). *Non-parametric statistics for the behavioral sciences.* New York: McGraw-Hill.

Sikorski, L. (2006). *Mastering effective English communication CD series* (5th ed.). Tustin, CA: LDS & Associates.

Sprent, P., & Smeeton, N.C. (2007). *Applied nonparametric statistical methods* (4th ed.). Boca Raton, FL: Chapman & Hall/CRC.

Sprinthall, R.C. (1994). *Basic statistical analysis* (4th ed.). Boston, MA: Allyn & Bacon.

Verzani, J. (2005). *Using R for introductory statistics.* Boca Raton, FL: Chapman & Hall/CRC Press.

Ware, W.B., Ferron, J.M., & Miller, B.M. (2013). *Introductory statistics: A conceptual approach using R.* New York: Routledge.

Yiu, D. (2011). *Are you a blabbermouth? A mixed-method study of personality and oral classroom participation.* (Unpublished paper, Graduate School of Translation, Interpretation, and Educational Linguistics, Monterey Institute of International Studies, Monterey, CA).

INDEX